# CHINESE
# POLITICS AFTER
# MAO

# CHINESE POLITICS AFTER MAO

## DEVELOPMENT AND LIBERALIZATION
### 1976 TO 1983

### Peter R. Moody, Jr.

PRAEGER SPECIAL STUDIES • PRAEGER SCIENTIFIC

**Library of Congress Cataloging in Publication Data**

Moody, Peter R.
   Chinese politics after Mao.

   Bibliography: p.
   Includes index.
   1. China—Politics and government—1976–
I. Title.
DS779.26.M66  1983      320.951      83-13925
ISBN 0-03-063527-6 (alk. paper)

Published in 1983 by Praeger Publishers
CBS Educational and Professional Publishing
A Division of CBS, Inc.
521 Fifth Avenue, New York, New York 10175 U.S.A.

© 1983 by Praeger Publishers

456789   052   98765432

Printed in the United States of America on acid-free paper.

# Contents

# CHINESE POLITICS AFTER MAO

# 1

# Introduction

When the Chinese dictator Mao Tse-tung died in September 1976, he was generally hailed abroad as one of the world's great leaders. This had certainly been the opinion of his own press at home, which had made him the object of one of this century's most remarkable personality cults. School children had at one time recited that Chairman Mao was dearer to them than father or mother; and at one time during the late 1960s, it was alleged that roving army medical teams were able, by thinking and applying the chairman's thought, to raise the dead. The thought was evidently unable to raise Mao himself, and within a month of his death his ambitious wife and three of her allies, the persons most closely identified with Mao personally and with his ideas, were placed under arrest and denounced as the "Gang of Four." Everyone knew how many were really in the Gang of Four and who the fifth member was. Mao's greatness may yet be confirmed by history, but when he died many of those he ruled were ready, if they could, to repudiate not only him but also the system he represented. This popular sentiment may be the basis for a radical transformation of that system.

Western students of Chinese politics have been impressed with the popular roots of Chinese communism. Yet, beginning in 1957, at periods of roughly a decade apart the Communist Party of China (CPC) has met with bouts of outspoken public criticism, to which it has responded by repression. It is likely that the Western (for the most part, United States') interpretation tends to take too cavalier a view of the Chinese people's affinity for totalitarianism. Certainly one of the more impressive aspects of communist rule in China has been the willingness of the people to protest againt it. Despite the relatively crude nature of dissident ideas in China as

1

compared with those in the Soviet Union, it is difficult to imagine anything like the T'ien-an-men riots of April 1976 taking place in Red Square; and within a few months after the death of Mao, vocal dissent against past policies moved beyond the intensity permitted in the Soviet post-Stalin thaw. However, the fact that this protest occurred shows there is some truth in the basic contention of communism's popular roots: in each of the protests, either against the regime itself or against aspects of its policy, some of the most radical criticism has come from members of the Communist Party itself. Political conflict in China, despite its basically elitist nature, is not simply infighting among the ruling group or a confrontation of the rulers and the ruled. At least to a limited degree, the conflicts among the rulers will have what the regime likes to call a social base. Some complaints of the ruled will be taken up by some of the rulers, and conflict among the rulers will at least indirectly reflect genuine conflicts in society.[1]

This may permit a *liberalization* of Chinese politics. This does not necessarily mean that Chinese politics will become genuinely liberal—that there will be, for example, a free press, competitive elections within a multiparty system, a legislature that truly legislates, a clear formal separation of administration and politics, and a real separation between the state and the ruling party. The term would imply, however, changes in a liberal direction and also changes that mark a structural break with totalitarianism. Such changes would be analogous to those in Hungary in 1956 or Czechoslovakia in 1968. They would be less thoroughgoing, perhaps, but in the case of China it is less likely that they would be stifled by foreign intervention.

Liberalization would mean more than simply those changes identified as "deradicalization"[2] or demobilization. The Brezhnev regime, for example, was deradicalized—post-totalitarian, we might say, but not really liberalized. The changes in China ultimately might amount to no more than that: in Maoist terms, China could become and remain "revisionist." But during the period from the death of Mao in the fall of 1976 at least up to the public trial of the Maoists at the end of 1980, Chinese politics seemed to be undergoing a deeper transformation. This change has two separate but related manifestations. The most obvious, of course, was the democratic movement of the winter of 1978-79, which still survives in potential and may revive whenever conditions permit. The second is an "official liberalization," sponsored particularly by what came to be the dominant force within the regime, Teng Hsiao-p'ing and those associated with his programs.

The most radical part of democratic movement demanded the transformation of the system into a democratic one. The official liberalization amounted, rather, to a "depoliticization," an awkward and ugly but perhaps accurate term. Depoliticization does not mean that life is becoming apolitical. Certainly more things are apolitical now than they were before but the inference should not be drawn that people are simply encouraged to concentrate upon their private lives and leave the politics to their rulers. Rather, depoliticization is itself a political program. A totalitarian regime is characterized by its ideological nature, its intolerance of passive obedience, and its need to mobilize its subjects behind its programs.[3] A deradicalized regime puts less stress on mass campaigns and more on bureaucratic routine, but it also emphasizes ideological orthodoxy. The ideology no longer provides much of a guide to action but becomes frozen into a dogma.[4] In China, however, this ossification of ideology had not taken place. Rather, the ideology seemed to be tapering off into a "mentality,"[5] to be becoming simply a synonym for pragmatic success: practice is the standard of truth.

Depoliticization in China meant that there came to be for a time official recognition of a legitimate diversity of political opinion and interest. There was also a refusal to deal with this diversity by the application, exclusively, of political and ideological criteria. There was less direct political pressure upon the population; the regime became minimally open to some genuine political participation from society. This openness, as well as a temporary tactical expediency, indicates affinity between the tendencies for depoliticization and the democratic movement. Yet those behind the official liberalization were easily able to participate in the suppression of the democratic movement once it had served its purpose, and the suppression of the democratic movement did not immediately halt the ongoing official liberalization.

During the 1970s outsiders tended to overestimate (to put it most kindly) the appeal of Maoist totalitarianism to those who had to live with it. From the current perspective, this seems too stupid even to refute,[6] although at the time students of Chinese politics had to take it seriously. Even then it seemed that opposition to the regime was tending to converge toward a liberal position, if only because when people cannot have everything their own way all the time they may still see some merit in a situation that allows a certain toleration of themselves.[7] If the liberalization of Chinese politics does occur, however, it will be not simply because it has broad appeal but also because it suits actual and current political interests—not merely the interests of abstract social categories but also of real persons, factions, and combinations.

After Mao's death the initial impetus toward liberalization came from officials who had endured the antibureaucratic animus of Maoism. Tensions among the post-Gang rulers led to the second rehabilitation of Teng Hsiao-p'ing. Teng and persons like him, unlike those in power when Mao died, had virtually no interest in preserving the practices associated with Maoism. Their own power would initially be at the sufferance of others, and to consolidate it they would have an interest in systemic reform.

Such functionaries would also have allies among the general population. These should include at least two segments of the amorphous category of educated youth. One would be the former Red Guards, who combine a radical hostility to rules and bureaucracy with at best an indifference and at worst hostility toward Maoist economic radicalism. Many of these felt betrayed by their "establishment" radical sponsors long before the purge of the Gang of Four.[8] The other category would be students and recent graduates particularly of technical schools and departments. These would-be technocrats will make their careers through the modernization of China and are threatened not just by a reassertion of radicalism but by any inclination to look upon political orthodoxy with more favor than professional competence. This potential alliance is not without its "contradictions." While the bureaucrats may fancy they favor the liberation of thought, they are not enchanted with the indiscipline that may accompany this and that the Red Guard-types (who seem to have predominated in the democratic movement) may be inclined to foster. At the time of Mao's death, there were four dominant tendencies among the elite: the radicals really "establishment" radicals, since they criticized the power structure even while benefiting from it themselves) headed by the Gang of Four; some nonradical leftists, originally allied with the radicals, with strong representation in the police system; the military; and the state bureaucracy, especially the segment concerned with managing the economy. The purge of the Gang of Four eliminated the establishment radicals and brought about a drastic change of tone in the regime and a definite moderation of policy. Tensions in the anti-Gang coalition brought about the return to power of the previously purged Teng Hsiao-p'ing. Teng may have had a genuine commitment to some kind of liberalization (although he certainly would have avoided the word) but also a definite political interest in changing the structure of the regime in order to make sure of his own base of power and to make himself independent of those who brought him back. Teng, therefore, cultivated his own "reform" group, persons having no vested interest in the system that had emerged from the Cultural Revolution. Teng and the reformers were able to outmaneuver and eliminate the leftists but in the process came into conflict with the military and the bureaucracy. The reformers have continued to push for reforms that would strengthen them against their enemies, and most of these reforms would tend to make the system more liberal. Yet the reformers have also been willing to compromise or turn against reform when this became expedient. The reform group has increasingly come to dominate the political system, but it may have reached the point at which this domination comes at the expense of reform itself. Chinese elites may be linked with the population, but they do not depend upon the population—upon a social base—for their position. The reformers share this fear of democracy with other elements of the elite. The reformers are much more willing to depoliticize than democratize. Further reform, however, may depend upon further democratization: reform may not really take hold unless the reformers come to need to retain the goodwill of the people, rather than that of their enemies in the elite.

If the structure of politics in China is becoming liberalized, this could have several rather important implications. World trends, despite the conservative temperament of the early 1980s, continue to encourage the growth of political power over both the person and the community, and it is about as clear as anything can be that no strong state, much less a totalitarian one, is going to be overthrown by popular revolution. If there is the possibility of a peaceful transformation of totalitarian systems, we might look to the future with more optimism than might seem justified on the face of things.

Such a transformation should in principle be possible, if only because totalitarianism is an incoherent, contradictory form of rule.[9] Hannah Arendt believes totalitarianism is built upon the notion that anything is possible (supplementing the nineteenth century proposition that anything is permitted) and that nothing is true.[10] If everything is permitted and more and more things are actually possible, there is no inhibition, moral or otherwise, to attempts at total control—but neither is there anything in which to ground control. Any rule requires predictability, order, and regularity—and these constrain the behavior of the ruler. Because totalitarianism is a contradictory concept it can have no stable empirical embodiment, although, obviously, there are unstable empirical approximations (this instability sometimes being confused with dynamism). Totalitarian rule seems typically to become stabilized as the "administered society,"[11] but totalitarianism may contain the potential for something else. Since every temporary consolidation of the totalitarian regime is opened to renewed dissolution, opposition and dissent form a sort of functional requirement of the regime.[12] This opposition is not institutionalized and is always subject to arbitrary and capricious repression. It works to increase general insecurity and unpredictability: no functionary is immune from arbitrary criticism, and no critic is immune from arbitrary punishment. The major long-term consequence of this is perhaps to generate a yearning for stable authority and an intolerance for troublemaking malcontents. In China, however, where radical Maoism stressed to an unusual degree the libertarian aspects of totalitarianism, the system may have nourished in at least part of the articulate population an anti-authoritarian ethos strong enough to prevent the easy consolidation of the post-totalitarian society. The liberalization of Chinese politics, such as it is, is part of a massive reaction against radical Maoism but if it goes beyond the first steps it may be because China has passed through Maoism.

The problem is not whether liberal ideas have appeal in China; they obviously do. But these ideas may continue to lack political relevance unless they become embodied in institutions. Whether and how liberal institutions will develop in China depends upon the play of political forces, and it is here, rather than on ideas as such, that the attention of this study should be. Much of the attention given to ideas should be to ideology, that is, to ideas as they function to rationalize actual or potential structures of power and privilege. This need not mean a thoroughgoing anti-intellectualism, however: there is always some interest in knowing what people will value, whether or not they ever get what they value; also, any power struggle is likely to be *about* something, to have some content, however vestigial.

The first part of this study describes the political structure in China at the death of Mao and analyzes the play of power at the center from the purge of the Gang of Four to the rise of supremacy of Teng Hsiao-p'ing in late 1978. The second part analyzes the liberalization produced by the power struggle: the "official" liberalization, both of the political structure and processes and of specific policies of the regime, and the social demands for liberalization manifested in the democratic movement. The next section resumes the analysis of the power struggle, tracing it from the suppression of the democratic movement to the apparently total victory of Teng Hsiao-p'ing over the post-Mao left and his at least partial victory over the antireform right.

## NOTES

1. Lucian Pye, *The Dynamics of Chinese Politics* (Cambridge, Mass.: Oelgeschager, Gull & Hain, 1981), argues that Chinese political alliances are not based upon policy, ideology, geography, institutional affiliation, and the like; they reflect, rather, the personal relationships of individuals in a hierarchy (pp. 7–9). This is a refreshing change from analyses of Chinese political behavior in terms of high-minded differences over principle or of analogies with, say, interest group politics in the United States. Yet not all political alliances in China seem to be based upon personal relationships (or, rather, the relationship may form after the alliance has been made in order to facilitate the alliance), and not all Chinese politics is factional, much less unprincipled. There is an analogy between the current situation and the interpretation of politics in traditional times by certain communist writers today. "In certain historical circumstances," factional struggle "can have a function of initiating political reform; this also is a form of class struggle." See Chang Ta-k'o, "An Attempt to Discuss the Chao-Hsuan Restoration," *Kuang-ming Jih-pao*, October 2, 1979.

2. Robert C. Tucker, *The Marxian Revolutionary Idea* (New York: Norton, 1969), p. 180.

3. Juan J. Linz, "Totalitarian and Authoritarian Regimes," in *Handbook of Political Science*, vol. 3, ed. Fred I. Greenstein and Nelson W. Polsby (Reading, Mass.: Addison-Wesley, 1975), pp. 175–411.

4. Tucker, *The Marxian Revolutionary Idea*, p. 193.

5. Linz, "Totalitarian and Authoritarian Regimes," p. 267.

6. Compare Paul Hollander, *Political Pilgrims: Travels of Western Intellectuals to the Soviet Union, China, and Cuba* (New York: Oxford University Press, 1981).

7. Peter R. Moody, Jr., *Opposition and Dissent in Contemporary China* (Stanford: Hoover Institution Press, 1977), p. 240.

8. Ibid., pp. 199–216; Hong Yung Lee, *The Politics of the Chinese Cultural Revolution: A Case Study* (Berkeley: University of California Press, 1978).

9. Peter R. Moody, Jr., "Law and Heaven: The Evolution of Chinese Totalitarianism," *Survey* 24 (Winter 1979):116–32.

10. Hannah Arendt, *The Origins of Totalitarianism*, 2nd ed. (Cleveland: Meridian Books 1958), passim, esp. pp. 382, 436–37.

11. Allan Kassof, "The Administered Society: Totalitarianism Without Terror," *World Politics* 16 (July 1964):558–74.

12. Moody, *Opposition and Dissent*, p. 239: John Bryan Starr, *Continuing the Revolution: The Political Thought of Mao* (Princeton: Princeton University Press, 1979), p. 222.

# 2

# Chinese
# Politics at
# the Death of
# Mao

In the early 1970s certain educated and well-to-do people from the wealthier parts of the world condemned their own societies for their soulless consumerism. Some claimed to see Maoist China as humanity's answer to the capitalist cancer. By the 1980s it had become more difficult to ignore the precarious nature of material prosperity and, therefore, more difficult to despise it. A similar new conservatism affected China as well. The Chinese people as a whole may not have been the enthusiasts for poverty their Western admirers once liked to believe they were, and in any case their rulers were rejecting the earlier vision of poverty communism. The Maoists—who later were condemned as the Gang of Four and its followers—wanted to bring about the wealth and power of the state in such a way that the modernization of China would be distinctly socialist. China would not be drawn into the capitalist world system but would find its own path, participating in the revolution of the peoples of the world against that system. This particular vision has been rejected with more brusqueness than the contemporary counterculture's vision of the United States, although in China as in the United States the rejection may have costs as well as gains.

## POLITICAL FORCES IN THE LOST DECADE

The last ten years of Mao's life were marked by chaos—a good thing, the chairman used to say. The Cultural Revolution had bequn in earnest in 1966, although there was argument and a few purges in 1965, and its origins reach back at least to 1956. Throughout 1967 different parts of the country were in turmoil. Superficial calm was restored in 1968, but to a large degree the institutional structure of rule had been destroyed and was not fully to be restored as long as Mao lived.

The Cultural Revolution has been considered, among other things, as an attack on rule by bureaucracy. But it did not eliminate bureaucracy, and its overall consequence may have been to strengthen the more conservative forces in society, particularly the bureaucratic structures of the state and the army. It did, however, damage or hinder the legitimation of political institutions, and from 1966 into 1977 political power in China, especially above the provincial level, may have been exercised on a largely ad hoc basis. This is perhaps one of those periods in which a "factionalism model" could be applied to Chinese politics, although not mechanically. There was, for example, rather little of the civility and self-restraint in power struggles that some theorists predict will be produced by a system of factional deadlock.[1] What civility there had been in the system prior to 1966 had eroded. Also, it is difficult to identify factions unambiguously, and the Chinese system may at times have tended to an almost Hobbesian individualism.[2] Rather than speak of specific (unless, of course, there is specific evidence, as in the case of the Gang of Four), it may be more in accord with the known facts to use vaguer terms—forces, categories, and the like.

### Party

Prior to the Cultural Revolution, the major ruling institution had been the Communist Party, but the party as a bureaucratic institution (not as an idea or as a vanguard of revolutionaries) was precisely the major target of the Cultural Revolution. The central organs of the party—the Secretariat and the various departments adhering to it—were ripped apart in 1966 and were not rebuilt completely until the 1980s. At the provincial level, the party organizations were replaced in the late 1960s by the revolutionary committees, which were in most cases simply covers for military rule. The provincial party organizations were rebuilt in the early 1970s as were, at a slower rate, the county party organizations. At that time, however, like the revolutionary committees, they tended to be dominated by soldiers. The CPC remained the largest communist party in the world, and membership in the party remained, for the lucky, a risky but almost only way to power and privilege. The party itself, however, became a sort of coalition of the politically significant groups in China and did not function as a cohesive instrument of rule.

The weakness of the party as such is seen in the succession to Mao. Typically in communist countries the advantage in the succession struggle has gone to the senior party secretary, the person in charge of the party apparatus.[3] When Mao died there was no such position in China. Hua Kuo-feng's power, to the extent it was not a result simply of personal and factional combinations, was based upon his position not in the party but in the *state*; he had succeeded Chou En-lai as premier, and this succession, to the extent that it had institutional rather than personal foundation, was based upon his control of the police as minister of public security. Teng Hsiao-p'ing had once held the position of China's top apparatchik: until 1966 he was the party's general secretary. But this did not do him any good in 1966, when he was purged. By 1980 Teng was rebuilding the central party organizations. His third rise to power, however, was brought about through his alliances with key leaders in the state bureaucracy, the military, and the provinces along with his subsequent ability to put his own supporters into similar positions. Neither he nor Hua controlled the party machinery, there was no machinery to control.

## State

During this period there did remain a state machine of sorts, headed until his death by Chou En-lai. Chou and his group on the State Council were perhaps more consistently antiradical throughout the years than the party apparatus. Chou, however, sided with Mao (or was permitted to side with Mao) against Liu Shao-ch'i, the founding father of the Chinese apparatus and something of its symbol. After the purge of Lin Piao, who was Mao's chosen successor and the head of the army, a struggle between Chou and the Gang of Four continued, the Gang vainly attempting to gain control of the state bureaucracy and Chou vainly attempting to discredit and eliminate the influence of the Gang. Chou was remembered admiringly in the late 1970s for his tact and diplomacy, qualities in his lifetime sometimes hard to distinguish from slipperiness. By refusing to confront Mao or, as long as they were sufficiently strong, the Maoists directly, Chou was able to preserve his own position, and the consensus has been that on the whole this was excellent for China. One wonders, however, whether more genuine prudence might have dictated that Chou be less passive. As it happened, Chou was unable to control his own succession. His choice, Teng Hsiao-p'ing, brought back from hell by Chou in 1973, delivered the eulogy at Chou's funeral and was purged before the ashes cooled.

## Army

Taken as a whole the army, while hardly untouched, was the institution least damaged by the Cultural Revolution, both in its regular chain of command and in its internal party organization. Were the army to act as a unit, it might have been able at certain times to have brought China under direct military rule. The army, however, perhaps more than other political institutions, has failed to act in a consistent manner as a cohesive unit. A plausible interpretation holds that the Chinese military continues to be divided into factions based ultimately upon the old field armies of the civil war period.[4] The period of Lin Piao's glory saw an increase in the number of persons in influential positions from his old Fourth Field Army. Many but not all of these were removed from office following Lin's demise. Other personnel changes hint that factional alliances in the army are rather incohesive and even that the unit of analysis should be the individual, not some faction.[5]

In any case, the major split in the army between 1966 and 1976 probably did not involve simple factional or personal hostilities. There was, rather, a division between the Center in Peking and the regional and provincial commands. During the Cultural Revolution, political power tended to gravitate toward the regional commanders as the army moved to suppress the Red Guards. This increase in military influence was, no doubt, expected by Lin Piao, who was then in overall command of the army as minister of defense and de facto head of the party's Military Affairs Committee. However, the increase in *regional* military influence did not work to Lin's advantage. Lin attempted to maintain an alliance with the radicals at the center, who in turn served as an inspiration for the various radical Red Guard groups throughout China, but Lin's alliance with the radicals excluded his complete endorsement of his subordinates' attempts to restore order. Lin was caught in the middle and antagonized both sides. When Lin plotted (or counterplotted) against Mao in 1971, the "big generals" on the Politburo who worked at headguarters were uniformly with him, but his support in the regions was limited, and few of the more politically important regional or provincial commanders joined him.

If only because of disharmony inside the army, China avoided military rule—but this meant that the military was not a dependable source of political control. While it is possible to speak of the local commanders as a category, the interest they share is a negative one. Were the commanders to act together they might constitute a powerful force, but they have little incentive consistently to act together except as a veto group. A sufficient condition for the fall of the Gang of Four may have been the close-to-unanimous distaste of the local commanders for that group. To the extent that local commanders are politically ambitious, however, they should be expected to be rivals of each other. They may have a common interest in maintaining at least local autonomy, but each will also have an interest in preventing the primacy of any of the others; and should some commanders achieve national power, they will have an incentive to cut down the autonomy of those they left behind. This basic divergence of political interest may have given the civilians leverage against the army. In 1973 the central authorities were able to bring about a massive reshuffle of the regional commands, with, in almost all cases, the commander of one region switching places with the commander of another. Prior to the 1973 transfer, the regional commanders had also been the first secretaries of the provinces in which the regional headquarters were located, which made the commanders minor satraps with military and political power concentrated in their persons. The transfers eliminated this formal basis for political power, although in some cases the influence of the former commander remained through the subordinates that were left behind.

## Bureaucratic or Police Left

Another category whose influence grew during the Cultural Revolution is what Jürgen Domes calls the Secret Police Left,[6] although the term *secret* here is not in all cases correct. Domes includes in this group Hua Kuo-feng, Wang Hung-wen (also, it turned out, a member of the Gang of Four), Wang Tung-hsing (commander of the 8341 Troops, Mao's bodyguard, and also a kind of military political police), and Chi Teng-k'uei (whose precise functions were always a bit unclear). Others in this category might include K'ang Sheng (before liberation he was head of the Social Department, the party's "special work" organization; he was a good friend of Chiang Ch'ing, Mao's wife, and a possible sponsor and patron of Hua Kuo-feng),[7] Wu Te (after the Cultural Revolution, he was first secretary of Peking), and Ni Chih-fu (in 1976 he was head of the urban militia in Peking, a police-type organization sponsored by the radicals partly in the hope of gaining an instrument of coercion independent of the army). This category had close ties with the Gang of Four; for that matter, it overlapped with it. One condition for the purge of members of the Gang was their betrayal by the police left. But while the police left was an important category, it was not a center of stable power. It could not have ruled China by itself. Before 1976 its members tended to work with the Gang. In 1976 they worked with the army and in 1977 they were forced to expand their coalition to include Hau Kuo-feng's rival, Teng Hsiao-p'ing.

## The Establishment Radicals or Inner Court

Another major force was, of course, the radical tendency, reduced at the top level by 1976 to the Gang of Four. Ten years earlier it had been embodied in the Cultural Revolution Group, but this had suffered from purges of its own members just as had other groups and tendencies. The radicals were clearly influential in Chinese politics while Mao lived, but equally clearly they did not dominate the system. The Gang more or less did dominate the agencies of propaganda. While they could not completely exclude the expression of other points of view, these had to be couched in the idiom of the Gang. The Gang thus controlled the tone of political discourse in China.

Members of the Gang, however, did not directly control much else. Their institutional power was limited. They had the city of Shanghai and the urban militias in other cities. More importantly, they had access to Mao himself. The Cultural Revolution Group had served as a kind of general headquarters for the more radical Red Guard groups (or, alternatively, a "radical" group may at times simply have been one that looked to the Central Cultural Revolution Group for support). These seem to have been attracted by the political, anti-authoritarian, antinomian aspects of Maoist idelogy, not by the affirmations of radical Great Leap Forward economic policies. The radical Red Guards were suppressed by the army in the 1968 restoration of order, and the Cultural Revolution Group, solicitous of its own skin, collaborated in this suppression. The Group abandoned political libertarianism and in later years came more and more to speak of "proletarian dictatorship," that is, the need to suppress enemies ruthlessly. The verbal commitment to radical economics remained, but it also remained largely verbal: because of the disastrous consequences of their past application, there was never a genuine systematic attempt to repeat the Great Leap policies. Control over economic management remained largely with Chou En-lai's people; but Gang control of the media prevented the official legitimation of the policies actually implemented.

The Gang did, however, have influence. Some of their supporters participated in the organizational rebuilding of the party in the early 1970s, but so did supporters of Chou En-lai and the local soldiers. Traces of the Cultural Revolution organizations remained. In 1977 the Gang's enemies spoke of a "gang system" (pang-p'ai t'i-hsi) permeating society, a "counter-revolutionary stewpot" of "renegades, spies, class aliens, new bourgeois elements, shameless literateurs, self-prostituting so-called old cadres, political opportunists of all shapes and sizes."[8] Among the productive sectors of the society, the radicals may have had a following among the so-called temporary workers in Chinese factories, workers without permanent contracts who are payed at a lower rate than the regular workers and are generally not given the bonuses that make up a not negligible proportion of the regular workers' income.[9] China was plagued by railway strikes and other labor unrest in 1974 and 1975, and the Gang (or its followers) was later blamed for this,[10] although popular unrest hardly ceased with the purge of the Gang. Members of the Gang also had residual and uneven support among young party members, which they had recruited during the Cultural Revolution, and perhaps among former Red Guards vegetating in the countryside.

## The System as It Functioned

Over all this was Mao Tse-tung, the unmoved pivot. In thought and sentiment he was probably close to the Gang of Four. His now famous alleged statement that gave them their name, "You must not become a gang of four," is not an attack on members of the Gang, but a warning to them that they had better modify their tactics lest they become isolated. The need to issue this warning shows, however it is taken, that Mao was no more in full control of the situation than were the other political forces.

It might be argued that if this description of Chinese politics is accurate the system was more pluralistic than totalitarian. It may have been incipiently pluralistic, and this pluralism would be a necessary condition for any subsequent liberalization. But there is nothing in the theories of totalitarianism requiring a genuinely monolithic structure of rule, and most of those who have discussed totalitarianism as an analytic concept have assumed some sort of factionalism. Totalitarian rule is arbitrary and recognizes no limitations. Hannah Arendt describes the instability of alliances and the insecurity of position in totalitarianism, as subordinates rise and fall at the whim of the leader. Lin Piao's son described the style in 1971: "Today he pulls in that one and beats this one down. Today he pulls in these people with honeyed words, tomorrow slanders them and sends them to the execution ground. His honored guest today is tomorrow a prisoner cringing beneath the throne."[11]

The *style* of politics in 1976 was totalitarian, as was the dominant ideological line. Totalitarian as well were the politicization of all aspects of life and the supervision and control exercised over the lives of ordinary people. There was not a strong totalitarianism in practice, however, because of the weakness of the leader both as a person and in his position. The totalitarian system may contain factional conflicts, but ideally the fate of each faction must rest entirely with the leader. Mao was hardly a negligible factor in Chinese politics, but neither was he everything. The various forces in China had some degree of autonomy not only from each other but also from him.

Mao's weakness as a leader, itself an unintended consequence of Maoist ideology, contributed to this incipient pluralism. Had Mao's control been more like Stalin's, the political structures inherited by his successors would themselves have been more stable, and his successors' prime concern would have been to bring about a little bit of security for themselves within those structures. They would have had an incentive to preserve the status quo, and after the power struggle would have settled down to a stable, repressive post-totalitarian rule. The chaos of Mao's last years may have been in its effect not much less vicious than the official terror in other totalitarian systems, especially since the chaos supplemented the official terror rather than replaced it. But chaos may allow an openness not present in a more stable system.

## POPULAR MORALE AND THE STYLE OF RULE IN THE AFTERMATH OF THE CULTURAL REVOLUTION

By 1976 China was ready for a turn away from radicalism. The party bureaucrats and the older intellectuals (despite the poses these latter had been forced to strike in the early 1970s) could not have been expected to have had good feelings about the Cultural Revolution. The Cultural Revolution also induced disillusionment with the radical status quo among those to whom radicalism might have been expected to appeal. The problem with Maoist radicalism was that it was really an "establishment" position, despite its masquerade as opposition. That it wore the masquerade, however, meant that it was also incapable of legitimizing the status quo.

Early in the Cultural Revolution, radical ideology contained a strong anti-authoritarian strain. Mao once said that the whole meaning of Stalin's life is summed up in the phrase, to rebel is justified. This became the slogan of the radical Red Guards. The targets of the rebellion were those persons in position of power in the established institutions, particularly in the party machinery. The anti-authoritarian ideology suited the Cultural Revolution Group until its members' themselves needed to consolidate institutional authority, and to the end the residual commitment to radicalism prevented them from doing that. Hong Yung Lee asserts: "It was the practice of the . . . Group to support the radicals from the lower strata of Chinese society." The Cultural Revolution Group itself would agree with this, but might not be happy with the interesting twist to Lee's argument: those groups in fact most dissatisfied were those defined by the regime and even by the Cultural Revolution Group as composed of the privileged—the children of "buorgeois" background.[12] The more radical students, Lee argues, were those who came from families that had lost status after liberation. It is not clear that Lee's thesis is universally valid, but it is certainly plausible. The hegemonic Marxist-Leninist-Maoist ideology meant that oppression had somehow to be defined along class lines, and the Maoist ideology of the Cultural Revolution was full of talk of class struggle. But by 1965 the landlords of China were oppressing no one, while the party bureaucrats were the lords of creation. The radicals' political rather than economic definition of class seems blatantly un-

Marxist, but in a society such as China's, or in contemporary society generally, it may be the only way in which class analysis can retain any utility.[13] Maoist ideology gave the genuinely deprived categories in Chinese society a "respectable" way to voice their grievances. As the Cultural Revolution Group absorbed itself into the power structure, its radicalism became hollow, but its effects on society lingered. That, on the whole, the Cultural Revolution resulted in the ascendency of relatively conservative forces (conservative in the sense of supporting the status quo), such as the army and the police, no doubt contributed to disillusionment with the methods of the establishment radicals, as well as with their persons.

Disillusionment was not confined to abstract disappointment. The youthful discontent mobilized by the Cultural Revolution seems to have been a result of psychological pressure from the heavily controlled and highly politicized school system and was in some ways ("changing what needs to be changed") analogous to the discontent among students in postindustrial societies at the same time. The Cultural Revolution brought real physical oppression—the fights and terror of the Cultural Revolution itself and the intensified rustication movement that was used to suppress it. This discontent fed a stream of protests from educated youth, whether in China itself or in exile, with the ideas built upon the radicalism of the early Cultural Revolution. The protest stressed political radicalism rather than economic collectivism and as the years wore on became increasingly wary of appeals to dictatorship.[14]

The Red Guard movement had become highly fragmented, but also showed a survival of the Chinese genius for forming far-flung, complex organizations based upon overlapping primary relationships. These groups and alliances were often linked one way or another with parts of the establishment, whether with the military or with the Cultural Revolution Group, but they were also autonomous organizations, not simply Leninist transmission belts. The military attempted to suppress these groups in a systematic fashion from 1968 on but does not seem in all cases to have succeeded. Rather, the Red Guard organizations survived underground (at times, perhaps, with the collusion of the allies of the Gang of Four, as part of the gang system), in the manner described in that interesting potboiler, *The Coldest Winter in Peking*.[15] This organizational style continued into the democratic movement of 1978 and 1979, and it is tempting to suspect that some groups in that movement were organized around illegal former Red Guard networks.[16]

Some assert that while revolution is costly in terms of liberty and in itself does little to improve the standard of living, at least it leads to a strengthening of community. The Chinese case gives little reason to think this is true. Rather, after the revolution all life becomes organized and all organizations politicized. This kind of totalitarian control might give the illusion of common feeling and singleness of purpose, but, whatever its mass base, in China it was control from above and had none of the spontaneity associated with the word community. In a classic formulation, the model social relationship was transformed from one among friends to one among comrades.[17] The Red Guard organizations and their descendants may mean the restoration of community at least among peer groups, but their appearance is a symptom of the loss of social control. The regime complains of undisciplined thought and behavior left over from the time of "Lin Piao and the 'Gang of Four.'" The crime rate is increasing in large and middle-sized towns. There is a growth of "gangsterism," and people were said to be forming links with "foreign countries and Taiwan."[18] The regime wishes to show that the democratic movement had been infiltrated by criminals and traitors, and not all of what it says needs to be taken literally. But the regime's allegations of social demoralization are perhaps not without objective basis.

The Cultural Revolution not only brought an increase in the open use of terror,[19] it is also held to have been a period of economic suffering. Workers' wages had been frozen since before the Cultural Revolution. Among the demonstrators in Peking in January 1979 were peasants, many of them rusticated youths or workers sent back to their native villages in the early 1960s during the famine that followed the collapse of the Great Leap. These peasants complained of lack of food in their home areas and of official indifference.[20] Stories of starvation do not acoord well with the impressions of foreign visitors before the purge of the Gang, and the demonstrators were persons who in any case would have preferred to have been living in the city. But it is possible they were not ignorant of economic conditions in the places where they lived.

The Cultural Revolution did benefit persons who otherwise might not have been able to achieve their ambitions, persons who became part of the so-called gang system. *People's Literature* published a kind of "non-fiction short story" about a woman in Heilungkiang who had allied herself with the rebel faction and so came to a position of authority in her county. "She discovered: there is nothing like political power to let you make all your dreams come true." The story describes how she and her sons were able to use patronage to develop a political machine and then use the political machine as the basis for a large-scale black market operation. The story's publication was no doubt designed to further rather specific political ambitions, but the hard language the author was permitted to use is perhaps testimony to social demoralization phenomena such as those he describes: "Oh, Fatherland, are these the masters of the People's Republic, the masters of the proletarian dictatorship? Is this our working class?"[21] Complaints about official corruption continue, and cupidity would seem to be no monopoly of the radical tendency.

Disenchantment may extend to the peak of the regime. In 1979 Ch'en Yun, long ago one of the most important men in the party, ignored for more than two decades because of the moderate nature of his views on economic policy, is alleged by the Taiwan regime to have said some blunt things after his return to the top. Peking claims, not very convincingly, that the speech is a fabrication, and it should therefore probably not be used to prove too much. But, according to Taiwan, Ch'en said:

> If I had known how for decades I would have been mistreated, I don't know about others but I, Ch'en Yun, would have run away from Yenan with Chang Kuo-t'ao and joined Chiang Kai-shek. The more comfortable we are, the more we fear. What are we afraid of? Of losing power . . .
>
> In the past we all used to say, "Class struggle in society must be reflected in the party." As a matter of fact, that's correct. But could it be that factional struggles, power struggles, in the party are not reflected in society? . . . If the common people remove the lid, we could lose our power.[22]

Ch'en's words, to put it mildly, express disenchantment in almost the literal sense of that term. The Communist Party is seen as a ruling group like any other, with all the faults of ruling groups, one which is in danger of being overthrown, and which, in fact, on the basis of its record to date may well deserve to be overthrown. Since the late 1970s, there has been malaise, with chaos in society and in the party mutually reflecting each other. Below is shrill impatience, above pusillanimous vacillation. Another part of the legacy of the lost decade, however, was a break in totalitarion control and a status quo that few if any had much incentive to maintain on its merits, apart from the fear of what would come with change.

## COMING TO A HEAD: THE POWER STRUGGLE 1975–76

Mao's second chosen successor, Lin Piao, was killed in 1971, supposedly following his attempt to murder Mao.[23] For about a year before this, there seems to have been an alliance between Lin and Chou En-lai, with the leftist tendency being gradually frozen from power.[24] For a year or so following the death of Lin, the rightist tendency continued to consolidate itself. In April 1973 Chou En-lai, already a sick man, brought about a rehabilitation of Teng Hsiao-p'ing, who had been purged at the beginning of the Cultural Revolution as China's number-two capitalist roader.

In 1973 the left began to recover strength. At the beginning of the Cultural Revolution, China's universities had been shut down. When they were reopened, entrance examinations were abolished on the grounds that it was bourgeois to judge students by academic aptitude or achievement rather than by political and ideological criteria. By 1973, however, Chou En-lai's people had managed more or less surreptitiously to reintroduce entrance examinations. This gave an advantage to those students just finishing high school at the expense of those who had spent the past few years up in the mountains and down on the farm, in conformity with Maoist policy. One of the latter, finding the physics test too difficult, turned in a blank answer sheet along with a letter denouncing the betrayal of the revolution. This captured the attention of Mao Yuan-hsin, the chairman's nephew and a party official in the indignant student's province, Liaoning.[25] The student became a media hero, someone who dared to resist the tide. Resistance to the tide—to Chou En-lai's bureaucracy and its increasing strength—became a theme of the Tenth Party Congress, held in August of 1973. This congress also marked the rise to prominence of Wang Hung-wen, the youngest of the Gang of Four. The major ongoing media event of 1974, the "criticism of Lin Piao and Confucius," was dominated by the left, although its beginnings in late 1972 may have been part of an attempt by Chou's group to discredit the left.[26]

The leftist drive seems to have dissipated by 1975. The regime's Fourth National People's Congress, held in January of that year, became Chou En-lai's last hurrah. In his political report to the congress, Chou stressed the need for planning to develop the economy and to promote the "four modernizations" (of agriculture, defense, industry, and science and technology).[27] The congress adopted a new constitution based upon a draft that had been circulating since 1969. It provided some formal regularity to state structure for the first time since 1966 and gave legal guarantees to the economic policies adopted in the wake of the collapse of the Great Leap Forward: limitations on the degree of agricultural collectivization, the right of households to private plots, and remuneration according to labor. Such policies would tend to encourage productivity, although perhaps at some cost to equality. These policies had been denounced by the Maoists, although their efforts to change them rarely came to anything. Mao did not attend this congress but had himself photographed elsewhere chatting with Franz-Josef Strauss, the hawkish anti-Soviet conservative German politician, presumably to demonstrate it was not because he was sick that he did not attend.

A leftist counterattack began at once. The March 1975 issue of *Red Flag* began with words of Mao to the effect that too rigid a definition of the state structure (as, we are to take it, in the constitution just adopted), too many set rules, and the like would allow a "Lin Piao-type to mount the stage and set up [*kao*] a capitalist system." This was followed by pages of quotations from Marx, Engels, and Lenin expounding proletarian dictatorship, dictatorship here being contrasted with rule through law (again, implicitly, as in the new constitution), which freezes the status quo and prevents further development.[28] The theme was elaborated in essays in this issue and the subsequent one by, respectively, Yao Wen-yuan and Chang Ch'un-ch'iao, who together made up the intellectual half of the Gang of Four. Their articles represent a return to the mood of the Cultural Revolution but without the mass movement. They attack empiricism, the word here having at least a double meaning. Most directly it is a slap at the old cadres who, unlike the people recruited into the party under the protection of the Gang, could vaunt themselves on their experience in life, revolution, and production. More pedantically it refers to reliance upon experience of what works, regardless of what Marxist (that is, Maoist) theory says should work. The attack on empiricism is a tacit admission that the moderate policies were successful, whereas the radical ones were not. But an empirical orientation will perpetuate China as a nation of "small producers" (peasants), over which the party will become a new ruling class. Strict dictatorship uninhibited by legalisms is required to prevent the emergence of this new class. Legal rights (*fa-ch'üan*) such as those embodied in the constitution (Yao and Chang leave this last phrase unspoken, of course, but their meaning is obvious) are perhaps necessary in the present stage of social and economic development but they are also transitory and are to be limited. They should not be treated as permanent or expanded. These legal rights form the basis for a new ruling class that spontaneously emerges from the party.[29] Behind the tortuous (but not totally invalid) reasoning was an attack on the institutional structure Chou En-lai was trying to build.

Yao Wen-yuan had called for *an-ting t'uan-chieh*, peace and unity. Chang, a month later, did not make the same mistake, since the phrase was tailor-made for the moderates, who lost no time in taking it up and accusing the radicals of bourgeois factionalism. By this time the struggle had perhaps passed Chou En-lai by, as he sickened to his death, and leadership of the moderate forces fell to Teng Hiao-p'ing.

Teng was no match for Chou in tact and craft, but he surpassed him in blunt courage. In the 1920s he had suffered at the hands of the Bolshevik faction in the party for his support of Mao, and after liberation he was not afraid to stand up to Mao himself. At the Eighth Party Congress in 1956, Teng more or less echoed Krushchev's criticism of the cult of the individual (Ch'en Yun says this was Teng's big mistake) but blandly claimed that China had never been cursed with that particular problem.[30] Teng's remarks may not have been directly anti-Mao, but they are an assertion of the supremacy of the party as a whole over its leader. As Teng's famous comment about the white cat and the black cat—who cares, as long as he catches the mice—shows, he was not an ideological zealot, but neither was he an easygoing liberal or a quasi-crypto-Social Democrat like Ch'en Yun. He was, rather, a disciplinarian and an organization man and, in the context of the 1950s, a lard-liner. Upon returning to power in 1977, after his second purge, Teng was to make much use of Mao's hundred flowers slogan. He was not, however, a supporter of the original campaign, and his main contribution to the political discourse of that time was a denunciation of the rightists, who took the slogan about blooming and contending too literally. Teng's remarks leave the impression that if he had had his way the liberalization would not have been tried in the first place.[31] His attitude toward dissent may have mellowed as a result of his own mistreatment, but even so his feelings about the democratic movement of the late 1970s were bound to be ambivalent.

Around August 1975 Teng caused to have circulated within the party a "General Program for All the Work of the Whole Party and the Whole Country." This was apparently drafted by Hu Yao-pang and Hu Ch'iao-mu, later Teng's close collaborators in the reform movement, but in 1975 still in official disgrace following their purge in the Cultural Revolution. The proqram denounces the Maoists (very indirectly, of course) and defends the moderate economic policies. Given the hegemonic position of radical ideology at that time, the program does not elaborate any principled attack on the Gang, and its criticisms are of the so's-your-old-man variety: "Waving the flag of antirevisionism they practice revisionism . . . ," etc., etc., etc. They are "new bourgeois elements, arising from [what else?] small producers." "In order to recognize political imposters one cannot be satisfied with their words, one must look also at their deeds." In other words, in those days the words of the Gang could only be held to be entirely proper. Teng also manages to adapt the radical slogan about opposing the tide: "Dare to lead and struggle against anti-Marxist class enemies, against those leaders who continue to practice bourgeois factionalism, against all erroneous tendencies which oppose the political line, policies, and measures of the Party."[32] Teng turns the radical rhetoric of defiance back against the radicals. This theme is to obey and dare to oppose those who refuse to obey.

This phase of the struggle culminated with the Tachai conference in the fall of 1975. Tachai, a village in Shansi province, was in those days the model of good agricultural policy. The peasants were said to work very hard and to rely on their own efforts, not the state; they worked for the love of the revolution and the people, not for money. Agriculture there was also more highly collectivized than was typical for most of China, although this aspect of Tachai did not receive as much publicity as its hard work and self-reliance. In general, Tachai was a symbol for anything desirable in agricultural policy, the content of what was considered desirable varying from time to time. The 1975 conference promised the "basic mechanization" of Chinese agriculture by 1980, a goal that was not achieved. With its emphasis on the economic infrastructure, improvements in the standard of living, and increased productivity, in general with all that the radicals affected to consider goulash communism, the conference, despite its grandiose promises, was a victory for the moderate tendency, if not a decisive one. Both Teng Hsiao-p'ing and Chiang Ch'ing spoke at the conference, but their words were not published. The major published speech was Hua Kuo-feng's, [33] his position probably being a compromise of the other two, but perhaps closer to Chiang Ch'ing's than to Teng's.

Hua, then minister of security and still nominally the first secretary of the Hunan provincial party committee, had spent most of his career as a party functionary in Hunan, Mao's home province. He himself, however, is not a native of Hunan. He held a variety of positions, and some analysts believe that he was an administrative "generalist" with his main competence in agricultural management.[34] His transfers from one unit to another rather regularly corresponded with purges in the unit he was being moved into, suggesting that in fact his main connection was with the police system. For what it is worth, a dissident pamphlet describes sordid relations between Hua's mother and K'ang Sheng, the late head of the party's police and espionage system, and K'ang is alleged to have acted as Hua's patron.[35] Again, for what it is worth, K'ang, who died in December 1975, continued to be praised as a great man during the period of Hua's ascendency, only to be denounced posthumously after the second return of Teng Hsiao-p'ing. Hua's first major promotion came during the campaign against right opportunism in 1959 under circumstances that suggest it was a reward for his timely betrayal of his superior.[36] During the Cultural Revolution, he was himself attacked by ultraleftist Red Guards, but these did not have the sympathy of the Cultural Revolution Group, and the attack did Hua no harm. In 1970 he became head of the reconstituted Hunan party committee, the first of the provincial party committees to be rebuilt following the Cultural Revolution. In 1971 he was brought to Peking, according to rumor to conduct the investigation into Lin Piao's crimes, and in 1973 he became a member of the Politburo. Hua seemed out of place in that company of tough soldiers and Long March veterans, skilled schemers, and hangers-on in the imperial retinue. On the whole he appears to have been a time-serving career bureaucrat, exhibiting no particular qualities in public that would raise him above the hundreds of thousands of his colleagues. Despite the cult he later attempted to develop around himself, he remains colorless. The cult praised him for his modesty. It would be easy to echo Churchill and say he has much to be modest about, but chances are this modesty is genuine. At the time of the purge of the Gang of Four, he seemed unexpectedly tough. But thereafter he was consistently outmaneuvered and outfought by Teng Hsiao-p'ing. Yet even after his many demotions and humiliations he remains, if not popular, at least not deeply disliked either by the population or by other members of the elite. He has the reputation of being one of the few in the hierarchy not to have used political power for petty material advantage for himself or his family. Hua's speech at Tachai is perhaps the outward sign that he was being groomed as counterheir to Teng Hsiao-p'ing, the more obvious counterheir, Chang Ch'un-ch'iao, being too closely identified with one faction to win general support before another major harrowing of the party.

The Tachai conference itself was a victory for the right, and this was followed in the propaganda field by a celebration of the Long March and the role of the party old guard in that retreat. The leftist counterattack came in a curious fashion. One of Mao's favorite books, the world had always been given to believe, was *Water Margin*, the story of good fellows forced into banditry by corrupt government. The conventional Marxist view had been that the book represents the popular outlook as opposed to that of the gentry. The anti-Confucius campaign had praised progressive peasant rebellions and *Water Margin* had been considered a literary treatment of peasant rebellion. In August 1975 a writer in the leading leftist intellectual journal, *Study and Criticism*, made these conventional points and added an equally conventional demurrer: the book does not, after all, present genuine revolution; the rebels "only oppose corrupt officials, not the emperor."[37]

A few days later the papers published a directive of Mao, using exactly the same words, but denouncing the novel as a negative example. The robber leader, Sung Chiang, was a "capitulationist": in return for an amnesty, he had surrendered to the emperor and had turned to fight other bandits.[38] As the denunciations of *Water Margin* accumulated during that dreary fall, it became as clear as this sort of thing ever is that Sung Chiang was a symbol for Chou En-lai, Teng Hsiao-p'ing, or both, although the precise nature of the charges being made against them, if they had a precise nature, was not pellucid.

By the end of the year, the left seemed to have prevailed. Teng's critique of the left of the previous summer was itself criticized as "strange talk and bizarre theories," *ch'i-t'an kuai-lun*.[39] A pseudo-Red Guard movement began at Peking and Tsinghua universities, although this time it was made clear that the big debate, as slander campaigns were called in Mao's day, would take place under the "monolithic leadership of the party": and there would be no disorder.[40] The faculties and administrations of the two universities were purged, as was the Ministry of Education. On New Year's day two poems by Mao, written a decade earlier, were published for the first time, condemning "goulash communism." Mao was later said to have said that the need for peace and unity (a slogan by then entirely coopted by the moderates) does not mean there should be no class struggle.[41] Chou En-lai died in early January, and if his rites were not quite as abbreviated as the enemies of the Gang later pretended, neither was he mourned with the enthusiasm that might have been thought appropriate for one of his historical stature. Teng Hsiao-p'ing disappeared from public view immediately after delivering Chou's eulogy, and in early February Hua Kuo-feng became acting premier.

The left had triumphed, but the left itself seems to have felt its triumph hollow. There was a later claim that Hua's promotion had aroused the jealousy of Chang Ch'un-ch'iao. Chang, is said to have written, apparently for his own edification, a little essay entitled "Thoughts on February 2" (the day Hua took office as premier):

> He comes on fast and fierce, and he will fall hard. A mistaken line will never work. It may have its way for a time and it will seem as if all under heaven is his, as if some new "era" were beginning. They always overestimate their strength. The people are the decisive factor. Those who represent the interest of the people, who plan for the interest of the people, who under all conditions stand on the side of the people, on the side of the progressive elements, these will prevail.

As even the denunciation of this essay makes clear, however, whatever they may have really thought, publicly the Gang supported Hua: "Their mouths said yes but their hearts said no."[42] Chang's brave words, whatever their specific import (it is far from obvious that their specific import is what the Hua regime was later to say it was), may indicate deeper misgivings; members of the Gang seem to have been well aware of their isolation and unpopularity.[43]

Chang soon received direct evidence, if he needed it, of how at least one articulate segment of the people felt about him and the other progressive elements. The Ch'ing Ming (bright and clear) festival falls in the spring, about two months after the Lunar New Year. On that day Chinese families tidy up the graves of their dead, pay their respects, and maybe have a picnic in the graveyard. On Ch'ing Ming 1976, wreaths had been placed on the monument to Chou En-lai in the main square of Peking. Many had been placed by "mass" organizations—groups formed independently of the party by people in factories, offices, and schools. The wreaths were removed by the police over the weekend, and on April 5 people began gathering in the square to protest their removal. The crowd eventually grew to about 100,000 persons, and the demonstration became a protest, if not against the regime itself, at least against the Maoist tendency. The targets of the protest included the "First Ch'in Emperor," Mao himself, and the "*hsiu-ts'ai*" or petty scholars who had "castrated Marxism-Leninism," meaning, in effect, the Gang of Four, or at least Chang Ch'un-ch'iao and Yao Wen-yuan. The protests spread in subsequent days to other cities, and in Canton there were attacks on the empress dowager, or Chiang Ch'ing. The demands actually made were mild compared with what was to come later, but the protest was unprecedented in the history of the People's Republic. The demonstration was broken up by the urban militia, with the army apparently remaining uninvolved (although the commander of the Peking troops, Ch'en Hsi-lien, was later to share the blame for the suppression). There was violence on both sides, and the more active demonstrators were jailed.[44]

The demonstration was perhaps more against the radicals than in favor of Chou En-lai, but it was also for Teng Hsiao-p'ing as the only alternative to the radicals. The regime at the time blamed Teng for the riots, a charge so absurd that when Teng had returned to power and the riots were rehabilitated he was not even able to take credit for them. Rather, as the beneficiaries claimed, the riots were spontaneous and no major leader or party organization had anything to do with them. The riots provided the pretext for the formal, public purge of Teng. Before the riots he had been attacked indirectly and by innuendo. Now he was denounced openly by name and removed from all his official positions, although the announcement of his dismissal noted that he retained his party membership.[45]

The main direct beneficiary of Teng's disgrace was, once again, not the Gang, but Hua Kuo-feng. Hua became the real not just the acting premier and later in April allegedly received the cryptic commendation from Mao, "With you in charge my heart's at ease." The riots caused a rallying of the previously divided elite. Teng was publicly denounced by the local political and military satraps, many of whom had been and were to be again his allies. The old soldier Yeh Chien-ying, the most active of the party's remaining *genro*, had disappeared from view in February. According to rumor he had retired to his home town to sulk about the way things were going. After the riots he returned to Peking. This rallying together of the elite served to limit the influence of the Gang, who were eager to extend the purge. The criticism remained restricted to Teng himself, without involving his supporters in official positions.

Teng, one suspects, rather more than most people must realize that politics is politics, although one might also wonder with what warmth inside he remembers how his friends picked at his wounds. This time, at least, Teng may have escaped physical abuse (although there was a rumor at the time that he had been shot while trying to force his way in to see Mao). According to stories, he was not put in jail but found refuge with Hsu Shih-yu, commander of the Canton military region.

As the criticism of Teng droned on during the spring and summer, nature seemed to take a hand. In late July a horrifying series of earthquakes hit northern China, devastating particularly the mining and industrial city of T'ang-shan. China had previously boasted of its ability to predict earthquakes, and one gathers that Chinese work in this field was the most advanced in the world. This time, however, there seems to have been no warning, and the death toll was enormous. The official response was, to put it mildly, tasteless. The earthquakes were held to be a glorious opportunity for people to demonstrate their ability to work miracles. One story told how miners buried for 15 days had been sustained by contemplating the thoughts of Mao. A major theme was the "linking" of relief work to the class struggle: if we were able to whip Teng Hsiao-p'ing, we are certainly able to whip the earthquake. The "masses" were improbably reported as saying: an earthquake only lasts a minute, but capitalist roaders in the party go on forever.[46] This callousness was later blamed on the Gang of Four, no doubt correctly.[47] It might also have been in part a subtle form of sabotage by journalists and censors.

In September nature struck again, Mao dying on the ninth day of that month. About a month later the Gang was arrested. The Gang may, as alleged, have been preparing a coup of its own. The weakness of the Gang's position meant that it had to take drastic action, and its failure only drives home how weak its position had really become.[48]

By the time Mao died China was ready for fundamental change. Perhaps ironically, the Gang was in the vanguard of those demanding change, sometimes even to the point of seeming to call for a revolution against the Communist Party. In 1976 the Gang cited an alleged statement of Mao's: "In making socialist revolution, don't you know where the bourgeoisie is? It is inside the Communist party, the power holders in the party walking the capitalist road."[49] Future dissidents in China will be able to draw upon Mao's "legacy of anti-authoritarianism."[50]

There is complexity here, however, since it was also Maoism that made change seem so desirable and gave people something to dissent against. The issue is not simply that of the Gang of Four or even Mao as persons, but of the system that had allowed members of the Gang and their leader to do what they had done. The major forces at the national level at the time of Mao's death were the establishment radicals, the police left, the military, and the rational modernizers on the State Council. The purge of the Gang meant the elimination of the establishment radicals by the other three forces. The Hua Kuo-feng regime was dominated by people who had benefited, or at least not greatly suffered, from the Maoist system. Could they have had their own way, they would probably not have pushed for basic change but would have settled for a tamed, watered down Maoism, a kind of routinized totalitarianism. Basic change, if it were to come, would have to come from those the Gang tried to destroy.

# NOTES

1. Andrew J. Nathan, "A Factionalism Model for CCP Politics," *China Quarterly* 53 (January/March 1973): 32–66.

2. Anthropoligical evidence indicates that Chinese "particularistic ties" tend to be diffuse and pluralistic. See J. Bruce Jacobs, "A Preliminary Model of Particularistic Ties in Chinese Political Alliances: *Kan-ch'ing* and *Kuan-hsi* in a Rural Taiwanese Township," *China Quarterly* 78 (June 1979): 237–78. When the Chinese act in politics, they, like everyone else, tend to act in concert with others, and Chinese political alliances may often rest on or entail the fictitious creation of personal ties (a phenomenon I suspect is not that rare elsewhere, regardless of what the theories of tradition and modernity may say). But identifiable and longstanding factions may be much less a general feature of Chinese politics than of, say, Japanese. Compare Chie Nakane, *Japanese Society* (Berkeley: University of California Press, 1970).

3. Myron Rush, *How Communist States Change Their Rulers* (Ithaca, N.Y.: Cornell University Press, 1974), p. 285.

4. William Whitson, "The Field Army in Chinese Communist Politics," *China Quarterly* 37 (January/March 1969): 1–30.

5. For example, Hsiao Hua had been Lin Piao's spokesman until he was purged sometime in the summer of 1967. Yang Ch'eng-wu was Lin's spokesman until he in turn fell in the spring of 1968. The two articulated somewhat different lines, but both lines were later attributed to Lin. Both were rehabilitated after Lin's death and as of 1980 both remained in good favor. Their stories somehow belie an interpretation of Chinese politics in terms of rigid factionalism.

6. Jürgen Domes, *China after the Cultural Revolution: Politics Between Two Party Congresses* (Berkeley: University of California Press, 1977). p. 200.

7. See the scurrilous attack on Hua and his poor mother circulated in Canton in 1977, translated in *China News Analysis* 1090 (August 19, 1977): 2–5.

8. Yü Ch'ing, "Thoroughly Smash the Gang System of the 'Gang of Four,' " *Jen-min Jih-pao* [People's Daily], August 6, 1977 (hereafter cited as *PD*).

9. Lynn T. White, III, *Careers in Shanghai: The Social Guidance of Personal Energies in a Developing Chinese City, 1949-1966* (Berkeley: University of California Press, 1978), pp. 101, 145.

10. *PD*, January 5, 1977.

11. " '571' Engineering Outline," *Chung-kung Yen-chiu*, July 1972, p. 101.

12. Hong Yung Lee, *The Politics of the Cultural Revolution: A Case Study* (Berkeley: University of California Press, 1978), p. 223 and passim.

13. Ralf Dahrendorf, *Class and Class Conflict in Industrial Society* (Stanford: Stanford University Press, 1959). I wonder, however, how much is really gained by treating relations between rulers and ruled as relations of *class*.

14. For an attempt at a systematic survey of this protest, see Peter R. Moody, Jr., *Opposition and Dissent in Contemporary China* (Stanford: Hoover Institution Press, 1977), pp. 202–36. On the "duplication, item by item," of the political grievances of the various movements, see Leo Ou-fan Lee, "Dissent Literature from the Cultural Revolution" *Chinese Literature* 1 (January 1979): 75.

15. Hsia Chih-yen, *The Coldest Winter in Peking* (Garden City, N.Y.: Doubleday, 1978).

16. For example, the "Society of Light," which was active in Peking in the spring of 1979, had first appeared in remote Kweichow province the previous fall. In 1979 its headquarters had apparently moved to Yunnan, and it was preparing to set up branches in all of China's major cities. See Agence France Presse, April 25, 1979 in Federal Broadcast Information Service, *Daily Report, People's Republic of China* April 26, 1979, p. L1 (hereafter cited as *FBIS/PRC*).

17. Ezra Vogel, "From Friendship to Comradeship: The Change in Personal Relations in Communist China," *China Quarterly* 21 (January/March 1965): 46–60. For a detailed description of the techniques of social control, see Martin King Whyte, *Small Groups and Political Rituals in China* (Berkeley: University of California Press, 1974).

18. *PD* January 29, 1980.

19. The famous Li I-che wall poster (Li I-che, "On Socialist Democracy and Legality," *Chung-kung Yen-chiu*, November 1975, p. 119) claims that 40,000 persons had been killed in Kwangtung province alone. Teng Hsiao-p'ing sponsored celebrations of persons murdered by the Gang in jail, particularly the dignified matron Chang Chih-hsin, who remained loyal to the party despite her heinous mistreatment (see *Kuang-ming Jih-pao*, June 5, 1979). The most famous of the democratic dissidents, Wei Ching-sheng, published an exposé of the conditions of political prisoners under the Gang: "A Twentieth Century Bastille: Ch'in-ch'eng Prison No. 1," *T'an-so* 2 (1978). Alleged descriptions of Chiang Ch'ing in her confinement do not generate confidence that prison conditions have become much more humane. See Tien Feng, "Chiang Ch'ing in Jail," *Cheng Ming* 8 (June 1978) in *FBIS/PRC*, June 7, 1978, pp. N2–N3.

20. Agence France Presse, January 14, 1979 in *FBIS/PRC*, January 15, 1979, pp. E1–E2.

21. Liu Ping-yen, "Between Man and Devil," *Jen-min Wen-hseuh* 9 (September 1979): 88, 94. Wang Shou-hsin, the poor villainess of the story, was executed in the spring of 1980.

22. *Chung-yang Jih-pao*, March 22, 1980.

23. Michael Y. M. Kau, ed., *The Lin Piao Affair: Power Politics and Military Coup*, (White Plains, N.Y.: International Arts and Sciences Press, 1975). I have drawn in my discussion of the politics of this period from the fine study by Jürgen Domes, *Politics after the Cultural Revolution*, although my interpretations often differ in details from his.

24. This is confirmed, in a way, by an article that attempts to show that Lin Piao and the Gang were exactly the same. It is conceded that after the second plenum of the Ninth Central Committee (late summer 1970, which was about a year before Lin's death) the Gang "pretended" to oppose Lin. See Shen T'ao-sheng, "The 'Gang of Four' and Lin Piao," *PD*, May 18, 1978. The ideological similarities between Lin and the Gang are clear enough, but the article also shows that Lin and the Gang represented distinct political forces, sometimes in alliance, and sometimes in opposition.

25. For example, see ibid., April 9, 1977.

26. This, at least, is what I once argued, although I cannot say that my interpretation has been unambiguously vindicated by later developments. See Peter R. Moody, Jr., "The New Anti-Confucius Campaign in China: The First Round," *Asian Survey* 14 (April 1974): 307–24. An attack on Yang Jung-kuo ("a certain professor"), who led this campaign in late 1972, restricts its criticisms to his activities in 1974 and implies that his position was in fact not exactly the same as that of the Gang. Rather, he capitulated to the Gang through a combination of conceit and fear. Shih Ch'un, "A Certain Professor's Ambush Historiography," *PD*, April 19, 1978.

27. *PD*, January 21, 1975.

28. *Hung Ch'i* [Red Flag] 3 (March 1, 1975): 1–19.

29. Yao Wen-yuan, "On the Social Base of the Lin Piao Anti-Party Clique," *Red Flag* 3 (March 1, 1975): 20–29; Chang Ch'un-ch'iao, "On Full-Scale Dictatorship over the Bourgeoisie," ibid., 4 (April 1, 1975): 3–16. Western analysts are particularly prone to stress the affinity between the CPC and the Chinese peasantry, but the communists themselves blame much of what they dislike about each other on the peasants. Some months before, Yao wrote that the Li I-che dissidents ("Socialist Democracy and Legality") developed a superficially similar argument but said it was the prevalence of the petty producer mentality that allowed China to develop leftist distortions such as the Lin Piao system—meaning the ideology of the Gang of Four. This argument, which has a long heritage in general Marxist thought, was

taken up by Teng Hsiao-p'ing's people in their 1980 drive against the left and the "restoration faction."

30. Teng Hsiao-p'ing, "Report on the Revision of the Party Constitution," *Jen-min Shou-ts'e* (1957): 26–37; for Ch'en Yun's comments, see *Chung-yang Jih-pao*, March 22, 1980.

31. Teng Hsiao-p'ing, "Report on the Rectification Movement," *Jen-min Shou-ts'e*, 1958, pp. 33–42.

32. *Teng Hsiao-p'ing and the "General Program"* (San Francisco: Red Sun, 1977), pp. 4–5, 17.

33. Hua Kuo-feng, "The Whole Party Should Mobilize, Do a Lot of Work in Agriculture, Fight to Make Universal Tachai-like Counties," *PD*, October 21, 1975.

34. Michel Oksenberg and Sai-cheung Yeung, "Hua Kuo-feng's Pre-Cultural Revolution Hunan Years, 1949–1966: The Making of a Political Generalist," *China Quarterly* 69 (March 1977): 3–53.

35. *China News Analysis*, August 19, 1977. A Hong Kong communist source, however, dates the association of Hua and K'ang only to 1970. See *Inside China Mainland*, March 1981, p. 15.

36. Oksenberg and Yeung, "Pre-Cultural Revolution," p. 29.

37. Hsu Yun-hsi, "An Informal View of a Little Literary History," *Hsueh-hsi yü P'i-p'an* 8 (August 18, 1975):59.

38. *PD*, September 4, 1975; for a convenient compilation of the criticism, see *Fan-mien Chiao-ts'ai "Shui-hu,"* edited by the Chinese department of Peking National University (Peking: *Jen-min Ch'u-pan She*, 1975).

39. *PD*, December 11, 1975.

40. Ibid., January 14, 1976.

41. Ibid., January 23, 1976.

42. Wei Hau and Tung Hsiao, "Iron Proof of a Plot to Usurp the Party," ibid., December 13, 1976. I have translated Chang's passage in a way to accord with the official interpretation. It is written in a terse style, however, and the citations of it are not given any context. The first sentence in the Chinese has no specified subject, for example, and what I have rendered as "he" could in reality be "they." For that matter the whole passage could be gloating over the defeat of Teng Hsiao-p'ing and not, as we are told, grumbling about the good fortune of Hua Kuo-feng.

43. For anecdotal evidence of this, see Ch'en Chung, "Put the 'Gang of Four's' Magazine *Study and Criticism* in the Prisoner's Dock," *Li-shih Yen-chiu* 1 (February 20, 1977): 29–39.

44. For contemporary material on the riots, see *T'ien-an-men Shih-chien Shuo-ming-le Shen-ma?* (Peking: *Jen-min Ch'u-pan She*, 1976). For the regime's second thoughts, see *PD*, November 16 and December 21, 1978.

45. *PD*, April 8, 1976.

46. Ibid., July 29, August 2, 11, 21, and 28, 1976.

47. Ibid., November 6, 1976.

48. For a reconstruction of events following Mao's death, see Andres D. Onate, "Hua Kuo-feng and the Arrest of the 'Gang of Four,' " *China Quarterly* 75 (September 1978): 540–64.

49. *T'ien-an-men*, p. 9.

50. Susan L. Shirk, "Going Against the Tide: Political Dissent in China," *Survey* 24 (Winter 1979): 113.

# 3

# The Era of
# Hua Kuo-feng:
# Politics, October 1976 to
# July 1977

Upon the overthrow of the Gang, the Chinese media began developing a cult of Hua Kuo-feng. The purge of the Gang was treated as a vindication of the policies of Mao, and the campaign to criticize Teng Hsiao-p'ing continued, albeit overshadowed by the campaign against the Gang. The Hua regime seemed initially confused about just what kind of line it should take; it seemed to desire to combine technological rationality within the limitations of basically leftist economic policies with a reassertion of discipline within the party and of the party's unquestioned hegemony over all aspects of social and personal life.

The logic of the situation, however, encouraged demands for a reevaluation of all past policies and would not rest with simple technological rationality. The Gang had been particularly strong in the cultural and education systems, and its purge led to pressure for greater intellectual freedom, particularly in science and technology but increasingly in the social and humanistic sciences as well. The new rulers called for order and discipline, but the ordinary person seemed to feel relief from the oppressive atmosphere under the Gang without recapturing the awe for authority undermined by the Gang's ideology and example. The ruling group itself was held together by a desire to displace the Gang and to hold onto power, not by any positive program of its own. In July 1977 a Central Committee plenum restored honor to Hua's rival, Teng Hsiao-p'ing. Hua retained his primacy but had lost, if he had ever had it, his supremacy.

## THE NEW RULERS

An examination of which persons and categories among the older elite gained and lost from the fall of the Gang should give a first approximation of the political changes resulting from the purge. Table 3.1 lists the members and alternate members of the Politburo for three three different times in 1976. The full lists are those of September 10 (Politburo members serving on the committee to arrange Mao's funeral) and October 25 (members attending the first public rally in Peking to celebrate the overthrow of the Gang). In the original of the September 10 list, members below Chang Ch'un-ch'iao are ordered not by party rank but by how many strokes of the pen it takes to write their names (one of the Chinese equivalents of alphabetical order). A comparison with the other two lists, however, allows a reconstruction of the actual party rank on September 10.

The most striking thing about these two lists is their similarity. Liu Po-ch'eng was listed in September but not in October: he was a very old

## TABLE 3.1:  Chinese Leadership, 1976

| April 27 | September 10 | October 25 | General Position |
|----------|--------------|------------|------------------|
| Hua Kuo-feng | Hua Kuo-feng | Hua Kuo-feng | State Center, police |
| Wang Hung-wen | Wang Hung-wen | | Gang |
| | Yeh Chien-ying | Yeh Chien-ying | Military Headquarters |
| Chang Ch'un-ch'iao | Chang Ch'un-ch'iao | | Gang |
| | Li Hsien-nien | Li Hsien-nien | State center, economic management |
| | Liu Po-ch'eng | | Old soldier |
| Chiang Ch'ing | Chiang Ch'ing | | Gang |
| Yao Wen-yuan | Yao Wen-yuan | | Gang |
| Ch'en Hsi-lien | Ch'en Hsi-lien | Ch'en Hsi-lien | Regional military |
| Chi Teng-k'uei | Chi Teng-k'uei | Chi Teng-k'uei | Local party, police? |
| Wang Tung-hsing | Wang Tung-hsing | Wang Tung-hsing | Military headquarters, police |
| Wu Te | Wu Te | Wu Te | Local party |
| | Hsu Shih-yu | Hsu Shih-yu | Regional military |
| | Wei Kuo-ch'ing | Wei Kuo-ch'ing | Local party |
| | Li Te-sheng | Li Te-sheng | Regional military |
| Ch'en Yung-kuei | Ch'en Yung-kuei | Ch'en Yung-kuei | Model peasant |
| Wu Kuei-sien | Wu Kuei-sien | Wu Kuei-sien | Model worker |
| Su Chen-hua | Su Chen-hua | Su Chen-hua | Military headquarters |
| Ni Chih-fu | Ni Chih-fu | Ni Chih-fu | Model worker, trade union leader, police |
| | Saifudin | Saifudin | Local party |

man and probably too weak to stand around for hours in public. Otherwise, the only difference in these two lists is that in October the Gang is no longer present. Their purge resulted in no other immediate major shakeup at the peak of the Chinese elite.

The April 27 list names those members attending the rally who congratulated the public security people for their fine job in suppressing the April 5 riots. These fall into several categories. There is, of course, the Gang of Four. The others are members who probably had something to do with the police system[1] and the Politburo's token "proletarians," these two categories overlapping in the person of Ni Chih-fu, supposedly a one-time model worker but in 1976 the trade union boss and head of the Peking urban militia. The April list might be taken as a rough measure of the leftist tendency on the Politburo.[2] Aside from the Gang (and probably including the Gang until October), the April list shows Hua Kuo-feng's closer allies. By the end of 1980, all of these persons had been criticized formally or informally, and all except Hua and Ni Chih-fu had been removed from office or were otherwise inactive.[3]

The remaining Politburo members fall into a limited number of categories. Yeh Chien-ying and Liu Po-ch'eng were old soldiers. In 1976 Yeh was serving as minister of defense. (At the onset of the Cultural Revolution, he had written a couple of articles in effect pledging his personal loyalty to Mao,[4] and during the Cultural Revolution, he had been protected from the Red Guards by Chou En-lai.) He was perhaps the last of the active grand old men of the party and was widely respected, particularly in the army. Aside from Su Chen-hua, the other Politburo soldiers in 1976 were regional commanders: Ch'en Hsi-lien (Peking), Hsu Shih-yu (Canton), and Li Te-sheng (Shenyang). Prior to 1973 Hsu had commanded Nanking and Ch'en Shenyang, while Li had been commander of the Anhwei military district. There were three provincial first secretaries on the 1976 Politburo (excluding Chang Ch'un-ch'iao, first secretary of Shanghai): Wu Te of Peking, Wei Kuo-ch'ing of Kwangsi, and Saifudin of Sinkiang. Only one Politburo member had special competence in economic management, the intelligent and skilled Li Hsien-nien.

While the "power structure" (insofar as it is reflected in lists such as these) was the same before and after the purge of the Gang (except for the subtraction of the Gang), within that structure there were no doubt changes in relative influence. Hua, one suspects, had been universally underestimated before his October coup, and while there was always something mildly ridiculous about the attempts to develop a cult around him, there was a period in which he seemed genuinely impressive. Perhaps as a balance to Hua, Yeh Chien-ying, who could serve as a symbol of continuity, came to enjoy an unprecedented prominence. He also probably symbolized increased corporate influence for the army. The press also gave much attention (without much detail) to the role of the 8341 Troops and the Peking troops in the overthrow of the Gang,[5] the coverage presumably reflecting increased stature for their commanders, Wang Tung-hsing and Ch'en Hsi-lien. Wu Te delivered the main speech at the October rally denouncing the Gang, explaining that Hua was Mao's legitimate and chosen successor, that members of the Gang were traitors, and that the criticism of Teng Hsiao-p'ing must continue.[6] Wu had been Teng's most vocal enemy, and he now seemed to be Hua's most vocal supporter.

The other immediate major beneficiary of the purge seems to have been Hsu Shih-yu. After the fall of the Gang, Ting Sheng, who had replaced Hsu as commander of the Nanking military region a few years earlier, dissappeared and was replaced in turn by Nieh Feng-chih, an old crony of Hsu. The effect may have been to give Hsu direct or indirect control of the military forces throughout southern and central China.[7] The city of Shanghai, which had been ruled by the Gang, was also purged after a brief delay. On October 25 Ma T'ien-shui, the ranking surviving member of the Shanghai apparatus, held a rally to express his joy at the overthrow of the Gang; a few days later he and his principal subordinates were themselves overthrown, and Shanghai was put under the rule of Su Chen-hua, Ni Chih-fu, and P'eng Ch'ung.[8] About a month later, Mao Yuan-hsin was dismissed from his position as a provincial secretary in Liaoning. He was called "the Gang's closest disciple in Liaoning"[9] but was not mentioned by name—perhaps because his surname was the same as that of his more famous uncle. Ch'ioa Kuan-hua, the foreign minister, was also purged, apparently not because he had any ideological or organizational affinity with the Gang but because his wife had been personally close to Chiang Ch'ing.[10]

## THE NEW LINE

Just as the purge of the Gang resulted in no immediate change in the formal power structure, other than the purge itself, neither did it bring a dramatic immediate shift in policy line. The new rulers seemed anxious instead to emphasize continuity. Under the Gang "left" (always in quotes), deviation had in theory been considered as bad an error as right deviation, but in practice all those who fell from favor came to be considered rightists. Hua Kuo-feng kept up this custom. According to him, members of the Gang, notwithstanding popular opinion to the contrary, were right wingers, just like Chiang Kai-shek.[11] A major theme of the early attacks on the Gang was its alleged similarity to those of the moderate tendency the Gang itself used to denounce. The gang were said to be like Liu Shao-ch'i, or like Chou Yang, the pre-Cultural Revolution literary tsar—or even like Wu Han and Teng T'o, the party intellectuals who had criticized radical Maoism in the early 1960s and who became, under the blows of the Gang, the first victims of the Cultural Revolution.[12] There was heavy-handed mockery of Chiang Ch'ing's somewhat shrill feminism (along with ludicrous assertions that she planned to have herself crowned empress), combined with tendentious arguments purporting to show that the opinions of the Gang were precisely the opposite of those they actually expressed[13] (a style of criticism that tends to vindicate the Gang's public line). The early criticism of the Gang was unprincipled, directed almost exclusively at their persons, not their policies or their ideas.

Condemnation of the Gang's line, not just their persons, was to become a major element of Teng Hsiao-p'ing's program after his second rehabilitation. Some criticism of the Gang line, however, crept even into Hua's practice. According to the story told by the victors, in April 1976 Mao had given Hua Kuo-feng three "instructions": "Go slowly; don't get excited"; "Act according to past directions" (*chao kuo-ch'ü fang-chen pan*); and "With you in charge my heart's at ease." The Gang is then said to have distorted the middle instruction, changing it to "Act according to the set directions" (*an chi-ting fang-chen pan*), presenting it as Mao's "last advice" (*chien-chung shu-fu*).[14] This, somehow, was the Gang's big crime. The article containing the "set directions" version was the last major expression of their point of view that the Gang managed to have published. There is no doubt that it is an attack on Hua Kuo-feng and objectionable to him on that account: "To usurp and change the direction set by Chairman Mao is to turn your back on Marxism, on socialism, on the great theory of continuing revolution under proletarian dictatorship."[15] The semantic difference between the two versions of the phrase is, however, the same in Chinese as in English: none. One critique of the Gang implies that to say "set directions" means that Mao did not creatively apply and develop Marxism-Leninism, although it is not explained why "past directions" is not open to the same objection.[16] The point, if there is one, is that the Gang quoted the set directions version without any context, as a kind of abstract absolute, but the regime placed the "past directions" version in a specific historical circumstance. The effect of the set directions slogan, then, might be to dogmatize Maoism, while the past directions slogan would imply the regime need not be bound so rigidly by the words of the dead. This difference, however, would come only from a difference in usage, not from any difference in literal meaning. The excitement over Mao's advice shows the vacuity of the early criticism of the Gang, but even this emptiness hints toward future content.

In economic policy the early changes were mainly those of attitude. The Gang had held that attention to efficiency and production for their own sakes was a mask for ideological inadequacy and would lead to the perpetuation of social stratification. The Hua regime, however, was unequivocally committed to technological rationality:

> The "Gang of Four" 1) did not engage in manual labor; 2) did not cultivate the fields; 3) did not fight war. They possessed neither truth nor following among the masses. They spent their days beating people with sticks and calling names. They produced nothing themselves and hindered those who did.

By their logic, "Sputnik climbs to heaven, the red flag falls to earth." They thought people should be able to "eat the northwest wind" (that is, that it did not matter whether there was enough food or not). No one wants production without revolution, but the Gang was composed of fake revolutionaries or, in Mao's words, "bourgeois elements who suck the workers' blood."[17]

The Hua regime revived the slogan about the hundred flowers blooming, the hundred schools contending, but tended to limit its application to scientific research. The new line in economic policy is perhaps best symbolized by the publication on December 25, the eve of Mao's birthday, of his 1955 speech, the "Ten Great Relations." The text of this had been revealed by the Red Guards and had circulated abroad for about a decade, but this was the first time it was officially published on the mainland. The speech marks a break with the Soviet model of economic development, proposing a "dialectical" approach to the problem, with the deliberate cultivation of tensions among economic sectors and the achievement of goals by roundabout ways. While this became part of the official policy of the Great Leap Forward, in 1955 Mao's specific policy proposals were very moderate, with much attention to problems of consumption and respect for the interests of those who work in different parts of the economy. The spirit of the speech is quite remote from Gang Maoism, but it does give Maoist sanction to economic pragmatism. The structure of the policy remained, however, what it had been. There was no hint, for example, that complete collectivization of agriculture was not the ultimate goal of rural policy. Hua's economic line was in effect the same as had been official regime policy in the early 1960s: a command economy with pragmatic and tactical concessions to limited economic freedom and consumer welfare. Now, however, those who implemented the policies no longer had to be on the ideological defensive.

A second major strain in the Hua line was an emphasis on authority and discipline. The Gang had been totalitarian, not authoritarian, and attacks on entrenched power and privilege were an integral part of their own ideological line. The Hua regime returned to an unequivocal affirmation of democratic centralism, something the Gang in its headier days had considered "slavism": the individual obeys the organization, the minority obeys the majority, the lower level obeys the higher, and the party obeys the Center.[18] Members of the Gang were called Trotskyites, believers in uninterrupted (pu-tuan) revolution. This theory had once been associated with Mao as well, but now was held to represent simply an unmotivated will to sabotage. The Gang, with never a thought to improving the lives of the people, spent all its time in factional intrigue. Just like Trotsky, its members accused the army and the old guard of being bureaucrats.[19] At one point the new rulers alleged that the Gang desired a "society of absolute freedom,"[20] which is news, one suspects, to those the Gang had imprisoned, tortured, and murdered.

The epitome of the new line is the fifth volume of Mao's *Selected Works*, published under Hua's auspices in the spring of 1977 after some "technical adjustments" (such as the removal of favorable references to Liu Shao-ch'i). It contains speeches and writings by Mao for the period from September 1949 through November 1957. During this time the party was consolidating its rule. Economic policy largely followed the Soviet model, although toward the end changes were being introduced. The alternative direction had not yet been set and the radical experimentation was still to come. Even the land reform program, however socially violent and radical, was economically conservative, and prior to 1958 efforts to collectivize the land were halfhearted and vacillating. Mao's economic pronouncements during the period—and especially those reproduced in the book—tended to be moderate, as was the policy of the party. The other main theme of the collection is the endless series of purges of the preliberation social elite and of intellectuals, a series culminating in the anti-rightist campaign of 1957. Like Mao V, the Hua line entailed technical rationality and political repression.

This position contained tensions. In early 1977 one of the pillars of the Gang line, the "dog-head general Chang Ch'un-ch'ioa," a theory of full-scale dictatorship,was denounced. Chang had argued that proletarian dictatorship should work to extirpate all nonproletarian influences in society. Now it was pointed out that the elimination of classes could come about only through the development of production. Classes rest upon a material base and cannot be eliminated by political dictatorship. Similarly, survivals of the old class system, such as remuneration by the amount of work done and, therefore, unequal remuneration, occur precisely because the productive capacity of the society remains too low to do without them. These all result from conditions of relative poverty and this does not change when the means of production are publicly owned.[21]

In terms of one version of classical Marxism, this is good social theory. In the context of Chinese politics at the time. however, it amounted to an apology for the perpetuation of privilege. Among those to receive privilege, it soon came to be intimated, were intellectuals, a category the Gang had compared to flies swarming around stinking fish.[22] The need to give privileges especially to intellectuals shows a tension between totalitarianism and technical rationality. The Hua regime wanted to indulge intellectuals because it needed technological and managerial skills and because it wanted to encourage scientific research. It may be logically possible to allow autonomy for technocrats or, for that matter, for intellectuals, without allowing it for anyone else. This may not, however, be possible in fact. The "new class" school of Eastern European dissidents has some similarities with Maoism, although the Europeans do not draw the same rules of action from their analysis. One argument from this school holds that in advanced socialist society the intellectuals come to constitute the dominant social class. The party political elite apes the ways of the intelligentsia and subordinates its goals to those of the technocracy. The technocrats differ in outlook and temperament from the creative intellectuals but come from similar backgrounds and run in the same circles. The technocrat cannot feel himself secure as long as artists and writers are subject to arbitrary persecution.[23] The dictatorship of the intellectuals may be no more appealing than the dictatorship of anyone else, but in China of 1977 the intellectuals had hardly achieved dictatorship. In the totalitarian context, the assertion of privilege is also an assertion of autonomy and of at least one sort of freedom.

The political structure of the Hua regime reinforced or may have been the efficient cause of the drive toward more intellectual freedom (or freedom for intellectuals). According to the Gang model, conflict is normal within the Communist Party. It develops spontaneously or (by Maoist voluntarism) should be artificially nurtured if it fails to develop spontaneously. These developing differences should then be crushed. This ceaseless struggle—continuing revolution under proletarian dictatorship— is the motive force of history. There is a more "bureaucratic" model of the party that can be derived from some of the writings of Liu Shao-ch'i. Here, too, differences within the party are taken as normal, but the function of the party is to resolve these differences in a harmonious fashion. The main crime is to push one's own interests or opinions to the point where the disciplined unity of the party is disrupted. Instead, there must be mutual adaptation of the various interests within the party, combined with a self-conscious submission to organizational discipline. Concretely, to criticize members of the Gang as anarchists and liberals is to condemn their pushing their attacks on others inside the elite without regard for party discipline and procedure.

Members of the Gang, despite their talk, were never in a position to impose their own dictatorship on the party. They were always simply one faction among many. When they and their mentor were gone, only separate interests or factions remained. Particularly given the damage done by the Gang to the party's organization, the major source of cohesion among the victors was their common loathing of the Gang and a fear of disorder. Given conditions in China in 1976—the purge of Teng, the April riots, the earthquakes, the death of Mao, the purge of the Gang—while there was potential for conflict among the survivors, open conflict may have been the one thing prudence would lead all the groups to avoid. Prudence dictated, if not abandonment of dictatorship, at least a backing away from "full-scale dictatorship." No one force should attempt to impose itself on all the others, however much limited conflict and marginal intrigue might continue. The Hua regime was tacitly, no longer just "incipiently," pluralistic. This was an oligarchical pluralism, to be sure, but also one that might allow the evolution of a more open and humane political process.

## THE HEROIC AND BRIGHT LEADER:
## THE CULT OF HUA KUO-FENG

There had been something like oligarchical pluralism in Mao's time as well. This pluralism worked, however, within the context of a hegemonic totalitarian ideology and under a totalitarian leader. This kind of leader may be a necessary condition for totalitarian rule: "The 'totalitarian' regime is essentially a leadership regime."[24] The successor regime also seemed at first to aspire to be a leadership regime as well, with perhaps a less impressive leader. The cult of Mao continued much as it had been before (and it was already considerably toned down from its high point under Lin Piao in the late 1960s), and Hua Kuo-feng derived his right to rule from his purported selection by Mao. This identification was sometimes carried to surprising links. Whereas previously Hua had sported a crew cut, by the winter of 1976 he had begun to style his hair to look like Mao's. Had he known how, he might have grown himself a mole on his chin. At the same time a cult of Hua was developing. Somehow he rapidly became party chairman, the "heroic and bright" (ying-ming) leader. The thwarting of Hua's ambition to become a great leader was perhaps the necessary condition for further liberalization.

A distinction should be made here. The crucial consideration is not the actual power exercised by any particular leader. Teng Hsiao-p'ing may well have more personal power (assuming we could measure it) than Hua ever had, and it would not even matter if Teng's power were greater than Mao's. But there was no "cult" of Teng as there had been a cult of Mao and as there seemed to be developing a cult of Hua. Teng's primacy, when he achieved it, was not justified by the glorification of his person, although, of course, the press said many nice things about him. Teng's regime may have involved strong leadership, but it was not a leadership regime.

Hua based his own legitimacy on his alleged designation by Mao, and he himself attempted to rule in the Maoist style. This set up a series of interconnections. Hua's own position would be harmed by any post-humous denigration of Mao, and any depreciation of Hua would tend to reflect back upon Mao. The structure of the leadership regime would depend not only upon Hua's ability to create a cult but also upon Mao's continuing good reputation.

Hua was presented as someone "limitlessly trusted by Chairman Mao," and Wu Te in particular was vocal in his praise for Hua's excellent qualities.[25] Hua became something of an artificial Mao. The late chairman was proud of his calligraphy, and those who know about such things find it eccentric but forceful, certainly of some artistic merit. For a time in 1977 the media featured samples of Hua's calligraphy,[26] and one does not have to know much about such things to pronounce it a third-grader's scrawl. Hua's writings were often presented alongside the more elegant and workmanlike brush strokes of other party big shots, such as Yeh Chien-ying, and it is not at all clear just what point was being made. Mao had also been something of a minor poet. The Chinese papers reproduced, in Hua's handwriting, a transcription of what they said was a Hunan folksong: "From the peak of the tall mountain I see the river stretching out, laughingly flowing along the mountain's side. In former days I walked beneath your feet, while today I bestride your head."[27] Some claim these last two lines (the second sentence in the translation) bespeak an over-weaning arrogance. Ever since the Cultural Revolution, it had been the custom of Chinese papers to carry on their masthead a thought of Mao for the day. This continued after Mao's death. Hua Kuo-feng had not previously been known as either an aphorist or a theoretician, but in 1977 the papers began featuring quotes from him in addition to quotes from Mao.

From the very beginning, there were hints of opposition to this new cult. Since the Cultural Revolution, Mao had been called almost exclu-sively "Chairman Mao," although prior to that he had as often as not been called instead "Comrade Mao Tse-tung." The use of the official title, obviously, serves to elevate Mao above the other comrades. Immediately following the purge of the Gang, the press began to talk about Chairman Hua. At the end of October, however, the military paper, *Liberation Army Daily*, published a piece on "Comrade Hua Kuo-feng, our party's worthy [wu-k'uei] leader." The paper says that the leader of a proletarian party is not self-appointed (although Hua in effect was) but, rather, becomes recognized by the masses in the course of the struggle. "The people, only the people"—in other words, not great leaders—are the motive force in history. "A great revolutionary struggle will create great revolutionary personages." Comrade Hua Kuo-feng's leadership reflects the needs of the revolution, the desires of millions of people, the necessity of history. All of this seems a politely bombastic way of hinting that Hua as a person is not really all that important, except as the emanation of a larger process. Only once in the article is Hua called chairman, and there the context stresses his formal position as head of an organization: the reference is to the "party center headed by Chairman Hua Kuo-feng."[28]

A few weeks later, the army published another article. This time the large type of the headline calls Hua chairman, although the text sometimes refers to him simply as comrade. The article itself stresses organizational discipline and democratic centralism—the individual obeys the organization—not personal leadership. It ostentatiously dilates upon Hua's modesty, his loyalty, and his trust in the masses.[29] The message one gets is that the army supports Hua, but Hua had better not begin to take himself too seriously. Those who made him—the "masses," "history," and the People's Liberation Army—can also break him.

There are also contemporary hints, albeit obscure, not only of resistance to the cult but of covert attacks upon Hua himself. The new rulers began the rehabilitation of several post-Cultural Revolution literary works condemned by the Gang (a policy, by the way, which did not imply any particular liberalization of literary policy), including a modern Hunan opera, *The Gardener's Song*. The rehabilitation claims that Hua, who at the time it was denounced in 1974 was first secretary of Hunan province as well as minister of public security, thought it was a good play and blames its condemnation on the person writing under the "stinking name of Ch'u Lan."[30] Ch'u Lan, the signature on several articles of literary criticism in the early 1970s, refers to Chiang Ch'ing, one of whose stage names had been Lan P'ing. The attack on *The Gardener's Song*, however, had *not* been initiated by Ch'u Lan, but by someone calling himself Hsiang Hui.[31] This name, which means something like "the glory of Hunan," appeared over several generally leftist articles in the years following Hua's takeover of the Hunan party committee, and if Hsiang Hui is not Hua himself it is certainly someone who speaks for him. The rehabilitation of *The Gardener's Song* neglects to mention the role of Hsiang Hui, but one wonders whether the point of the rehabilitation is not an indirect rebuke to Hua for his former collaboration with the Gang.

The main resistance to the cult, however, was through its dilution. On January 5, the anniversary of Chou En-lai's death, the Chinese press began a prolonged celebration of the former leader. Given the way of the world, the glorification of Chou could only serve to dim that of Mao and, of course, of Mao's chosen successor. Chou was presented as warm and approachable, something Mao had not been. Praise for Chou also served to discredit the leftist line and brought home what was no doubt obvious all along, the hostility between Chou and the Gang.

Hua was rarely able to hold the stage alone. As noted above, samples of his calligraphy were shown together with the superior work of others. Yeh Chien-ying in particular came to function as Hua's shadow, tagging along wherever Hua might go. In April 1977 a teacher at Peking Normal noted, in a very banal context, "Recently Chairman Hua and Vice Chairman Yeh have issued an important summons to grasp the study of party history."[32] The content of this boring summons is neither here nor there; the interesting point is that Yeh is pictured as sharing in the issuing of it, with the implication that Hua's words carry greater weight if they are endorsed by Yeh. Perhaps this may be taken as symbolic of Hua's failure to make himself into a Great Leader.

## TENG HSIAO-P'ING

The public report of the Central Committee plenum held in July 1977 says that in March of that year Hua had proposed to the party that Teng Hsiao-p'ing be brought back to work and that Teng had agreed to return in May.[33] By April the public was given a clear hint that Teng had been forgiven. The fifth volume of Mao's *Selected Works* contains several friendly, if passing, references to Teng: he was being repersoned. "Just as Comrade Hsiao-p'ing has explained," we should be willing to work with comrades who have erred; "our Comrade Hsiao-p'ing" gave a good dressing down to an obstreperous university student; "Comrade Hsiao-p'ing" has explained that we should preceed in a dialectical fashion.[34]

By the time of the publication of the fifth volume of the *Selected Works*, there was little public discussion of Teng at all, and this in itself indicates some sort of change. Chinese purges since 1968 followed a regular pattern: the last victim would receive the bulk of media attention. When a new victim came along, attention would be shifted to him, the older sinking deeper into the morass to make way for the new, like the souls of the corrupt popes in hell. The earlier villains would continue to be denounced, although less frequently. From 1968 into 1971, Liu Shao-ch'i was the source of all evil in the world. In 1971 pride of place was taken by a "Liu Shao-ch'i type political swindler," or Ch'en Po-ta. Before Ch'en was denounced openly by name, Lin Piao fell and became the Great Satan, although Liu and Ch'en continued to receive some share of the vilification. In early 1976 Lin sank deeper, and Teng began receiving the bulk of the publicity. By the fall of 1976, everyone was excited about the Gang, but the criticism of Teng continued.

The last direct public attack on Teng was uttered by Wu Te and published on December 1. By the middle of that month, the tone had begun to change. The Gang was said to have abused the criticism of Teng movement by trying to turn it into a general purge. Luckily, Hua Kuo-feng had prevented this.[35] According to a Taiwan source, on December 30 Hua himself asserted that no one cares much to talk about the criticism of Teng any more, and people in fact doubt whether Mao had anything to do with initiating the movement. Teng and the Gang opposed each other, Hua says, but their revisionist lines are exactly the same. While we still oppose Teng, this is no longer the major contradiction. "This is what Chairman Mao's theory of revolution by stages teaches us."[36] In January the "problem" of Teng was redefined as a "contradiction among the people."[37]

The question should arise: just who desired Teng's return? Publicly the regime chose to present the whole thing as Hua's idea, but it seems more plausible to hold that the rehabilitation was forced, first by the military component of the new regime (at a guess, by Yeh Chien-ying and Hsu Shih-yu) and secondly by the economic bureaucrats, whose importance within the regime was then increasing. There was talk at the time to the effect that Teng was prized for his administrative ability. There were plenty of people in China able to keep files in their proper folders and not to get account numbers mixed up. Teng's political style had heretofore been bureaucratic, but he was important not as an administrator but as a politician. In 1975 he had made himself the symbol of opposition to the left and his public return would be a visible rejection of the left. This rejection would be particularly dramatic since Teng's 1977 rehabilitation would seem to be the first for a Chinese leader attacked publicly by name (not just by code words) in the central media (prior to his 1973 rehabilitation, Teng, unlike Liu Shao-ch'i, had not been criticized by name).

Teng's return might have been motivated in part by the perception of his powerful supporters that he himself would be weak. He had not previously shown himself to be an effective leader. There can be no doubt about his courage but much about his political sagacity. Although he was general secretary of the Central Committee from 1956 to 1966, he had been overshadowed in that period by the second-ranking secretary, P'eng Chen. His purge in 1966 seems to have required no great effort; it was an afterthought to the purge of Liu Shao-ch'i. A politician in disgrace is not always in a position to build a power base, and one brought back to office by others will be initially weak. In 1976, for example, Teng's political life was coextensive with the physical life of his sponsor, Chou En-lai. According to one story, in 1976 Teng found refuge with Hsu Shih-yu in

Canton,[38] and in 1976 Hsu seemed to be extending his influence throughout southern and central China. Perhaps he thought Comrade Hsiao-p'ing would make a useful stooge.

Teng, however did not want to be anyone's patsy. According to the transcript of an improbable conversation betwen Hua and Teng that, whether authentic or not, did circulate among students in Peking during 1977, Teng made Hua crawl before consenting to his own rehabilitation. In particular, Teng is supposed to have demanded the explicit revocation of the decrees purging him—the very decrees that formalized Hua's position. Hua is supposed to have said: "Don't get excited, Comrade Hsiao-p'ing." The trouble is, the decrees were authorized by Mao, and "Whatever Chairman Mao has decided cannot be reversed. That is a matter of principle." "Don't think," rejoined the gracious and affable Teng Hsiao-p'ing, "that because your coup succeeded you can piss on my head. The majority of the cadres in the party, administration, and army are on my side. They certainly won't stand with you, Hua Kuo-feng, when the time comes for the reckoning of old debts." Poor Hua is then supposed to have explained: "Although Wu Te, Ch'en Hsi-lien, Chi Teng-k'uei, and I myself went along with the Gang of Four, we really had no alternative."[39] Again, there is no guarantee that this is anything like an authentic text of a real conversation. It is likely, however, that Teng's rehabilitation neither resulted from gratuitous goodwill nor brought about a great reconciliation.

In early July the *People's Daily* berated the Gang's attack on Teng's 1975 General Program, claiming the Gang's real target was Hua Kuo-feng—an assertion at least as improbable as the conversation cited above. The General Program was on the whole correct, although not without a few "mistakes and defects."[40] This was the last public reference to any mistakes and defects of Teng's.

Hua's coup had eliminated the establishment radicals as a force in Chinese politics. The victorious coalition was composed of the police left, the army, and the rational modernizers on the State Council. All had interests both in toning down radical Maoism and also in avoiding other major social or political changes. All were committed to the technological rationalization of the economy. Despite the common interests within it, the coalition was unstable. The circumstances of the coup tended to make Hua perhaps more powerful than his colleagues thought he should have been, while Hua's need to consolidate his power led him to stress the continuity of the Maoist heritage and to attempt to develop a leadership cult around himself—moves that his allies probably saw as threatening. On a deeper level, Hua's program was contradictory: he would seem to have desired technological modernization, a continuation of Maoism, relief from the constant round of campaigns and purges and no further change in the structure of power. The incoherence both of the program and the alliance brought about the return of Teng Hsiao-p'ing, the army ahd the bureaucrats being more instrumental here. Teng, however, to secure his own position required reforms more radical than any of those desired by the other leaders. Teng was soon to find himself in conflict not only with Hua Kuo-feng but with those who had brought him back.

Later that month the Central Committee restored Teng to honor. He became a member of the Politburo Standing Committee, a vice-chairman of the Central Committee, a vice-chairman of the Military Affairs Commission, a vice-premier, and chief of staff of the People's Liberation Army. Opposition to Teng was added to the list of crimes of the Gang, and the Gang's individual errors were sorted out: Chang Ch'un-ch'iao was a Kuomintany agent, Chiang Ch'ing a renegade, Yao Wen-yuan a class alien, and Wang Hung-wen a new bourgeois element. When Teng was purged, he had been allowed to retain his party membership. The Gang, however, was expelled from everything, forever.[41]

# NOTES

1. Chi Teng-K'uei was a second secretary of the Honan party committee and a commissar of the Peking military region. He spent most of his time in Peking. A mysterious figure, he was virtually unknown before 1969 when, for reasons unexplained to the world outside, he became a member of the Politburo. His real work was probably within the police system. Wu Te, the head of the Peking party committee, and Su Chen-hua, officially deputy commander of the navy and at one time the navy's political commissar, may also have had police connections.

2. Saifudin, while not at the rally, should probably be counted as a leftist.

3. Su Chen-hua's loss of influence, however, should be attributed to his death in 1978.

4. Yeh Chien-ying, "Great Strategy Decides the War," Jen-min Jih-pao [People's Daily], August 30, 1965 (hereafter cited as PD); "Raise High the Red Banner of the Thought of Mao Tse-tung and Manage Schools after the Style of Resist-Japan University," ibid., August 2, 1966.

5. Ibid., October 22, 1976.

6. Ibid., October 25, 1976. During the Great Leap Forward, Wu, then an apparatchik in the Kirin province, had voiced strong support for the Maoist emphasis on red over expert (see Appendix A). Wu Te, "Liberate Thought; Greet the Technological Revolution," ibid., May 24, 1958.

7. Ming Pao, August 23, 1978, citing what purports to be an inner party document, alleges that Ting Sheng had colluded with the Gang. See Foreign Broadcast Information Service, Daily Report, People's Republic of China, August 30, 1978, p. E29. The allegation is also a part of the formal indictment of the Gang.

8. PD, October 26, and 30, 1976.

9. Ibid., November 30, 1976.

10. Cheng Ming 13 (November 1, 1978); Foreign Broadcast Information Service, Daily Report, People's Republic of China, November 3, 1978, p. N3.

11. See, for example, Hua Kuo-feng's speech at the second Tachai conference, PD, December 27, 1976.

12. Ibid., November 26, 1976; ibid., March 31, 1977.

13. Ibid., November 26, 1976.

14. Ibid., December 17, 1976. This supposedly correct version of the phrase was not revealed until the supposedly false version had been under criticism for a month or so.

15. Liang Hsiao, "Always Act According to the Directions Set by Chairman Mao," *Kuang-ming Jih-pao*, October 4, 1976. Liang Hsiao, by the way, says this is Mao's advice, but he does not call it Mao's *last* advice.

16. T'ien Ch'ing, "Part of the Record of the 'Gang of Four's' Failure in Their Struggle to Usurp the Party," *PD*, November 14, 1976.

17. Jen P'ing, "A Gang of Pernicious Vermin Who Harm the State and Injure the People," ibid., November 14, 1976. The phrase about Sputnik is quoted from Chang Ch'un-ch'iao, "On Full-Scale Dictatorship over the Bourgeoisie," *Hung Ch'i*, 4, April 1, 1975, pp. 3–16.

18. Hua Kuo-feng, December 27, 1976.

19. Cheng Lien, "The 'Gang of Four' and the Trotskyites," *PD*, January 27, 1977.

20. *Kuang-ming Jih-pao*, March 10, 1977.

21. Wang Hui-te, "A Counterrevolutionary Quack," *PD*, January 22, 1977.

22. Ibid., February 22, 1977.

23. George Konrad and Ivan Szeleny, *The Intellectuals on the Road to Class Power* (New York: Harcourt Brace Jovanovich, 1979).

24. Leonard Schapiro, *Totalitarianism* (New York: Praeger 1972), p. 70.

25. *PD*, December 1, 1976; also Chang Ch'un-po, "Fake Criticism of Confucius, True Usurpation of Power," *Kuang-ming Jih-pao*, December 14, 1976.

26. *PD*, March 25 and April 23, 1977.

27. Ibid., March 25, 1977.

28. Ibid., October 31, 1976. The term *wu-k'uei* (or, depending upon its grammatical function, *pu-k'uei*) may call for at least a comment. *K'uei* means shame, and *wu* or *pu* mean not, or without. Hua is not, however, the shameless leader, but the leader who has nothing to be ashamed of. The official rendering of the term is *worthy* when applied to a person. This term came into common use in the Chinese press in the summer of 1976 in rather funny contexts, and I wonder if its currency did not originally derive from a personal speech habit of Hua Kuo-feng's. At the Eleventh National Party Congress in August 1977, Hua said: "Our party is not ashamed [*pu-k'uei*] to be a proletarian party with a long and mature experience of politics." Who said it should be ashamed of this? "Our army is not ashamed to be the army personally created and commanded by Chairman Mao; our people are not ashamed to be a people armed with the Thought of Mao Tse-tung." Ibid., August 23, 1977.

29. Ibid., November 23, 1976.

30. Ibid., November 10, 1976; *Kuang-ming Jih-pao*, November 22, 1976.

31. Hsiang Hui, "Criticizing the Hunan Opera, *The Gardener's Song*," *PD*, August 2, 1974.

32. *Kuang-ming Jih-pao*, April 19, 1977.

33. *PD*, July 23, 1977.

34. *Mao Tse-tung Hsuan-chi*, vol. 5 (Peking: Jen-min Ch'u-pan She, 1977), pp. 301, 355, 361. There are, in fact, more references to Teng in the volume than to any other single communist leader. Chi Hsin, *Teng Hsiao-ping: A Political Biography* (Hong Kong: Cosmos Books, 1978), p. 133. The use of the given name without the surname carries an intimate, affectionate connotation.

35. Chang, "Fake Criticism of Confucius"; comments by Ch'en Yung-kuei, *PD*, December 24, 1976.

36. *Chung-yang Jih-pao*, February 26, 1977.

37. Harry G. Gelber, *Technology, Defense, and External Relations in China, 1975–1979* (Boulder, Colo.: Westview, 1979), p. 16.

38. *Chung-yang Jih-pao*, December 6, 1978.

39. *Far Eastern Economic Review*, January 20, 1978, p. 23. Hua's position in this conversation is reflected in the *PD* editorial, February 7, 1977.

40. *PD*, July 7, 1977.

41. Ibid., July 23, 1977.

# 4

# The Third Coming of Teng Hsiao-p'ing: Politics, August 1977 to December 1978

The changes in the Chinese political style were presaged in Hua's time, but they became most evident only after Teng's return. The changes came about, as changes in politics generally do, in a context of continuing struggle for power and influence. Later chapters deal with the substance of the changes; this one concentrates simply on the background, on the political struggle itself, from the time of Teng's return until the end of 1978, when the struggle among the elite spilled over into society with the democratic movement.

## THE ELEVENTH CONGRESS

The CPC convened its eleventh national congress in August 1977, electing a new Central Committee and Politburo and adopting a new constitution. This congress coincided with an intensification of the purge. Attacks were no longer restricted to the Gang and its immediate followers but came to be extended to a diffuse "Gang system" throughout society.[1] This social purge was probably not solely a product of the "line" struggle at the center but was also an expression of the concern by the central rulers with the spread of crime, indiscipline, and corruption. This seems to have gone along with renewed worry about the power of local soldiers. The previous chapter speculates that certain local commanders, particularly Hsu Shih-yu, were instrumental in bringing Teng back to work. But by his past record Teng could not be expected to look with favor upon any local military autonomy, and Hua, at this point in his career, would not either.

The new constitution contains a warning against "bureaucratism, commandism, and warlordism," followed by appeals for party discipline and warnings against factional activities, defiance of authority, and anarchy.[2]

Teng's restoration was no doubt intended to symbolize a dramatic repudiation of the leftist line, but this repudiation, however dramatic, was far from total. There was even ambiguity in the public praise for Teng at that time. Shortly before the congress, for example, a discussion of Teng's activities during the civil war also lauds Hsieh Fu-chih, China's minister of public security from 1959 until his death in 1971. During the Cultural Revolution, Chiang Ch'ing had commented that although Hsieh had once been one of Teng's supporters, in 1966 Hsieh was the first to expose him.[3] In 1980 Hsieh was revealed as one of the great leftist villains, one who, like K'ang Sheng, had he still been alive, would have been put on trial with the "Lin Piao-Chiang Ch'ing cliques." Whatever point was being made in 1977 by coupling praise for Teng with praise for Hsieh, it was probably not a point Teng cared to have made.

At the eleventh congress, Hua Kuo-feng seemed determined to salvage as much as possible of the leftist line and of his own prestige. He began with a commemoration of the Grand Old Men of the party who had passed on, including the soon-to-be execrated K'ang Sheng. He called the defeat of the Gang the party's eleventh struggle over line. According to Maoist analysis, the Lin Piao affair was the tenth line struggle; so Hua excludes the second purge of Teng from his list. But this way of counting tacitly includes the Cultural Revolution, the ninth line struggle (meaning the 1966 purge of Liu Shao-ch'i and Teng Hsiao-p'ing), and generally vindicates the Maoist interpretation of party history. Hua says the February 2, 1976 decision that he become acting premier was made by Mao, as was the decision of April 7 formally purging Teng and making Hua the official premier of the country. Hua keeps to the theme of class struggle, reviving the slogan Mao had used against Chou and Teng in 1975:

> Peace and unity does not mean there is no class struggle. The first Great Proletarian Cultural Revolution has come to a victorious conclusion, but class struggle has not reached its conclusion and continued revolution under proletarian dictatorship has not reached its conclusion.

Cultural revolutions will continue until the advent of communism.[4] This was the first official recognition that the Cultural Revolution had in fact ended (for all practical purposes it was over by 1969), but Teng Hsiao-p'ing might not have looked forward with such relish to the cultural revolutions to come; from Teng's perspective, the first Great Proletarian Cultural Revolution was one more than was desirable.

Eleven new members were added to the Politburo, including Teng Hsiao-p'ing (see Table 4.1). No old members were removed, although Saifudin suffered a covert rebuke: he was the only old alternate member not promoted to full membership. The new members included four long-time economic managers and planners. The most impressive of these was Nieh Jung-chen, one of the few among the older elite who might qualify as a true technocrat: he was a German-trained engineer as well as a skilled military field commander; before the Cultural Revolution, he had been in charge of supervising China's scientific establishment. The new Politburo also showed evidence of the regime's renewed interest in the outside world. Keng Piao had been head of the Central Committee's International Liaison Office, while Fang I, before moving up to general direction of economic planning, had been in charge of foreign trade. His former subordinate and successor in that ministry, Ch'en Mu-hua (the Politburo's only female member, later to gain a reputation for callous bureaucratic arrogance)[5] became an alternate member. The appointment of the commander of the air force, Chang T'ing-fa, also shows the general interest in technological modernization.

The appointment of P'eng Ch'ung is worth at least parenthetical comment. His joining Su Chen-hua and Ni Chih-fu on the Politburo meant that, as under the Gang of Four, the three ranking Shanghai party secretaries were members of the party's highest decision-making body. No other locality was so represented.

The August 1977 Politburo was thus a relatively conservative one but it was not necessarily dominated by Teng Hsiao-p'ing. The economic managers in those days no doubt agreed with Teng on most points of policy, but their affiliations were more with Chou En-lai than with Teng.

**TABLE 4.1:  Additions to Politburo, August 1977 (by stroke number order)**

| Name | General Function |
| --- | --- |
| Ulanfu | Nationalities work? |
| Fang I | Economic management and planning |
| Teng Hsiao-p'ing | Policy leadership |
| Yu Ch'iu-li | Economic management |
| Chang T'ing-fa | Military headquarters |
| Keng Piao | Military headquarters, international affairs |
| Nieh Jung-chen | Economic management, military |
| Hsu Hsiang-ch'ien | Military headquarters, old soldier |
| P'eng Ch'ung | Local party |
| Ch'en Mu-hua (alternate) | Economic management |
| Chao Tzu-yang (alternate) | Local party |

Unlike Teng, they had not been purged during the Cultural Revolution, despite their lack of sympathy for radicalism. The outstanding surviving Politburo figure of this group was Li Hsien-nien, who was about one year younger than Teng, easily as competent, and with as much seniority in the party. It would be surprising if Li did not feel some jealousy toward Teng.[6] Teng, on his part, needed departures from the past more radical than those the former Chou En-lai group could comfortably tolerate.

Among the new members, I speculate that those most sympathetic to Teng might include Ulanfu, Chang T'ing-fa, and certainly Chao Tzu-yang. Ulanfu, a sinified Mongol prince and lifelong member of the CPC, had once acted as a kind of spokesman for the interests of minority nationalities within party councils. Before 1966 he held the top party, state, and military positions in Inner Mongolia and was accused during the Cultural Revolution of fostering Mongol separatism. He had resumed active political life in the early 1970's, long before Mao died, although he was not restored to his Mongolian satrapy. Chang, an air force officer, disappeared during the Cultural Revolution and did not reappear until after the purge of the Gang. He then became air force commander; the man who had occupied that position in turn disappeared. Chao had once been part of the system of cadres associated with T'ao Chu in the old South-Central Regional Bureau. He had been purged in 1967, but following the death of Lin Piao he became de facto head of Kwangtung province. In 1975 he was transferred to Szechuan, where he presided over the implementation of the radically reformist economic policies that province came to symbolize. In 1980 he succeeded Hua Kuo-feng as premier. In 1977, however, his main connection may have been with a kind of "southern gang" under Hsu Shih-yu and Wei Kuo-ch'ing.

Ch'en Yun did not become a Politburo member in 1977, but he did become more active, perhaps symbolizing the growing aggressiveness of the right. Along with Nieh Jung-chen, he began to stress the slogan, seek truth from facts—a proverb historically used in People's China during periods of retrenchment from grandiose leftist projects. Nieh, using somewhat intemperate language (the Gang is "a bunch of bad eggs; they piss and defecate on the heads of the masses"), spoke of a system of "institutionalized lies," while Ch'en began to criticize "left dogmatism" (specifically, however, that of Wang Ming, the leader of the old "Bolshevik" faction within the CPC).[7] Nieh also delivered the first rather mild hint that the prestige of Mao himself was to be reduced, scolding those who "take phrases of Marxism-Leninism, the Thought of Mao Tse-tung, treating them as dogmas apart from time, place, and circumstance." Mao, Nieh says, always opposed this kind of metaphysics. He did not consider his own thought to be the peak of Marxism-Leninism nor did he consider that it had absolute authority. A few days later, the *People's Daily* echoed

Nieh's words in an edition commemorating the first anniversary of the chairman's death. This same edition contains a most unattractive color portrait of Mao's cadaver in its crystal coffin. According to the text, the Gang used to "choose random words from the works of Chairman Mao, distorting them according to their hearts' desire." They "mechanically applied phrases of Chairman Mao's works in abstraction from concrete time, place, and circumstance."[8]

In addition to this very mild symbolic anti-Maoism, during the period immediately following the eleventh congress there came to be more outspoken and straightforward defenses of the principle of material incentives, of remuneration according to labor, than had been possible under the Gang.[9] This issue, however, shows the somewhat ambiguous nature of the rightist victory. Under the Gang moderate arguments had to be couched in leftist terms. By the fall of 1977, leftist arguments had to be disguised by moderate words. The Gang of Four used to criticize what it called the "theory of nothing but production forces," *wei sheng-ch'an-li lun*, the idea that socialism comes about because of changes in the economic base and that, therefore, there is no need to worry about ideological indoctrination. In September 1977 someone signing himself Lin Feng contrasted true Marxist theory with what he called the "vulgar theory of nothing but production forces," the import of the argument being that the Gang was comprised of corrupt people, but on this point their analysis was correct: it is not enough simply to pay attention to the forces of production.[10] All of this is rather arcane, but so is most political discourse in China. The Lin Feng article also plays with certain code words. On September 5 Nieh Jung-chen had mentioned the evils of Lin Piao and the Gang but not those of Liu Shao-ch'i. On September 10 the *People's Daily*, in the same article in which it echoed Nieh, condemned the Gang for calling the old cadres "democrats," or, in other words, persons who had not progressed to a socialist mentality (socialism being an advance on ordinary democracy). Lin Feng, on September 7, reminds us that Mao quite properly criticized Liu Shao-ch'i for being unwilling to advance beyond the democratic revolution. A few days later, the State Planning Commission congratulated itself for having resisted Liu's policy of "consolidating the social order of new democracy."[11] This article probably reflects the views of the main planners, Li Hsien-nien, Yü Ch'iu-li, and Fang I, and is thus evidence of the then embryonic rift between the old Chou En-lai group and Teng Hsiao-p'ing.

One intended implication of the slogan, seek truth from facts, was that this was something the Gang and radicals generally did not do. But rightist slogans, as long as they remained only slogans, could also be advanced in advocacy of a leftist line. In October the one-time peasant Ch'en Yung-kuei talked of the need for caution in planning and of the need to increase the material well-being of peasants: to fail to do this, Ch'en says, will give the class enemy a pretext for complaint. Ch'en was voicing rightist themes but not for exactly the same reasons as the regular rightists. He also grudgingly accepted the principle of remuneration according to work, going on, to say, however, that people should not be intimidated by any talk of the "wind of communism," *kung-ch'an feng*, a hoary rightist code word for radical egalitarianism. Ch'en in effect says that the wind of communism is not so bad: we live under socialism at the present, but we look forward to communism.[12] The Gang would have put the point a little more viciously as, for that matter, would have Ch'en himself a few years earlier. But the policy he advocates is precisely that of the Gang: there must be tactical concessions to the interests of the more productive peasants, but the general bias of the policy should be toward the elimination of these "inequalities" and toward increasing the scale of collectivization. Almost a year later, Mao Chih-yung, then first secretary of Hunan (and no doubt a cousin or nephew of the great Mao), celebrating the twentieth anniversary of the commune system, continued to attack Liu Shao-ch'i for wanting to decollectivize agriculture. Mao explicitly praised Hua Kuo-feng for resisting this.[13] But a few weeks after Mao Chih-yung's article, Ch'en Yung-kuei's own Tachai model began to be called into question.[14]

Some of this assertion of the left took personal forms. As part of the 1977 commemoration of Mao's death, three days after Nieh Jung-chen's implied denigration of Mao, the 8341 Troops published a long essay praising Mao and, by reflection, Wang Tung-hsing (not named, but styled "the working personnel at Chairman Mao's side"). The article describes how Wang not only protected Mao against Chiang Ch'ing but also plotted with Mao against Lin Piao. The Gang and Lin Piao advocated "doubt everything." "But can one doubt the existence of the sun?" or of Mao's brilliance (something the Gang and Lin publicly never did doubt). The article is less a criticism of Lin Piao and the Gang than of those persons at the time of publication who were beginning to dismantle the Maoist system. The article also reminds us that Mao said there would be a need for many more Cultural Revolutions,[15] something Hua Kuo-feng had said also less than a month earlier, which those of the Teng Hsiao-p'ing and Chou En-lai affiliations scrupulously avoided saying.

Wang and Hua may have been allies, but an even closer relationship probably existed between Hua and Wu Te. In October the Peking press gave lavish publicity, complete with color photographs, to a rather pointless visit by Hua and Wu to a chicken farm in the Peking suburbs. Hua wrote one of his not very elegant scrolls urging improvements in the mechanized raising of chickens and pigs and gave the farmers some advice about learning foreign methods. His visit was treated as if he were an angel from heaven. Wu Te, it will be remembered, had been Teng Hsiao-p'ing's most vocal antagonist and also Hua's most vocal supporter. By the fall of 1977, Wu was under heavy wall poster attack. Hua no doubt needed all the friends he could get but his drive out to the chicken farm with Wu may also have been a handsome gesture of support for a loyal ally in trouble.[16]

The tone of the period around the eleventh congress, then, was conservative but not unambiguously so. The rhetoric and assumptions of the Maoist period continued to linger, as did old fears that the moderation was temporary and that those who had adapted too early and too easily would come to grief when the pendulum swung back. The newspapers urged: "Those comrades who still have fear in their hearts, who stare to the east and west, to the left and right, who equivocate and procrastinate— these no longer have the slightest pretext or reason to waver."[17] Rather, more would have to be done before the comrades were really convinced.

## THE THIRD CAMPAIGN

Toward the end of 1977, the military paper, *Liberation Army Daily*, announced the opening of what it called the "third campaign," directed against the "counterrevolutionary line of the 'Gang of Four.' " The focus of the vilification was moving increasingly away from the Gang's persons to their "line," the ideology they embodied. The specific line the army then had in mind was the Gang's notion that "old cadres are democrats and democrats are capitalist roaders," an idea, as we have just seen, still somewhat current in the fall of 1977. The military paper had two major concerns: first, it was indignant over the Gang's erstwhile search for capitalist roaders inside the army; and secondly, it worried that the army had become insufficiently responsive to the will of the party center.[18] Talk of the third campaign soon dissipated, but the focus of the discourse thereafter continued to be on radicalism as such, with the Gang more and more becoming a metaphor for currently active rivals.

Despite the initiation of the third campaign, at the beginning of 1978 the advantage seemed to be with the left. Before the turn of the year, on the late chairman's birthday, the *People's Daily* published a statement he had made in 1964: "Within not too long a historical period our country will be established as a strong, modernized socialist state. This is what we mean when we talk about a great leap forward. Could it be that this can't be done? Is this just a lot of bull, just shooting off a big gun? No . . ."[19] As Mao well knew, great leap forward had more connotations than those he chose to mention there. In 1964 the Leap Forward was discredited within the party generally, although the Maoists wanted to revive it, and Mao's statement, in its "time, place, and circumstance," is a very defensive defense of the radical line. The words "great leap forward," however, would function as a symbol of radicalism, and in the new year the press continued to promise a "new leap forward." By the year 2000, China "will in most respects approach, in a few respects surpass, the levels at that time of the most developed capitalist countries,"[20] which is a somewhat more modest version of the sort of claim that had been made during the original leap forward in 1958.

In 1978 there was, to be sure, none of the radical voluntarism of 20 years earlier. This shadow of the Great Leap Forward mentality, however, may have contributed to the rather grandiose economic projections of 1978, projections later retracted. Some opportunism may have been involved in this Leap Forward boomlet: support from it seems to have come from the old Chou En-lai group even more than from those around Hua. Li Hsien-nien encouraged talk of China's becoming a modern socialist state by the year 2000: this is a "historical necessity no reactionary force can block." Li also said the economy was developing faster and better than the planners expected (another echo of 1958, when Li had in fact been among the more cautious of China's rulers)—something that later turned out simply not to be true. Yü Ch'iu-li around the same time promised, like Hua Kuo-feng at the 1975 Tachai conference, basic agricultural mechanization by 1980.[21] Yu, three years closer to the set goal and with a sounder knowledge of economic development, had even less excuse for this than Hua.

Talk of the Great Leap Forward petered out before the end of January. The slogan of the first Leap Forward had been: much, fast, good, cheap (*tuo, k'uai, hao, sheng*). The recitations of this phrase in 1978 came increasingly to urge that quality and economy not be sacrificed to quantity and speed, as had happened in the original Leap Forward;[22] this in itself was enough to reduce talk of the Leap Forward to a harmless platitude.

Another aspect of the first Leap Forward had been "politics takes command," the virtually total politicization of economic activity. This mindset continued to receive support into the spring of 1978. A contrast can be detected, for example, in the approaches taken by Teng Hsaio-p'ing and Hua Kuo-feng at a science conference in March. Teng still had to pay lip service to what, a couple of years later, he could dismiss without argument, the Maoist-Great Leap Forward notion of the primacy of the human over the material factor in production; but even in 1978 in the process of paying lip service he negated it:

Our party says, man is the most vital factor among the forces of production. The "man" spoken of here is man with a certain degree of scientific knowledge, with experience in production and the ability to use the tools of production, who is able to bring about material production.

Hua, for his part, was equally committed to modernization, but he emphasized the political side of the concept: "In the world every line has its own kind of modernization," capitalist, imperialist, revisionist, and social imperialist. We want socialist modernization, "modernization upholding continued revolution under proletarian dictatorship."[23]

If the left had the initiative early in 1978, it soon lost it. Beginning in January, the *Liberation Army Daily* began publishing a series of entertaining articles about various "factions": (1) the wind faction, who go along with whatever is currently in power, who "steer according to the wind"; (2) the "slippery" faction, persons who once seemed more radical than anyone else but who now scratch their heads and innocently murmur, "Did I write this"; (3) the quake faction, who ran wild under the Gang and caused big disturbances but who now blend into the slippery faction; and (4) the cover-up faction, persons involved in the errors of the other three factions but who stubbornly deny all culpability. "In any case," they say, "mine is a contradiction among the people." These articles no doubt have a specific referent; most narrowly, they are probably part of an internal struggle within the army, an attack by supporters of Hsu Shih-yu upon Ch'en Hsi-lien.[24] But they also have a more general implication. The "factions" here probably do not refer to organized cliques as such but to patterns of behavior or, if it comes to that, to the same pattern of behavior. The general target of the "faction" series is persons still in power who had done well under the Gang and the object of the series to implicate these persons in the crimes of the Gang. Almost anyone not purged by the Gang could legitimately be depicted as a member of any or all of the factions, and the only major leader with an unmixed interest in the publication of the articles would be Teng Hsiao-p'ing'

These essays pointed to a widening of the scope of the struggle. There were those who wished to restrict it. Fang I said at the end of December 1977, "In criticizing the counterrevolutionary line of the 'Gang of Four' and in investigation work we should, as stipulated by the party center, emphasize the period since the tenth congress [August 1973], especially the period since the criticism of Lin and Confucius [ca. January 1974]."[25] Fang's restrictions would preclude any raking over of the Cultural Revolution or any systematic criticism of the general Maoist tradition. On May 18, 1978, this alleged stipulation of the party center was aggressively violated by a writer signing himself Shen T'ao-sheng. Lin Piao and the Gang, Shen says, are "foxes on the same hill." He does not claim they were always in collusion and many of the facts he cites tend to show they were not. But while Lin and the Gang may not always have worked together, according to Shen they committed the same error of line.[26] Both, in fact, were radical Maoists, and in linking Lin's line with that of the Gang the struggle became a direct confrontation with the Maoist heritage.

In June Hua again told some soldiers about the "victorious conclusion of the first Great proletarian Cultural Revolution" and used language once he popularized by Lin Piao: "Politics is the commander, the soul." He rejoiced in the smashing of Liu Shao-ch'i, Lin Piao, and the Gang.[27] To introduce Liu here is to dilute the impact of linking Lin and the Gang, for what were once held to be Liu's errors are obviously different from those of the others. In Hua's construction, Lin and the Gang become simply two separate entities in a long list of enemies and villains. Speaking to the same meeting, neither Teng Hsiao-p'ing nor Wei Kuo-ch'ing (who had become head of the army's General Political Department) mentioned Liu, but both linked Lin and the Gang. Wei also denounced Lin's "spiritualism," perhaps an oblique criticism of Hua's speech.[28] After June mentions of Liu Shao-ch'i became rare. A review of the history of intraparty struggles published on the eve of the anniversary of the party's founding talks about "Khrushchev-type ambitionists and plotters," which may or may not be a reference to Liu Shao-ch'i (once "China's Khrushchev") but it does not explicitly name him.[29]

   *Red Flag*, then controlled by Wang Tung-hsing, published an editorial in September conceding that Lin and the Gang should be linked and rather truculently calling for a truce. We cannot tolerate error, but "we welcome those who make a sincere self-criticism." "Those who, being misled committed serious mistakes should be dealt with mainly through thought education. We should not pursue individual responsibility," and we should not "reopen old historical accounts." "We absolutely must not plot individual revenge, nor should we engage in struggles for individual power. We should look ahead and concentrate all our hatred on the persons of Lin Piao and the 'Gang of Four.' "[30] Teng was apparently not inclined to show much mercy, nor did he seem particularly intimidated by the accusation that he was concerned only with personal power and revenge. The *People's Daily* immediately denied that linking the Gang with Lin was reopening old accounts or that it was a negation of the Cultural Revolution (apparently another current criticism). A month later the point was made even more strongly: "In the past it was said that the 'Gang of Four' 'inherited' the mantle of Lin Piao. This manner of speaking is incorrect." The Gang inherited nothing; Lin and the Gang were always exactly the same in line. Also, it is wrong to say that members of the Gang had no theory (that is, that they were corrupt people but that Maoism is above reproach): they were counterrevolutionary revisionists. Some comrades remain fellow travelers of the Gang and are getting so nervous about the continuing criticism that they even start to blather about "defending the accomplishments of the Cultural Revolution." But without a thorough criticism, there is no protection against the reemergence of even more Lin Piaos, Gang-type plotters, ambitionists, and fake theorists.[31]

Thorough criticism of the Gang's line, rather than mere hatred for their persons, implied a repudiation of Maoist radicalism. Although radical policies had rarely in fact been implemented since the collapse of the Great Leap Forward, radicalism remained the hegemonic ideology. Even under Mao leftist errors were officially held to be as bad as rightist ones, and cadres were criticized for believing that "left" is better than right. But cadres were prone to this error precisely because conditions encouraged it. If the only leftism to be criticized was "leftism" in quotation marks, the implication would be that leftism in itself is good, and only fake or so-called leftism bad. Hua Kuo-feng consistently classified the Gang as extreme rightists, not leftists in any sense.[32]

Publicly labeling the Gang as left would serve further to discredit the Maoist line as well as to discredit Hua. Here Hua seems to have been able to maintain a tenacious fight. In April 1978 the *People's Daily*, liberally quoting various dicta of Hua's, called for exposure of the "fake leftism" of the Gang, which enabled them to deceive people. This implies that genuine leftism is so attractive that even its counterfeit has some appeal. In June the Gang was denounced for "extreme 'leftism,'" but this turns out to be precisely the same thing as rightism.[33] It was not until 1979 that leftism itself was criticized. It was then tediously pointed out that while it is not incorrect to say that members of the Gang (and Lin Piao) were fake leftists and true rightists, it is more to the point simply to call them leftists. Talk of "fake 'leftism,'" in fact, is often merely a way of excusing leftist errors. Just because some people act in bad faith does not mean they cannot be leftwingers. We need to look at the essence of the error itself. "Since the founding of our state thirty years ago we have suffered much more from 'leftism' than from rightism—and we have suffered enough."[34]

In addition to criticizing other people, Teng also developed his own particular line. In the spring of 1978, he introduced his notion that practice is the sole criterion of truth.[35] The wider implications of the stress on practice are discussed in the next chapter. In effect, if taken to its extreme the slogan renders nugatory any formal ideological doctrine. Here it is enough to point out that the slogan in its context demystifies Maoism and, for that matter, Marxism (the words of Mao or Marx may be truth itself, but they cannot be the standard of truth)[36] and removes some of the patina from Hua's claim to be Mao's successor. The slogan functioned in a way some find rather contrary to its spirit: to mouth the slogan was one way of pledging allegiance to Teng Hsiao-p'ing.[37] *Red Flag*, perhaps too busy at the time protesting the reopening of historical accounts, refused throughout the fall of 1978 to publicize the thesis that practice is the standard of truth.

## THE PURGE OF PEKING

Mao Tse-Tung once said that one of his ways of bringing about the destruction of his chosen successor was to "dig up the cornerstone." By the fall of 1978, Hua's cornerstone was perhaps pretty well undermined, but his position had not yet collapsed.

In July the Tientsin Party committee had been purged. Its most heinous crime was that it had "taken the lead . . . in slandering Vice Chairman Teng by name. What is more intolerable, until November, 1977, they were still publishing and distributing extremely reactionary [materials] maliciously to attack Comrade Teng Hsiao-p'ing."[38] Lin Hu-chia, who conducted this purge, was again transferred in October to become first secretary and "mayor" of Peking, Wu Te then being removed from that post.[39]

Around the same time, there were many reports from Peking and Hong Kong that Ch'en Hsi-lien had been dismissed as commander of the Peking military region. This was not in fact official until January 1980, but whatever his nominal status Ch'en was clearly in trouble and probably not in actual charge of his military region throughout 1979.[40] Also during 1978 there were rumors of a rift within the military, particuiarly between a southern block led by Hsu Shih-yu and a northern group led by Ch'en Hsi-lien. If this is true, by early fall a split in the northern block seems to have developed.

In September 1978 Hsu Shih-yu published a rambling, garrulous piece, ostensibly a commemoration of Mao but in fact a crude and blatant exercise in self-promotion—so crude and blatant that it is almost innocent. Hsu says many strange things. He says that in 1965 Mao warned him to be wary of revisionism, especially revisionism emerging from the center. "He asked me: If there is revisionism at the center, what will you do? I answered: If the center becomes revisionist, I'll march north with my troops and protect Chairman Mao, protect the party center! Chairman Mao laughed and said: It won't come to that." Hsu apparently would lead a coup if things were not going properly in Peking. Although, to all indication, Hsu had been one of Teng's strongest supporters, these words would imply his support for Teng had its limits. In the then still official, if neglected, version of history in 1978, the second-ranking revisionist at the center in 1965 had been Teng Hsiao-p'ing. Hsu moves on to explain, however, that the real revisionists are not the ones the Gang of Four considered revionists. The Gang thought the old cadres were revisionists but the old cadres are all fine fellows. Revisionism will never come from them. There are, however, "so-called 'old cadres'" who belong to the wind faction. These are "self-seeking and utterly shameless. Day and night they passed through the gates of Lin Piao and the 'Gang of Four,' hoping to run with their filthy feet right up to the azure clouds, riding on the heads of the masses for the sake of their own power and joy."[41] This, one assumes, is Hsu's considered opinion of poor Ch'en Hsi-lien.

Hsu has more positive words for Comrade Li Te-sheng, a fine fellow. Li had looked after Hsu's daughter when the girl came to work in Peking. Li, the commander of the Shenyang military region, had been commander of the Ahwei military district during the Cultural Revolution. He was technically subordinate to Hsu, then commander of Nanking. Hsu, however, was constantly quarrelling with the radical Red Guards, while Li remained on good terms with the Central Cultural Revolution Group. After that Li had his ups and downs. At one time he had been a member of the Politburo Standing Committee but was later demoted to regular member. Before replacing Ch'en Hsi-lien in Shenyang, he had been briefly in charge of the army's General Political Department, until Chang Ch'un-ch'iao decided to take that job himself. Li was perhaps the most leftist of the regional commanders. The day after Hsu's article was published, Li, who seems to be an altogether more suave character, also published a piece. Li's eulogy of Mao contains the most advanced views of the Teng line and sounds almost as if it had been written by the Li I-che dissidents of 1974. Bureaucratism has not, says Li Te-sheng, been opposed enough. Some of our leaders (Ch'en Hsi-lien?) act like patriachs. They never consult with others and never admit mistakes. Socialism in China, Li says, is distorted by the 2000-year-old feudal tradition and by the lack of a capitalist phase. Sometimes Chinese socialism has been no better than fascism. Democracy and a legal system is needed. The days of no law and no heaven are gone. "Chairman Mao always taught us to talk about democracy, to talk about legality," Li says, perhaps with a straight face.[42]

The purge of Peking was perhaps completed by the firing of Chi Teng-k'uei as commissar of the Peking military region.[43] Concurrently there were purges in northern China, with the removal of the first secretaries of Liaoning and Inner Mongolia.[44] The other big leftists on the Politburo, Wang Tung-hsing and Ni Chih-fu, were criticized on wall posters and within the party, but their positions did not suffer at that time. Also, while Wu, Chi, and perhaps Ch'en lost their jobs, they were not then publicly humiliated and they remained nominally members of the Polit-buro.

The local authorities in Peking had been directly responsible for the suppression of the April 1976 riots, and their removal served as a preliminary for the "reversal of verdicts" on that incident. Since this incident had been the occasion for Hua's formal assumption of the premiership, the reversal was a direct slap at him. The reversal was also perhaps the first official endorsement in People's China of a genuinely spontaneous political act, and it thus added to the momentum of the developing democratic movement.

## THE THIRD PLENUM

The formal rehabilitation of the T'ien-an-men incident began very soon after the change in the Peking party committee. In October *China Youth* remarked that the incident had been an expression of the will of the people; on November 16 the new municipal committee pronounced it to have been "entirely revolutionary."[45] In December, immediately before the closing of the third plenum, the *People's Daily* printed a detailed evaluation of the riots. The then dominant tendency in the party attempted to arrogate to itself as much credit as it could: the incident shows that the "masses" love Chou En-lai and the "old cadres" (especially Teng Hsiao-p'ing, we gather, although this is left tacit), and the old cadres, on their part, are not ashamed of (*wu k'uei-yü*) the esteem the masses hold them in. The exercise as a whole is what might be called Maoism, Teng Hsiao-p'ing style. Part of the idea of the Cultural Revolution had been that the people should act both as a check on and a goad to the party. Teng was now giving specific endorsement to popular checks against the leftist establishment. The incident is said to show the need for the party to have roots among the people. "Anti-people, anti-democratic forces [Hua Kuo-feng?] often become impacted within our party and our organs of proletarian dictatorship and obtain some power in the party and the state." Sometimes these evil forces even manage to equate themselves with the party leadership. The people need to be able to protest against this. We believe the people "will not permit wicked persons to take the opportunity" of licensed protest to cause chaos. Also, the party will continue to decide for itself the specific merit of the ideas expressed. "To protect the people's democratic rights we must establish a socialist system of laws." Democracy, however, is prior to law, and law cannot be allowed to become an instrument of oppression.[46]

The dominant forces had no patience then with the argument that appeals to the people would disrupt unity. The deeper the criticism goes, they purported to believe, the more unity becomes consolidated. Teng's group was in fact threatening to enlarge the purge further: those who repent will be forgiven, but those who "remain stubborn to the end will not have a pleasant fate."[47] As it happened, the third plenum of the Eleventh Central Committee (which met from December 12 to December 21) did not purge anyone but made a few promotions, as indicated in Table 4.2. Ch'en Yun, the party's outstanding economic moderate, had not been purged during the Cultural Revolution but had been for the most part ignored since the late 1950s. He now became a member of the Politburo Standing Committee. Hu Yao-pang had been head of the Youth Corps prior to the Cultural Revolution and had also been one of Teng's few personal supporters. He was now to become one of Teng's closest collaborators, a counterheir to Teng, along with Chao Tzu-yang. Wang

## TABLE 4.2:    Additions to Politburo, December 1978

| Name | General Function |
| --- | --- |
| Ch'en Yun (to Politburo Standing Committee) | Economic management |
| Teng Ying-ch'ao (widow of Chou En-lai) | Women's work |
| Hu Yao-pang | Central apparatus; formerly, youth work |
| Wang Chen | State bureaucracy, agriculture |

Chen, the minister in charge of state farms, was an old Chou En-lai bureaucrat, and the treatment of Teng Ying-ch'ao, Chou En-lai's widow, should be seen as honorific.

Teng Hsiao-ping may have had even more direct support among the new appointees to the Central Committee. The plenum restored the good name of P'eng Te-huai, who had been purged as minister of defense in 1959 for his opposition to the Great Leap Forward; and of T'ao Chu, former boss of the South-Central region and generally an economic moderate, who had had a meteoric rise and fall in the summer of 1966.[48] Former supporters of P'eng (Hsi Chung-hsun) and Huang K'o-ch'eng, who had been chief of staff under P'eng and of T'ao (Wang Jen-chung) were now put back on the Central Committee. Also reappointed were followers of the pre-Cultural Revolution mayor of Peking, P'eng Chen. P'eng had been the second-ranking man on the central secretariat and was perhaps Teng's main rival in those days. During the 1960s his supporters had been the most articulate critics of radical Maoism, and they had been purged several months earlier than Liu Shao-ch'i. Now it seems that the rivalry, if there had been any, was forgotten. Former followers of P'eng Chen (whose own rehabilitation still had to wait several months) restored to the Central Committee include Sung Jen-ch'iung, Huang Huo-ch'ing, and Hu Ch'iao-mu. Also promoted to the Central Committee was Ch'en Tsai-tao, the soldier who had led the so-called Wuhan mutiny against the radicals in the summer of 1967. The plenum set up the Disciplinary Inspection Commission, presumably giving Teng institutional leverage over life within the party. The leadership of this organ was dominated by the newcomers: Ch'en Yun, Teng Ying-ch'ao, Hu Yao-pang, and Huang K'o-ch'eng.

The public report of the plenum was the least ambiguous antiradical party pronouncement since the fall of the Gang. The major concession to the left is the announcement that the mass movement to criticize Lin and the Gang had reached a "basic conclusion." In 1979 the party will concentrate on "socialist modernization" rather than these political campaigns. This concession is vitiated by the announcement later in the document that in some places the campaign had not been very thorough;

in fact, in 1979 criticism of crimes and errors continued unabated. In addition to being a bow to the left, however, and an insincere signal that the purges had come to an end, this may also have been evidence of a "basic" intention to be done with Maoist-style rule by campaign. The public report also begins the reevaluation of the Cultural Revolution. It says the party must not be overly hasty in reevaluating the Cultural Revolution, which would seem to mean that everyone knows the Cultural Revolution was a disaster but it is not yet expedient to say so too clearly. The report makes the curious claim that the main target of the Cultural Revolution was Soviet revisionism, although every previous statement about that set of events had indicated the main worry was revisionism inside the CPC. The report condemns egalitarianism in economic policy but otherwise commands equality before the law. The most politically significant part of the report, at least for purposes of tracing the power struggle, is the treatment of Mao and the cult of the individual. "Comrade Mao Tse-tung" turns out to have been a great leader, a great Marxist. He had a scientific attitude about everything, himself included, and was well aware of his many shortcomings. "Comrade Hua Kuo-feng" gave a speech stressing collective leadership. He thought there should be less boasting about individuals and also believed that titles such as chairman are inappropriate for ordinary use. Citizens should call each other comrade. And no comrades should take it upon themselves to issue directives in their own name (as Mao had done and as Hua had done until then). Hua's face was, just barely, saved.[49]

The third plenum also encouraged the growing democratic movement. At first glance it is not obvious why it should do so. If he had to, Teng would certainly wish to mobilize public opinion in his favor; but if articulate public opinion were allowed to have its way, it is equally certain that it would soon go beyond what Teng was willing to tolerate. Also, while from Teng's point of view the democratic movement was, at least among other things, one of the weapons he could use to beat his enemies, it did not really begin to flourish until Teng had achieved a seeming triumph.

In fact, even at the end of 1978 Teng's victory was incomplete. In terms of his ability to set the official line, he may have obtained almost all he wanted, but he had not been able to get rid of his antagonists. The left had been weakened, but it was not eliminated.

As Teng's reforms became more radical and as his position became more secure, opposition to both also grew even among persons with no particular affinity for the leftist tendency. Yang Ch'eng-wu, Lin Piao's chief of staff from 1965 until 1968, for some reason rehabilitated after Lin's death, is said to have complained that every time Teng liberates one of the victims of the Cultural Revolution, he purges someone else.[50] Even some of Teng's original supporters seem to have been drawing back—a possible interpretation of the curious performance of Hsu Shih-yu on the occasion of the anniversary of Mao's death. The State Council bureaucrats also betrayed signs of discontent.

It should be recalled that it was not just the leftists but also those responsible for bringing Teng back in 1977 who had benefited, or at least not been greatly harmed, by the Cultural Revolution. To free himself from dependence upon those who had brought him back, Teng had to push for a change in the status quo, through the change creating a new basis for his own position. By 1979 he seems increasingly to have called upon the services of politicians purged during the Cultural Revolution and not rehabilitated during Mao's lifetime—persons with no interest at all in protecting the reputation of the Cultural Revolution. At the same time, Teng could call upon the Maoist legacy of mass activism in order to legitimize his own actions before he could consolidate his new base. As long as articulate public opinion was in his favor, Teng has no reason not to milk it. At the end of 1978, he still had an incentive to further the democratic movement.

## NOTES

1. Yu Ch'ing, "Thoroughly Smash the Gang System of the 'Gang of Four,' " *Jen-min Jih-pao* [People's Daily], August 6, 1977 (hereafter cited as *PD*).

2. *Hung Ch'i* 9 (September 4, 1977): 34. In the spring of 1978, the Military Affairs Commission complained that army discipline had been neglected for a decade (*PD*, April 10, 1978). Around the same time, a wall poster asserted that a political alliance of the northern military regions had formed against an alliance of the southern regions (*Chung-yang Jih-pao*, May 17, 1978). If true, this would reflect a rivalry between between Hsu Shih-yu and Ch'en Hsi-lien. On the other hand, later commentaries on the social purge substitute formalism for warlordism in the trinity with bureaucratism and commandism (e.g., *PD*, August 3, 1978).

3. *Kuang-ming Jih-pao*, August 8, 1977; Peter R. Moody, Jr., *The Politics of the Eighth Central Committee of the Communist Party of China* (Hamden, Conn.: Shoestring Press. 1973), pp. 58–59.

4. *PD*, August 23, 1977.

5. *Cheng Ming* 22 (August 1979); Foreign Information Broadcast System, *Daily Report, People's Republic of China*, August 9, 1979, pp. U1–U2 (hereafter cited as *FBIS/PRC*).

6. A Taiwan source claims Li opposed Teng's return to power. *Chung-kung Wen-t'i Tzu-Liao* 52 (September 29, 1980): 24.

7. Nieh Jung-chen, "Restore and Develop the Party's Excellent Style," *PD*, September 5, 1977; Ch'en Yun, "Uphold Seeking Truth from Facts," ibid., September 28, 1977.

8. Ibid., September 10, 1977.

9. Li Hung-lin, "Is Distribution According to Labor a Socialist or a Capitalist Principle?" ibid., September 27, 1977. The Gang has said it was a concession to a residual capitalist mentality. The line now was that it was no concession at all, but just pure socialism.

10. Lin Feng, "The Struggle of Marxism against the Vulgar Theory of Nothing but Production Forces," ibid., September 7, 1977.

11. Ibid., September 12, 1977.

12. Ibid., October 12, 1977.

13. Mao Chih-yung, "Earnestly Allow the Party's Economic Policy to Take Root and Fully Mobilize the Peasant's Socialist Activism," ibid., August 30, 1978.

14. Ibid., September 22, 1978. See ibid., February 12, 1981 for the formal repudiation of the Tachai model.

15. Ibid., September 8, 1977.

16. Ibid., October 7, 1977. The great event had actually taken place, however, on September 22.

17. Ibid., November 19, 1977.

18. Ibid., December 28, 1977.

19. Mao Tse-tung, "A Great Leap Forward Will Appear in China," ibid., December 26, 1977.

20. Wu Hsu, "Welcoming a New Leap Forward," ibid., January 3, 1978.

21. Ibid., January 28 and 29, 1978.

22. Ibid., January 27, 1978.

23. Ibid., March 22, and 26, 1978. Fang I, of the old Chou En-lai group, took a position similar to Teng's. Science as such has no class character. In a bourgeois society scientists work for the bourgeoisie; now they work for us, the proletariat. Ibid., March 29, 1978.

24. For the articles, see ibid., January 6, 10, 16, and February 22, 1978. For an analysis from the perspective of the pro-Teng people in Hong Kong, see Cheng Chao-mao, "A New Struggle Unfolds in Communist China?" *Cheng Ming* 4 (February 1978) in *FBIS/PRC*, February 3, 1978, pp. N2–N6. Tanjug identified Ch'en Hsi-lien as the head of the wind faction. Later developments show, I think, that this is probably true. In the meantime a Peking wall poster around January 1978 described Li Te-sheng in terms that make him sound like a member of all the factions. *Chung-yang Jih-pao*, March 8, 1978. Ch'en and Li may then have been members of a northern military combination against Hsu in the south, and I argue below that quite possibly in the fall of 1978 Li sold Ch'en out. The article on the slippery faction mentions those who manage to slip away into Papaoshan, the graveyard serving the party elite. This is perhaps the first of the covert attacks on K'ang Sheng, whose ashes were soon to be removed from that place.

25. *PD*, December 30, 1977.

26. Shen T'ao-sheng, "The 'Gang of Four' and Lin Piao," ibid., May 18, 1978.

27. Ibid., June 4, 1978. Yeh Chien-ying, perhaps even then becoming anxious about Mao's reputation, also mentioned Liu. Ibid., June 6, 1978.

28. Ibid., June 6 and 8, 1978.

29. Ibid., June 30, 1978.

30. *Hung-ch'i* 8 (September 3, 1978): 63–65.

31. *PD*, September 7, 1978; ibid., October 4, 1978.

32. Ibid., December 27, 1976; ibid., March 7, 1978.

33. Ibid., April 18, 1978; ibid., June 28, 1978.

34. Chin Wen, 'Thoroughly Criticize the Bad Faith Implementation of the 'Left' Opportunist Line by Lin Piao and the 'Gang of Four,' " *Kuang-ming Jih-pao*, January 23, 1979; also Chang Hsien-yang and Wang Kuei-hsiu, "On the Nature of the Line of Lin Piao and the 'Gang of Four,' " *PD*, February 28, 1979.

35. Teng's speech outlining his notion was not published, but the gist is given in *Kuang-ming Jih-pao*, May 11, 1978; see also Teng's remarks to the military conference, *PD*, June 6, 1978.

36. For example, *PD*, September 22, 1978.

37. *Cheng Ming* 13 (November 1, 1978), in *FBIS/PRC*, November 3, 1978, p. N1.

38. Tientsin radio, July 28, 1978; *FBIS/PRC*, August 1, 1978, p. K6.

39. Taiwan reports that Lin Hu-chia is the husband of Ch'en Mu-hua, a Li Hsien-nien protégé. *Chung-kung Wen-t'i Tzu-liao* 56 (October 27, 1980): 24. If so, the replacement of Wu by Lin would be a way of removing support for Hua Kuo-feng in Peking without giving the capital entirely to Teng Hisao-p'ing. Lin was removed from his Peking positions in late 1980 after a long criticism of the mishandling of building and improvements in the city, particularly of carrying out construction without regard for historical or aesthetic considerations. He was not, however, disgraced and soon found work with the central government.

40. Agence France Presse, October 14, 1978; *FBIS/PRC*, October 16, 1978, p. E1. When Ch'en's purge finally became official, he was treated the most leniently among the "little Gang of Four." By 1980 it seems that relations between Teng Hsiao-p'ing and Ch'en's main antagonist, Hsu Shih-yu, had in their turn soured.

41. Hsu Shih-yu, "Chairman Mao Will Always Live in Our Hearts," *PD*, September 8, 1978.

42. Li Te-sheng, "Deeply Penetrate Reality, Link Up with the Masses," ibid., September 9, 1978. A month later (ibid., October 10, 1978) a news story headline says Li endorsed the principle that practice is the criterion of truth. Perhaps this is what Li meant, but the story does not quote him using the words. In both his September and October pronouncements, Li does use the locution, seek truth from facts. The critique of feudalism became a major theme in 1980, with Teng's simultaneous assault on the Hua Kuo-feng left and on the old Chou-En-lai bureaucrats.

43. *Chung-yang Jih-pao*, November 23, 1978.

44. Agence France Presse, October 14, 1978; *FBIS/PRC*, October 18, 1978, p. E1.

45. *Kuang-ming Jih-pao*, October 22, 1978; *PD*, November 17, 1978. The Youth Corps was then in the forefront of Teng's reforms. *China Youth* had just resumed publication, having been suppressed in 1966. Wang Tung-hsing had attempted to block the publication of the first new issue, since it contained articles questioning Mao's ominiscience. *Ch'i-shin Nien-tai*, November 1978, in *FBIS/PRC*, November 9, 1978, p. N3.

46. *PD* December 21, 1978.

47. Ibid., November 18, 1978.

48. Peter R. Moody, Jr., "Power and Policy: The Career of T'ao Chu, 1956-1966," *China Quarterly* 54 (April/June 1973): 167–93. Some of T'ao's group had returned to public life before Mao died—for example, Chao Tzu-yang and Chang P'ing-hua, who had in the meantime tied his fortunes to those of Hua Kuo-feng and was repurged in 1979. Chao later praised T'ao as the embodiment of all that was fine in traditional Chinese statesmanship. See Chao Tzu-yang, "The Exalted Virtues of a Communist," *PD*, March 23, 1979. For the story of P'eng Te-huai's sorry treatment, see Huang K'o-ch'eng, "Pure in Heart, He Gazes at the Sun and Moon: His Moral Courage Will Endure a Thousand Autumns," ibid., January 3, 1979.

49. *PD*, December 24, 1978.

50. *Chung-yang Jih-pao*, November 2, 1978. Yang himself received an indirect criticism at that time. *PD*, November 2, 1978 attached those who would "greatly and particularly" (*ta-shu t'e-shu*) establish the "absolute authority" of Mao and Mao's thought. This inelegant phrase had allegedly been coined by Ch'en Po-ta, but it was Yang who popularized it. Yang Ch'eng-wu, "Greatly and Particularly Establish the Absolute Authority of the Great Supreme Commander Chairman Mao, Greatly and Particularly Establish the Absolute Authority of the Great Thought of Mao Tse-tung," ibid., November 3, 1967.

# 5

# Official Liberalization: Political Ideology and Institutions

The context of the democratic movement was an official liberalization undertaken by the regime itself. This chapter and the next explore the nature and the limitations of this official liberalization. The present chapter discusses the liberalization of political practices and institutions, while the next deals with specific policies. Since the democratic movement was itself a political phenomenon, it is expedient to examine separately the regime's political reaction to it. This chapter, therefore, is limited to a discussion of changes taking place up to the third pleum, which gave brief official sanction to the democratic movement.

At a minimum, to the extent that a totalitarian movement ceases to be totalitarian, to that extent it liberalizes. The following are some of the standard attributes of totalitarian politics: (1) totalitarian regimes are leadership regimes; (2) rule is carried out through an ideological party, the ideology in principle having something to say about every aspect of life and the party having the competence and the authority to enforce the ideology anywhere it chooses; (3) the regime is not, however, bound by any literal construction of its ideology, nor is it bound by its own laws and regulations—it is, rather, a "movement" regime; (4) like a liberal regime, a totalitarian regime is founded upon popular support—but rather than reflecting public opinion, the regime defines and shapes it. This listing suggests we should look for changes in the nature and function of the ruling ideology, in the evaluation of the leader and the leadership principle, in the function of the party, in the role of law as an instrument of rule, and in the treatment of political participation by those outside the elite.

## IDEOLOGY

The great sacred phrase of Mao's last decade and more was class struggle. All truth was held to be conditioned by class, and everything had to be seen from a class perspective (although the Maoist tendency was to define class in terms of agreement with the ideological line). The Gang of Four would not agree that it was opposed to the modernization of China; rather, the Gang wanted to be sure that it would be *socialist* modernization. The development of productive capacity by itself, they alleged, would produce "bourgeois" modernization leading, for example, to rule by a privileged stratum of technocrats. Socialist society is still class society and develops by means of class struggle. The influence of old ways remains strong and must constantly be suppressed by dictatorship. To treat any aspect of life as irrelevant to politics is, precisely, to turn it into a weapon of bourgeois politics.

Class struggle is, therefore, related to another Maoist derivation from Leninism—politics takes command. The assertion of political over technological or other criteria may serve well as a means to justify unlimited party dictatorship, it may also hinder technological development. By the time that Mao died, this was no longer a price the dominant groupings among the elite were willing to pay, and from the time of the purge of the Gang there were moves to deideologize at least policies having to do with economic development, at least to a degree.

The early Hua regime paid lip service to the Maoist tenets but ceased to give them practical effect. Hua was wary of loosening *controls* and in his time a concern for technological rationality went along with ideological orthodoxy and affirmation of the continued need for dictatorship and the repression of dissent. The logic of Hua's regime was more nearly Stalinist than Maoist.

After the eleventh party congress, this pragmatism in economics began increasingly to encroach upon ideological orthodoxy. By the fall of 1977, the old moderate slogan, "Seek truth from facts," was being repeated to the point of tedium and was more frequently and explicitly accompanied by its codicil warning against the radical propensity to tell lies. By the spring of 1978, this trend had evolved into a questioning of the radicals' dichotomy between politics and economics, as the regime became more inclined to the classical or scholastic Marxist position that politics is shaped by the level of economic development, rather than the Leninist-Maoist theory that politics should take command. A *People's Daily* editorial of April probably reflects what had come to be the views of Hua Kuo-feng; at least it quotes Hua liberally. "Only socialism can save China," it asserts. "Our standard in the modernization of China must be the socialist road." By implication this is at odds with the alternative slogan that Teng Hsiao-p'ing had already introduced within the party—that practice is the criterion of truth. But the editorial also quotes Hua as saying: "Socialism cannot be separated from the four modernizations."[1] By June, when Teng had grown stronger, the same newspaper asserted the validity of the idea that politics should take command but continued: "Marxism holds that economics is the basis of politics, while politics is the collective manifestation of economics."[2] Good politics becomes whatever contributes to the health of the economy.

Teng, meanwhile, had claimed that practice is the sole criterion of truth. Some comrades think this weakens the role of theory, but it is only through practice that one can discover that some theories are false, thereby protecting true theories. The Gang, exaggerating the role of individual geniuses, took the thoughts of Mao as the standard of truth, in the process distorting the thoughts. If Mao's thoughts are true, it is because it stands up to the test of practice.

Teng's slogan was itself a quote from Mao, and this opposition to dogmatism was certainly a part of Mao's thought, at least until the 1950s. Mao also tended to assert a radical relativism: there is no absolute truth since our knowledge is always developing. Teng too made use of this sort of relativism.[3] An argument between Marx and Engels was cited to show that not everything in the Marxist canon could be true: if the two men contradict each other, they cannot both be right. It was also asserted that Marxism was itself incomplete and in need of development.[4]

The function of practice was different for Teng than for Mao, however. Maoist relativism served to underpin a revolutionary voluntarism critical of classical Marxism. Teng tended at least verbally toward the deterministic aspect of Marxism, stressing the limitations on human will imposed by objective constraints.[5] Mao's relativism served to feed the permanent purge: one can perceive truth only by taking the proper class perspective and, since things are always changing, so also is the proper perspective. For Teng relativism was simply a result of the normal limitations of human knowledge; truth itself was declared to be without class character.[6] Maoist pragmatism, in short, was a form of totalitarian antinomianism. Teng's was a way of freeing policy from vulnerability to criticism on grounds rising from theory.[7]

There is, of course, more than a little truth to the Maoist analysis. There is no such thing as practice in the abstract, but only practice directed toward some end; and to serve one end may mean to neglect another. Another version of Teng's slogan ran: *successful* practice is the standard of truth. But what, then, is the standard of success? Maoists, for example, would not see Teng's practice as successful, even if it were economically efficient. Teng's pragmatism worked to justify, among other things, increased power and privilege for experts and technocrats, while the pragmatism of the Maoists would benefit other categories. Which is correct, of course, is a matter of political choice and power, not of some mechanical measurement of truth by the standards of an abstract practice.

Another function of the practice slogan was to serve as a token of the utterer's fealty to Teng. The skeptical observer is moved to comment upon the dogmatic critique of dogmatism, whereby pragmatism becomes one more repressive ideology.[8] It would obviously not have been shrewd in those days to claim, for example, that practice had demonstrated the validity of the ways and views of the Gang of Four. Teng Hsiao-p'ing is no more Voltaire than Mao was, as the democratic movement found out.

Yet it may be one-sided to dismiss the practice slogan as just another smelly little orthodoxy. The slogan does not point to the affirmation of any particular mode of practice but, if taken to its logical conclusion, to the rejection of ideological politics as such. It is irrelevant to this function that it also in its context threatened rough treatment to those who would continue to conduct politics in an ideological manner.

Here we begin to see the outline of what the official liberalization of Chinese politics really was. It was not an expression of political liberty but, rather, a *depoliticization*. In totalitarianism all things are potentially matters for political concern, and Maoism entailed nearly the total politicization of life. The practice slogan implies a recognition of the autonomy of some aspects of life. It need not imply a renunciation of overall political control by the regime: one assumes one motive for depoliticization is to increase the efficiency of control by curbing its more outrageous ambitions.[9] But it does mean at least a limited recognition of the legitimacy of spontaneous public and private behavior and a determination that control will not take the form of an attempt to direct everything through political power. This, in turn, implies a change in the nature of the regime. Marxism in China could become a mere word or could turn from an ideology to a *mentality*, a vague set of attitudes and ideas that have no particular consequences but are accepted as a way of acknowledging the regime's legitimacy. Given that the People's Republic has been an ideological regime and given the Leninist heritage of those who rule it, it is doubtful that this change is irreversible or that it can take hold without friction. It is not really surprising that since 1980 the regime was complaining about a crisis of faith.

## THE PARTY

The ruling party plays an ambiguous role in a totalitarian regime. In such regimes there has been tension between the role of the party and that of the leader. The ideology provides some kind of guide for the total transformation of society, and the party consists of the disciplined eli that implements the ideology. But the party is also an organization and like any effective and enduring organization requires rules, structure, and routine. Rules and routine limit the totality of the change, and those who fill positions in the party structure become a new ruling establishment with some interest in keeping things as they are. The intensification of totalitarian rule is sometimes marked by an attack on the party from within, from its own leadership. These attacks—the Night of the Long Knives, Stalin's Great Purge, the Cultural Revolution—not only bring to grief individual party members but also disrupt the organizational functioning of the party. The prime target of the Cultural Revolution had been persons in power inside the *party*, not, say, ideological moderates as such. Ideological moderates, themselves, of course, party members, who worked for the state bureaucracies or for the army came out of the Cultural Revolution relatively well. The Maoist position was caricatured during the Hua and Teng regimes as "kicking out the party committee to make revolution,"[10] and the Gang would sometimes speak of the party as something to make revolution against.

The Cultural Revolution brought chaos to the party organization everywhere except possibly inside the army, but the Cultural Revolution could do what it did only because the party was already vulnerable. In 1956 Liu Shao-ch'i and Teng Hsiao-p'ing had attempted to institutionalize the leading role of the party. A couple of years later, however, the Great Leap Forward led to an expansion of the functions of the party, as the party organizations directly took over the work of state institutions and the transmission belt "mass organizations." This enlargement of the scope of the party went beyond the normal Leninist model whereby the party organization within each unit sets the policy direction of the unit in conformity with general party policy. This at least arguably results in what can be called party control. In China, however, as those worried about the trend put it, the party was tending to replace the state (and the process was in fact accompanied by the slogan about the withering away of the state, although Marx probably did not have what was then going on precisely in mind). The party became in effect the totality of the political structure and could no longer be said to control that structure. It contained within itself all the relevant political cleavages in Chinese society (because those it did not contain could be ignored until mobilized by one group or another within the party). The central party bureaucracy became largely superfluous, and the party as a whole fractionalized. It was easy to overthrow the central party organization in these conditions.

The rebuilding of the party at the provincial level began in 1970, when Hua Kuo-feng became first secretary of the new Hunan party committee. The central party machinery remained vestigial until at least

1980. Even the local party organizations remained in disarray, at least if we believe the Hua-Teng analysis. Contemporary material from the 1970s indicates factional strife inside local organizations. A post-Gang description of the Shanghai party, while no doubt tendentious, makes that organization sound like a federation of special interest groups held together by agreements among gangsters. The basis of the organization at the beginning, it was said, had been the revolutionary rebels—Wang Hung-wen's "little brothers," composed of lumpenproletariat thugs sworn to personal allegiance to Wang—allied with hack intellectuals. The criminals and the intellectuals constantly bickered with each other, and this allowed opportunistic old cadres once purged by the rebels to regain influence. These three groups "treated party membership as if it were a gift," allocating new memberships and official positions according to factional quotas.[11]

The Gang had provided a theoretical basis, if not for the freewheeling factional divisions alleged to exist in Shanghai, at least for some kind of factional activity within the party. Maoism entailed one version of the "new class" argument. In the absence of a thoroughgoing dictatorship, the party constantly and spontaneously breeds "new bourgeois elements." These could sometimes come to dominate the party, and thus the good communist, as Wang Hung-wen said in 1973, dares to oppose the tide.

The Hua regime insisted upon a return to democratic centralism, with the emphasis on centralism. Teng was able later to dismiss the Maoist theory of a bourgeoisie within the party, although, at one point, he flirted with the idea of retaining it for his own purposes. Hua, with his residual commitment to Maoism, initially had to be more equivocal. Mao, Hua noted, said a bourgeoisie arises within the party, and Mao was right. Examples include Liu Shao-ch'i, Lin Piao, and the Gang of Four. Capitalist roaders of this ilk can take power inside the party. But, Hua explains, Mao never meant to assert that the party itself contains or produces a bourgeoisie.[12] For Hua, the trouble is simply that bad individuals can gain control of the party, not that the party need contain class antagonisms.

Hua did not expect an automatic concord of opinion within the party, even in one purged of the bad people. Democratic centralism itself implies a recognition of internal disagreements. Hua asserted from the beginning of his rule that there should be freedom to express differences of opinion. On his return to grace, Teng Hsiao-p'ing preached a brief homily on democratic centralism stressing its democratic side. The party must maintain discipline, but it should not violate the peace of mind of those who, in good faith, disagree with party policy.[13] More generally, disagreements within the party should be conducted and resolved in a civil manner. A thought of Mao was discovered: "If you let people speak out the sky won't fall, nor will you yourself be overthrown. If you don't let people speak out, eventually it will be hard to avoid being overthrown."[14]

Toleration of dissent within the party is not the same as toleration for public expression of that dissent nor for public dissent from those outside the party—although the Teng line eventually came to encourage this. The Hua-Teng line on the party, prior to the third plenum, was basically a return to the Chinese version of Leninism developed especially by Liu Shao-ch'i[15] but also by Mao in his preradical days. The Chinese party had always been dominated from the top, and problems within it were perhaps rarely handled in the benign and reasonable fashion the party manuals describe. The theory asserted, however, that while there were no objective grounds for factionalism inside the party, differences of view were to be expected. Struggles within the party could legitimately take place over issues of principle (but not over power, privileges, perquisites, and the like—and presumably it was the party leadership that decided which complaints were based upon the principle of good faith). These disagreements were to be resolved within the party in a routine and civil manner, with special attention to the needs of party discipline and the willingness of the members to subordinate their own views to those of the organization. Party members should be allowed to do or say what they want as long as their words and deeds are not "antiparty" or antisocialist, as long as they do not form cliques, and as long as they do not defy discipline. Disagreement and criticism are not to be held tantamount to opposition to the leadership.[16] These criteria may no doubt admit flexible application, but their spirit is different from that prevailing during the Maoist era.

Since the party's central organization had not played the role in China that it had in other communist regimes, its crippling during the Cultural Revolution was not as disastrous in its consequences as might have been thought. Strenuous efforts to rebuild the central organization were postponed until 1980. In 1978, however, at the third plenum, the Disciplinary Inspection Commission was set up, which was probably a revival of the old central Control Commission. As its name implies, it was charged with supervising the enforcement of party discipline.[17]

The rebuilding of the party has mixed significance for the theme of liberalization. The party was limiting its ambitions for total control, but this was for the sake of exercising more efficiently what control it could. By 1980, however, there was even the expressed intention of making more explicit the separation of party and state, a policy the Chinese sometimes rather inappropriately compare with the United States' separation of powers. This theme was reemphasized in 1982, when the party was reorganized to make its form similar to that of the Soviet and Eastern European parties, whereby the top position in the hierarchy is held not by the chairman of the Central Committee but by the secretary general. This reform in itself should in fact enhance the institutional predominance of the party, although supposedly the party would have to exercise its dominance through the institutions of the state and in accord with the laws of the state, rather than directly against the nonparty ordinary citizen. There are limits, it would seem, to how democratic any single-party regime can become. Despite the CPC's apparent determination to tolerate dissent within itself and despite constant exhortations to "consult with the masses," there was no mechanism for popular control of the party. Things could change if there is a genuine separation of party and state along with a genuine democratization of the state structure. But even if the rationalization is for the sake of control, rationalization in itself implies limits, and the picture of the party in 1977 and 1978 is different from totalitarianism either as that concept has been reconstructed in the West or as it has been applied in China. The rationalization of the party combined with a loosening of the ideology and a general depoliticization could be one more aspect of liberalization.

## THE CULT OF MAO

Typically in totalitarian regimes the party and the leader provide alternative foci of legitimacy. Since one-person rule is less likely to be bound by routine than is party rule, totalitarian leaders have worked to undercut the institutional strength of the party, and periods of strength for the party organization have tended to coincide with periods of lower approximation to the totalitarian model. This is another reason why the rationalization of the party could mean a liberalization. Hua Kuo-feng based his position upon his supposed selection by Mao and had an interest both in the perpetuation of the cult of Mao and the creation of a cult of himself, but the leadership principle was decisively repudiated at the third plenum. The proper evaluation of the roll of Mao remained a major pretext for the continuing struggle within the party. The most vigorous drive against Mao took place in 1979 and 1980 (after which it abated) and is thus outside the limits imposed on this chapter, but the later themes were already visible before the third plenum.

It is certainly possible to glorify a leader who is in fact impotent, and during the Cultural Revolution the cult of Mao had become less an instrument of Mao's personal power than that of Lin Piao and, to a lesser degree, the Gang of Four. The more ludicrous excesses of the cult ended pretty much with the death of Lin Piao. There is nothing to indicate that this limited "de-Maoification" did not take place with the chairman's full approval or even at his initiative.

There was only a limited abandonment of the cult during Mao's lifetime, however. Although the words of Mao were no longer thought sufficient to raise the dead, they were still considered something sacred. In the press the words of the chairman were printed in heavy black type. To make this less crass, so were the sayings of Marx, Engels, Lenin, and Stalin, but Mao was quoted constantly, while the others were not.[18] Beginning around the fall of 1977 Mao's more casual comments began to be printed in regular type, the black type reserved for his weightier sayings. By the spring of 1978, the heavy type had disappeared. Around the same time the newspapers' daily masthead quote from Mao—which was increasingly becoming a quote from Hua—also vanished.

By the first anniversary of Mao's death, the Gang was being attacked for having treated Mao's thought as a dogma, universally valid without regard to time, place, or circumstance. In part this was a reversion to an interpretation of the thought that had prevailed at times when Mao was alive. The original interpretation of Mao's thought was that it was not itself a universal truth but the application of the universal truth of Marxism-Leninism to the concrete problems of the Chinese revolution. While Mao was still alive, it was also possible to intimate from time to time, with due caution, that he was after all a human being, not a god. By the fall of 1977, hints that Mao might have been fallible became more common, although the public was not then given details of precisely what his failings might have been.

In 1978 Wei Kuo-ch'ing, then head of the army's General Political Department, said that Mao did not really know much about modern warfare.[19] The fall saw a return to the themes of a year earlier: those who say Mao never made mistakes are bad people. Denunciations of the Lin Piao-Gang position that every word of Mao's is truth became part of the affirmation that practice is the criterion of truth.[20] Even then, however, the world at large was not regaled with descriptions of Mao's faults.[21] General prudence, the political balance, and even perhaps a due respect for the regime's origins dictated that the question of Mao be treated delicately. By the end of 1978, however, the regime had denounced the leadership principle. This in itself does not mean liberalization, but it does mean a partial breaking away from totalitarianism.

## REHABILITATIONS

A more subtle way of depreciating Mao was to restore the good names of the objects of his wrath. To begin once again to praise a figure who has been subject to calumny does not always mean a turn toward greater honesty. Aleksandr Solzhenitsyn writes, "In totalitarian states the restoration of historical truth is viewed as the most subversive of activities."[22] The post-1977 evaluation of the victims of Mao's irritation may have been closer to historical truth than the Maoist attacks on them had been. But if justice was being done, it was being done selectively: the truth was being told when it would contradict the official Maoist interpretation of things.

The most dramatic and significant rehabilitation in this respect was, of course, that of Teng Hsiao-p'ing, since what little evidence we have tends to indicate that the two men loathed each other during the last 20 years of Mao's life. The flood of rehabilitations did not really begin until after the third plenum, but the few that came before illustrate the emerging trend. Thus the second most dramatic rehabilitation was a posthumous one, that of Liu Shao-ch'i, symbolizing the formal repudiation of the Cultural Revolution. Liu's rehabilitation did not take place until 1980, but it was forecast, among other things, by the reappearance of his wife in 1978.[23] In early 1979 the coalition that had once centered around P'eng Chen was rehabilitated, and many of the surviving members were given high positions. These rehabilitations were preceded in 1978 by that of the Ming dynasty statesman, Hai Jui, who had been the P'eng Chen group's symbol for their opposition to Maoist agrarian policies.[24] These rehabilitations were themselves no doubt matters of political controversy, and there was probably no masterplan known and agreed to by all members of the elite. As late as August 1978, for example, Nieh Jung-chen was still gratuitously attacking his old commander, P'eng Te-huai.[25]

The rehabilitations were not, however, indiscriminate. Rather, they served to reflect discredit upon Mao's policy or to dilute his historical importance. One of Mao's insights, for example, had supposedly been that he realized the revolutionary potential of the peasantry. But P'eng P'ai had organized peasants several years before Mao did. During the late chairman's lifetime, P'eng P'ai's contribution had for the most part been ignored and, according to the renewed attention given him in 1978, his family was mistreated.[26]

Not all past monsters were rehabilitated. Former rivals of Mao who might be seen as traitors or renegades to the party remain villains. Chang Kuo-t'ao who in the late 1930's abandoned the party for the Kuomintany and Wang Ming, who fled to Moscow in 1958. So do the first victims of post liberation party purges, Kao Kang and Jao Shu-shih. Perhaps this is because they, too, were pro-Soviet or, more likely, because whatever they may have been to Mao at the time of their purge they were a more direct threat to Teng Hsiao-p'ing. The radical Maoists—Lin Piao and the Gang of Four—continue to be execrated. Indeed, during 1980 additional Maoist villains were added to the list posthumously, including the police bosses K'ang Sheng and Hsieh Fu-chih.[27]

The key rehabilitation of 1978, that of P'eng Te-huai, was also the last major one of that year.[28] P'eng was purged in 1959 for his opposition to the Great Leap Forward. At that time he had the tacit support of the party functionaries and intellectuals affiliated with the first secretary of Peking, P'eng Chen. After 1959 Te-huai, through his surrogate, Hai Jui, was used as a symbol by the P'eng Chen group of courageous resistance to tyranny and folly. The Cultural Revolution began in 1965 with the Maoist counter-attack, led by Yao Wen-yuan, on the symbol of Hai jui, with this initial stage of the Cultural Revolution culminating in the purge of P'eng Chen. The rehabilitation of P'eng Te-huai was a prelude to the rehabilitation of the P'eng Chen group, and these amounted to a joint repudiation of both the Great Leap Forward and the Cultural Revolution—with the later rehabilitation of Liu Shao-ch'i only making this more obvious.

Since the rehabilitations were political tools, they do not fit comfortably into the pattern of depoliticization identified above. They do, however, serve further to undermine the leadership principle. Also in 1978, along with the rehabilitations there was a growing tendency to discuss historical figures in terms of universal values—their moral or physical courage, honesty, intelligence, and the like—rather than in terms of their ideological opinions and factional affiliations. To the extent that this means some autonomy of some values from political expediency, it is at least a partial depoliticization. The regime continued, however, the Leninist practice of presenting persons out of favor as monsters and demons in human form. While there may have been fewer demons around than previously, the required emotion concerning Lin Piao and the Gang of Four remained hatred!

## LAW

The radical tendency in China has been hostile to the idea of rule through law (not even to speak of a rule *of* law). A legal system freezes the status quo and brings social development to a halt. Law restricts the will of the masses and creates a new ruling class. The communists had been in the process of drafting law codes in the 1950s. In 1957, however, the hundred flowers rightists blamed the party for being too slow in codifying laws and for ignoring those laws it had codified. The upshot was that active legal development ceased until 1979. The last fully developed campaign during Mao's lifetime was directed against "bourgeois legal rights," *tzu-ch'an chieh-chi fa-ch'üan*. In 1975 the radicals said that rights—private plots, remuneration according to labor, and the like—all supposedly guaranteed by the new state constitution adopted by the regime in January of that year may be necessary, given China's low level of development. As long as these rights remain, however, China is not much different from a bourgeois state and, whatever happens, at every opportunity these rights must be restricted and never expanded. The campaign against *fa-ch'üan* had economic rights limiting collectivism as its specific referent, but it symbolized a generalized Maoist distaste for legality. Those who opposed the radicals complained, in terms used to protest tyranny in traditional times, that they were living in a world of no law and no heaven. In 1974 former Red Guards in Canton argued that to overthrow "feudal fascism" China needed to adopt a system of rule by law. In order to shape, control, and protect the legal system, China should also adopt democracy.[29]

The question of law points to an endemic contradiction in totalitarianism. A political system governed by law need not be liberal, democratic, humane, just, or even fair, but it cannot be totalitarian, since a system of law will restrict as well as regularize the exercise of power. No system, however, can be ruled over a long period of time in an entirely unpredictable and arbitrary manner. Therefore, any enduring system will probably be found to have evolved, if not open and codified law, at least a set of routines and customary practices that will function in a fashion analogous to law—if not to the point of guaranteeing due process to subjects, at least making the behavior or rulers predictable.

The line about legal rights did not change immediately with Mao's death and the purge of his followers, but neither did it occupy much of the attention of the new rulers. One assumes that Hua Kuo-feng, here as elsewhere, was less ready than Teng Hsiao-p'ing to make an open break with the old line, and the formal codification of law did not resume until after the third plenum. One also gets the impression, however, that on the abstract question of whether China needed some kind of formal commitment to legality, there was not much at issue between Hua and Teng.

At the eleventh party congress in August 1977, Hua did not have anything good to say about the concept of bourgeois rights itself, but he did criticize the *Gang's* attack on it. The Gang was said to have treated what Hua delicately calls the "difference in distribution" between party big shots and ordinary people, that is, the wealth and privileges enjoyed by the elite, as if it were an instance of class exploitation. This shows the malicious purpose of the Gang in trying to limit bourgeois rights.[30] In December a translation committee pointed out that in Marx the word rendered *fa-ch'üan* was *Recht*. *Fa-ch'üan* literally means *legal* rights or powers, but Marx's *bürgerliche Recht* only means bourgeois *rights* and has no necessary connection with the idea of a legal system. Marx's meaning is, therefore, better rendered by *ch'üan-li*, a more general word for right, privilege, power, ability, and so forth.[31] The effects of this sophistry is to deprive the concept of legality of any necessary "bourgeois" connotations (and therefore to allow public advocacy of legality as something a real proletarian might go for), while reducing the criticism of bourgeois rights to platitudes against special privilege.

By the spring of 1978, even the concept of rights found approbation. Hua Kuo-feng told the National People's Congress, in the course of a discussion of the need to strengthen political control, that one job of the police is to protect the rights of the people and to handle violations of people's rights according to law.[32] At that time human rights was a cant phrase in U.S. diplomacy and therefore not a popular concept with the Chinese regime (even though the United States lacked the motivation or the moral courage to apply it to China). Also, the CPC has traditionally shared the Marxist aversion to human rights since, if the implications of the concept are rigorously thought through, it implies there is an unchanging human nature. Marxists prefer to believe that in a class society there is no human nature as such, only class nature (or, there is no human nature, but only the human condition). The United States' vulgarization of the concept of human rights, however, created an atmosphere in which the idea could be taken up by Chinese dissidents and used against the rulers in Peking. But while the regime chose to avoid the issue of human rights, it did begin to speak of *civil* rights, defined and protected by the constitution and the laws. Yeh Chien-ying, perhaps because he was explicating the regime's new constitution, went into more detail about this than Hua. Yeh discovered a thought of Mao: "Legality must be observed." As the delegates to the National People's Congress pondered this profundity, Yeh explained that the law must be obeyed and that the constitution guarantees personal freedom, democratic rights, and legal economic rights.[33]

By the summer the regime had evolved what was to be its official position on legality, a diluted version of that of the 1974 Canton dissidents. A *People's Daily* "special commentator" noted: "A legal system is a tool of the ruling class; it is the expression of the class will of the ruling class." If this is true, there is no reason why the current ruling class, the proletariat, should not rule by means of law. Lin Piao and the Gang of Four, representatives of the feudal comprador class, quite naturally hated socialist legality. Suppression and dictatorship were much more to their taste. They could get away with what they did because "our socialist society was born from old China, a semi-feudal semi-colony without democratic traditions." The purge of the Gang must therefore be a purge of feudal attitudes. The special commentator does not develop an overly crude view of the class nature of law, however. Even in feudal times, he says, there were plenty of officials who respected the rights of the people. Although ultimately serving the ends of their own class, these officials selflessly upheld the law without fear or favor.[34] The reason the special commentator says this, apart from its being true, is, probably, to present legality as a good in itself, even abstracted from its class content, and also to indicate that socialist legality will entail a genuine legal system and not simply be a parody masking a capricious tyranny.

The question is whether this amounts to anything more than words. The laws themselves, when introduced, were harsh. "Counterrevolution," for example, was defined as a crime. The 1979 dissidents were tried by procedures looser than those provided in the law codes that were already published, since the laws had not yet been formally put into effect. The advocate of democracy, Wei Ching-sheng, and those like him were at least tried, and this is an advance over the Maoist practice, when people simply disappeared. The trial of the Gang of Four was unpleasantly reminiscent of the Stalinist show trials, which followed the promulgation of the "most democratic constitution in the world." In form, at least, the remnants of Lin Piao's group and the Gang were being tried for specific acts and not for political attitudes, and to all indications they had actually done more or less what they were accused of; so the analogy with the Moscow trials is not exact. Given the rudimentary nature of the law when the defendants were in power, the trial may violate the principle that where there is no law there is no crime, but this violation of elementary fairness in the present case is perhaps more disturbing in theory than in fact. If members of the Gang were really guilty of crimes, to put them on trial would be to vindicate the rule by law. The trouble is, however much the Gang may deserve punishment and whatever the formalities of the trial were (and there were not many), there was no way their trial could be fair.

## DEMOCRACY

The People's Republic has always claimed to be democratic, just as it has always claimed to be a dictatorship. There was no pretense of formal or "bourgeois" democracy. Rather, the Chinese rulers claimed to represent and carry out the true interests of the vast majority of the laboring people. The Chinese rulers also claimed to follow the mass line. The leaders would conduct investigations among the "masses," discover their needs and opinions, systematize and summarize these, condense them into policy, and then educate the masses so they would perceive that the policy truly met their needs and interests.[35] Western analysts have the incorrigible impression that the mass line was taken more seriously by the radicals than by the moderates,[36] but here they probably confuse the moderates' propensity for technocratic or bureaucratic control with a lack of concern for the opinions of or impact upon those affected by the policy. In fact, a standard moderate criticism of the radicals had been that the radicals acted on the basis of formalistic or wacky theories without determining the nature of the concrete situation, the actual possibilities, and the real needs and desires of the people.[37] A stock criticism of the Gang from the very beginning had been that they ignored the mass line.

The mass line does not give any real popular control over the rulers. To the limited extent that this has been achieved anywhere it has been through formal democracy, that is, through a system of legally guaranteed civil liberties and competition among organized parties in elections. Aspects of formal democracy formed a part of the demands of the democratic movement and are even, in a rudimentary way, part of the Teng program following the third plenum. Some elections were held, with the number of candidates exceeding the positions vacant. A limited expansion of formal democracy was part of the structural reform movement Teng sponsored in the closing months of 1980.[38] Prior to 1979, however, the main aspect of democratization remained a reaffirmation of the mass line with, perhaps, more genuine content than it had had before. At the same time, the regime's public pronouncements came to emphasize the concept of popular severeignty and to take up the one-time dissident theme concerning the relationship between democracy and the rule through law.

As in the past, the post-Gang talk of the mass line assumed that leaders who go "among the masses" will be able to avoid "subjectivism."[39] On the other side, the masses should be encouraged to tell what they think of what is going on.[40] Again, because in 1978 Teng Hsiao-p'ing could be confident that mobilized public opinion would favor him, this second theme became quite prominent. Popular opinion could find expression not only on wall posters but also through letters to the editors of newspapers.[41] Comments carried in the official media tended, not surprisingly, to be either specific suggestions or complaints about specific abuses, not general critiques of the regime and its policies. But in at least one case, public protest may have caused a moderately important policy change. Since the 1950s the regime has been trying to "simplify" the Chinese characters, supposedly to promote literacy. There seems to be a dearth of empirical evidence on whether this works, but one's impression is that while the new characters are certainly easier to write than the old, they are not necessarily easier to read or to remember.[42] In 1978 the regime published its third official list of simplifications; many of the new characters are grotesquely ugly and without etymological, philological, or even phonetic justification. Public comment on the new list was allowed, and few had anything good to say about it.[43] The egregious 1978 simplifications were soon withdrawn.

This is trivial in terms of any impact on the locus of power. But there was also some evidence that the party's official attitude toward its relationship with the people was undergoing a change. According to Taiwan, in the summer of 1979 Ch'en Yun rambled on to the Politburo, reminding the comrades that the CPC rules by power (*ch'üan*), by its control of the police and the army. "But don't forget the people have the right [or power—the word here, too, is *ch'üan*] to choose whether they want this rule or not." They might instead choose to be ruled by the KMT or by some other political party. Also the party has discussed how, had the rule of Lin Piao and the Gang of Four continued, it might have evolved into a fascist organization. The party should watch itself and start acting less like a ruler and more like a servant. "China can't be destroyed, but the party can,"[44]—a theme of the hundred flowers rightists of 1957.

In an unusual step, regime spokesmen took the trouble to deny the authenticity of this report but the denial rings less true than the text. In 1978, however, the regime seems to have been in the process of considering itself less a revolutionary vanguard and more the representative of all the people, anticipating Ch'en Yun's later critique. At the same time, there was less of a tendency to make the tautological identification of the good of the people with the good of the party. The Maoist notion of dictatorship itself was finding less favor among the regime; it was not explicitly repudiated, but the appeal of dictatorship was more and more being attributed to the feudal mentality of the Gang of Four.[45]

Like the 1970s dissidents, the party coupled democracy with law.[46] Without a framework of legal guarantees, talk of democracy is just talk. China is perhaps more likely to attain a genuine rule of law more easily than it will achieve formal democracy. Yet the official position on the eve of the third plenum was that law and democracy mutually support each other, with law only the means and democracy the end. Law serves to "protect the people's democratic rights." Democracy is prior to law, and law should never become a formula to oppress the people.[47]

## NOTES

1. *Jen-min Jih-pao* [People's Daily], April 18, 1978 (hereafter cited as *PD*).

2. Ibid., June 22, 1978.

3. In early 1978 the Chinese press showed much interest in Albert Einstein, a scientist considered a charlatan by the Gang because his model of the universe did not accord with that of Engels. A defense of Einstein asserts that he must be correct because both Lenin and Chou En-lai, two who ought to know, spoke highly of him, and also argues that the theory of relativity supports a theory of relative truth. Ibid., January 13, 1978.

4. Lin Ching-yao, "The Revelation of an Argument between Marx and Engels," *Kuang-ming Jih-pao*, July 29, 1978; ibid., September 19, 1978.

5. Ibid., September 19, 1978. The Gang "fanatically exaggerated the role of spirit, holding that will could not be bound by objective reality, that it could decide everything." This is "an extremely reactionary subjective idealism."

6. Chang P'en-ssu, "Does Truth Have a Class Character?" *PD*, November 28, 1978.

7. For a comparison of Mao's and Teng's pragmatism, see Wang Jo-shui, "Marxism and the Liberation of Thought," ibid., August 1, 1980. Since Maoism upsets things and causes change and since in the post-Mao period it was the left that would lose the most through change, there are often more similarities on the theoretical plane between Maoism and Teng's line than between Maoism and the post-Mao left. In 1979, for example, Hua Kuo-feng appears to have been much more eager than Teng to assert that class antagonisms had ceased in China—since it was Hua who was in danger of being labeled a class enemy. See Chi Hsin

(a Hong Kong apologist for the Teng line), "The Class Situation and Principal Contradiction in Mainland China—An Important Theoretical Issue at the Second Session of the Fifth NPC," *Ch'i-shih Nien-tai*, August 1979, in Foreign Broadcast Information Service, *Daily Report, People's Republic of China*, August 13, 1979, pp. U1–U5.

8. Brantly Womack, "Politics and Epistemology in China Since Mao," *China Quarterly* 80 (December 1979): 788.

9. Compare Kenneth Lieberthal's vindication of Hua Kuo-feng's curious idea that members of the Gang were really right wingers, since their policies were so disruptive that the regime became unable to prevent the reassertion of traditional culture and social patterns. See Lieberthal's *Revolution and Tradition in Tientsin, 1949–1952* (Stanford: Stanford University Press, 1980), p. 185.

10. See, for example, Hsu Hsiang-ch'ien, "The Party Must Always Control the Gun," *PD*, September 19, 1977.

11. *Kuang-ming Jih-pao*, November 23, 1977. The old boss of Shanghai, K'o Ch'ing-shih, who died in 1965, had been a strong Maoist, and I suspect that the bulk of the Shanghai apparatus already had affiliations with the left.

12. *PD*, August 23, 1977. This line was taken up again in 1981, in response to the contention of elements of the democratic movement that the party created a bureaucratic ruling class. *Hung Ch'i* 5 (March 1, 1981): 12–18.

13. *PD*, August 26, 1977.

14. Ibid., July 2, 1978.

15. The classic work is Liu Shoa-ch'i, *On Inner Party Struggle* (Peking: Foreign Language Press, 1951).

16. Chu Yen, "The Party's Organization Departments Must Carry Out the Party Constitution in a Model Fashion," *PD*, September 3, 1978.

17. The public report of the third plenum does not say what the function of the organization is, but see the new party constitution finally adopted in 1982. Ibid., September 9, 1982.

18. Mao once commented on something his wife had said: "Fart! That misses the whole point." After her purge this was printed in type suggesting it had issued from a burning bush. Ibid., December 24, 1976.

19. Ibid., June 8, 1978. Teng Hsiao-p'ing, ibid., June 7, 1978 expresses his complete agreement with Wei and makes the same points without directly implicating Mao. As these dates indicate, Wei's speech was not published for several days after it had been delivered, and then only excerpts were made public.

20. Yang I-chen, "To Extirpate Chaos and Restore Rectitude It Is Necessary to Liberate Thought," ibid., August 23, 1978.

21. The first direct contradiction of Mao did not come, I think, until 1980. An article that year dismissed as false Mao's contention that the question of the minority nationalities was essentially a question of social class. Ibid., July 5, 1980.

22. Aleksandr Solzhenitsyn, "The Courage to See," *Foreign Affairs* 59 (Fall 1980): 199.

23. *PD*, September 1, 1978.

24. *Kuang-ming Jih-pao*, November 15, 1978.

25. *PD*, August 8, 1978.

26. Ibid., August 31, 1978.

27. The inclusion of these two among the villains was probably a slap at Hua Kuo-feng more than anything else. As noted earlier, K'ang may have been Hua's patron. Hsieh Fu-chih became head of public security in 1959, as part of the purge of P'eng Te-huai. His predecessor, Lo Jui-ch'ing, at that time became Lin Piao's chief of staff. Lo was purged by Lin in 1965. His formal rehabilitation came before Mao's death and has not, therefore, been discussed in this section. During 1978, before his death, Lo did receive an inordinate amount

of publicity, the gist of it being that under Lo the police had really been run properly. See ibid., March 23, 1978 and the obituary, ibid., August 9, 1978. Lo's tenure as police boss was in fact as brutal and as arbitrary as that of K'ang or Hsieh, and the major point of glorifying him would seem to be to detract from the achievements of Hsieh's successor, Hua Kuo-feng.

28. Ibid., December 24, 1978.

29. Li I-che, "On Socialist Democracy and Legality," *Chung-Kung Yen Chiu*, November 1975, pp. 117–31.

30. *PD*, August 23, 1977.

31. Ibid., December 12, 1977.

32. Ibid., March 7, 1978.

33. Ibid., March 8, 1978.

34. Ibid., July 13, 1978.

35. For a rather idealized description of the process, especially as it was supposed to have functioned after the Cultural Revolution, see Richard M. Pfeffer, "Serving the People and Continuing the Revolution," *China Quarterly* 52 (October/December 1972): 620–53.

36. Lowell Dittmer, "Chinese Communist Revisionism in Comparative Perspective," *Studies in Comparative Communism* 13 (Spring 1980): 6.

37. For example, Li Hsien-nien, "How to Look at Reform in the Management System of Finance and Trade in the Rural Areas," *PD*, January 17, 1959; Lu Li, "Leadership in Agriculture Must Begin from Reality," ibid., November 12, 1960.

38. Feng Wen-pin, "On Questions of Socialist Democracy," ibid., November 24 and 25, 1980.

39. Ibid., March 14, 1978.

40. Ch'en Pei-hsien, "Leading Cadres Must Let the Masses Speak," ibid., July 26, 1978.

41. Ibid., June 12, 1978.

42. For an exhaustive but politically tendentious study of communist language reform policy, see Wang Hsueh-wen, *Chung-kung Wen-tzu Kai-ko yü Han-tzu Ch'ien-t'u* (Taipei: Kuo-chi Kuan-hsi Yen-chiu-so, 1970).

43. *Kuang-ming Jih-pao*, June 12, 1978.

44. *Chung-yang Jih-pao*, April 26, 1980.

45. *PD*, September 21, 1978.

46. Ibid., July 13, 1978.

47. Ibid., December 21, 1978.

# 6

# Official
# Liberalization:
# Cultural and Economic
# Policies

The changes in the structure of politics are more relevant to liberalization than are particular policy changes. The "function" of the political structure, however, is to produce policy. The present chapter discusses the liberalization of policy, specifically by examining the extent to which selected social interests have been indulged by being freed from political constraints. The chapter examines the general policy toward intellectuals, not because intellectuals are the most important people in the world but because it is they who will articulate political ideas. The policy toward literature will be discussed in more detail. Literature does not directly contribute to the modernization of the state, and the regime may have its own reasons for maintaining political control. Policy toward literature, then, may be one indication of how genuine the liberalization is. To see what liberalization might mean in the daily life of the ordinary citizen, economic policy in general and policy toward agriculture in particular will be analyzed. The chapter also briefly examines the policy toward youth, religion, and population control since these raise issues involving social interests that the regime finds it inexpedient to indulge. Policy here, as in the case of creative writing, can serve as a test of the limits of liberalization.

The discussion in this chapter does not confine itself to the period before 1979. In the previous chapter, it seemed appropriate to determine how far liberalization had gone before the democratic movement began demanding ever more liberty. But for the policies discussed in this chapter, many of the more radical breaks with the past come well after the suppression of the democratic movement.

## INTELLECTUALS

In classic Marxist-Leninst theory, intellectuals are a stratum, not a class. They bear no distinct relationship to the forces of production but attach themselves promiscuously to groups that do. In general intellectuals are spokesmen for whatever the ruling class of a particular society may be. One line of Eastern Europe dissident thought argues that intellectuals have come to constitute a class in and for itself, and the post-Stalin communist state is the agent of the class power of the intellectuals.[1] This more or less accords with the Maoist analysis as well. In Mao's last years, intellectuals were held to be inveterate carriers of bourgeois vices who, in the absence of full-scale dictatorship, would come to hold predominant power in the state. The Hua-Teng regime reverted to the more classic doctrine, and then rapidly went beyond it. Soon intellectuals were being defined as components of the proletariat proper—even, perhaps, the most prole- tarian of all proletarians. The Teng regime, at least superficially would seem to corroborate the contention that the post-totalitarian communist state is the instrument of rule of the intellectual class.

The initial impetus for loosening the controls on intellectual activity and increasing the wealth and status of intellectuals themselves was, of course, the regime's desire for modernization. An early celebration of the rule of Chairman Hua (as Lenin points out, "History proves great revolutionary struggles produce great personages") hailed him for ending the "fascist dictatorship" over intellectuals.[2] Scholarly journals resumed publication, and certain kinds of intellectual activity, at first, research in the natural sciences, were now held to be without "class character." The discovery of truth was said to have its own logic, which was autonomous from politics—an insight, given the times, less banal than might be thought. Marxism is no substitute for atomic theory or electronics. Marxism is based upon science, not science upon Marxism.[3]

Particularly after the return of Teng Hsiao-p'ing, scientists came to be relieved of burdensome political duties. Small group political indoctrina- tion sessions had become a ritual in People's China. In 1978, however, Teng endorsed the principle that scientists should spend at least five-sixths of their time on their regular work, not on political or administrative chores. Some argued this left *too* much time for politics.[4] The five-sixths system might be all right in general, some asserted, as long as it was not construed to mean that one-sixth of the *time* had to be spent on political things.[5] Attempts were made to find work for specialists in fields for which they had been trained, and scholarly journals were no longer to carry political editorials.[6]

The slogan used in this context was to let a hundred flowers bloom, a hundred schools contend, and it was pointed out that the slogan did not mean anything unless the weeds were allowed to grow along with the flowers.[7] In the earlier blooming and contending in 1957, intellectuals who had responded too eagerly to the party's summons had been persecuted as rightists, forced to make degrading confessions, sent to labor education camps, and otherwise abused. In November 1978, immediately following the reevaluation of the April 5 riots, the "rightist label" was finally removed from this 1957 cohort. This was not openly intended as a vindication of the 1957 criticism or even as any admission of error on the party's part. Rather, it was argued that the 1957 repression had served to consolidate the dictatorship of the proletariat, but the rightists had now learned their lesson and had changed their ways. Mao and Chou En-lai, it was said, had thought about a general amnesty in 1975, but the Gang had sabotaged this.[8] In 1978 and 1979 the more prominent Chinese intellectuals did not on the whole repeat their denunciations of tyranny of two decades earlier; the democratic movement came from a lower social and intellectual stratum. Whether or not the higher intellectuals had reformed their thought, they had at least learned prudence.

Prudence had its rewards. By 1979 intellectuals were no longer spoken of as a stratum that could attach itself to any dominant class: they were instead a part of the proletariat. Even in the old society, according to the new line, they were a part of the proletariat: proletarians who labor with their brains.[9] As Mencius says, some labor with their hands and some with their brains; those who labor with their hands feed those who labor with their brains, and those who labor with their brains rule those who labor with their hands. Mencius perhaps put it too starkly for the party's taste, but the party had come around to his point of view. Sporadic outbreaks of anti-intellectualism continued, but intellectuals were considered by some to be not merely a part of the working class, but its very vanguard.[10]

## LITERATURE

It is easy enough to understand why the regime might wish to lift restraints upon scientists whose work contributes directly to the wealth and power of the state, or even why it might, if it can afford to, indulge pure science and scholarship. There is probably no direct relationship between national power and literary excellence, however, and it would seem to be possible at least in the abstract to allow the free play of scholarship while literature serves narrow propaganda ends. For if literature does not contribute directly to national power, it can certainly play a political role. Stalin used to call writers the engineers of human soul, and Teng Hsiao-p'ing is charmed by this metaphor.[11] The liberalization of literature has been less thoroughgoing than that in other areas.

Published literature in the years prior to Mao's death had been dominated by the Gang, and after the purge of the Gang if were there to be any literature at all there would have to be some kind of liberalization. Certain post-Cultural Revolution works condemned by the Gang (although very much in the Gang style) were rehabilitated. The hundred flowers slogan was interpreted to mean that the regime should tolerate a diversity of literary styles. In May 1977, the *Kuang-ming Daily*, in what I think is the first editorial of its own that it had printed since 1966, called for a greater variety and higher quality of literary works.[12] "Old works," meaning mainly leftist works published prior to liberation but also some works from imperial times, were republished,[13] and their old authors, such as Mao Tun and Pa Chin, who were pointlessly persecuted by the Gang, were allowed to reappear and were treated with honor.[14] The authorities came to understand that people can get tired of a Stalinist uplift and gave their imprimatur to love stories and to tragedies.[15] This halfhearted liberalization was accompanied during 1977 by a continuous picking at the scabs of earlier literary purges. The media once again attacked poor Hu Feng (imprisoned for counterrevolution in 1955), Feng Hsueh-feng (purged in 1957), the Three Family Village and Chou Yang (purged in 1966).[16] One essay found Teng T'o, the leader of the Three Family Village and a party intellectual who had satirized radical Maoism in the early 1960s, to be precisely the same sort of person as the dog's-head general, Chang Ch'un-ch'iao.[17] Mao Tun, until 1949 (when his inspiration apparently went dry) one of China's major novelists and until 1966 the regime's figurehead minister of culture, was brought back—in order to renew attacks on Hu Feng.[18] Inertia might account for some of this continuing vituperation. It is interesting, however, that all the persons mentioned above were later rehabilitated.[19]

The new minister of culture, Huang Chen, a workhorse from the diplomatic and espionage system, outlined his view of literary policy in the spring of 1978. Huang perceived a "new high tide of socialist culture." Culture was the field in which the Gang had the deepest roots; so there must be a "mass movement" to dig these out. Writers should develop a greater variety of themes but should concentrate especially upon "contemporary revolutionary themes" (a phrase also associated with Chiang Ch'ing, although Huang does not point this out). Literary work should support the party line. There should be a mass movement for literary production by ordinary people outside of working hours—what Huang calls the application of the Tachai model to culture. In this way literature will serve the worker-peasant-soldiers. A hundred flowers should bloom, but all the flowers should meet the test of orthodoxy.[20] The new high tide would seem to be the same old Gang stuff, now stodgy and boring rather than vicious and shrill.

Change was already beginning, however. About a month later Hsia Yen, China's leading contemporary playwright and another victim of the Gang, argued that writers, to have anything to say, need some experience of life. But young writers have only the experience of the 1960s and 1970s, a big blank when China was in chaos and cut off from world influences.[21] Writers increasingly came to take this barrenness and chaos itself as their theme, writing about the evils perpetrated under the Gang, a "scar literature" that allowed for naturalistic, rather than socialist, realism and not at all encouraging to revolutionary romanticism.[22] By 1980 the official encouragement extended to the literary treatment of atrocities committed during the post-Gang period when Hua Kuo feng was still on top.[23]

After the third plenum, supervision of literary policy reverted to Chou Yang, who was until his purge in 1966 the regime's chief literary inquisitor. The Maoists had improbably charged him with a soft, easy-going tolerance for error and diversity. As part of the anti-Maoist combination, Chou had in fact taken a tactical and temporary liberal position in the early 1960's and he was himself a cultured man, reputedly less fierce in private than in public. In a speech of December 1978, not published until the following February, Chou said that censorship was still required, but that it should be slackened. The regime should control writers more through "social opinion" than by "administrative methods."[24]

Given the popularity of tales of the evils of radicalism, this slackening would work to the advantage of Teng. It could also help discredit the entire system, however, and some critics began to wonder whether writers might not tell a little more about what is right with China. By the summer of 1979, even persons probably associated with Teng were becoming nervous. The *Kuang-ming Daily* said that while there were no "forbidden zones" and while it is perfectly proper to write about the dark side of things, there should be still no exposure for the sake of exposure.[25] Critics in a provincial journal went further, arguing that writers were distorting the official line and attacking socialism. Writers should praise virtue, not concentrate simply upon lack of virtue. This dissent against liberalization, however, met with official disfavor (and may have been a setup from the beginning). Those protesting the liberalization were said "really to terrify people, since this is something seldom seen since the collapse of the 'Gang of Four.' "[26] One wonders whether this incident indicates that "administrative methods" were still in order against those unhappy with the new line.

Adherence to Teng's line can hardly be counted as an unequivocal depolitization of literature, but it did bespeak a certain liberalization. By 1980 there was sentiment for a deeper depoliticization. Part of the Gang line had been that the 17 years prior to the Cultural Revolution had seen nothing in the way of creative writing but bourgeois trash. The early critique of the Gang asserted, on the contrary, that those were 17 wonderful years. In 1980, however, critics were saying that if truth were told there had been very little of literary merit published prior to the Cultural Revolution, and the Cultural Revolution decade was, of course, an unmitigated waste. Continued demands for party leadership of literature only stifle creativity.[27] A writer's choice of style was held to be in itself a matter of political indifference.[28] The regime published an anthology of short stories from Taiwan. Given the morbid stylistic and thematic preferences of serious writers there, the stories do not give an unduly rosy picture of life on that island; but these are genuine Taiwan writings, not propaganda screeds against the Chiang bandit gang.[29] One critic bemoaned the popularity of Gone With the Wind but did not suggest that it should be banned. He concludes, rather, on a wistful note: "There are all sorts of reasons readers read the books they do—social, personal, all kinds of reasons. As to how to make literary creativity flourish, there are all kinds of questions there, and I can't talk about them here."[30]

The Maoist slogan that literature should "serve politics" was replaced by a rather cryptic guideline: literature need not serve politics, but it should still serve the people and serve socialism.[31] This means that political considerations will continue to limit how matters may be treated—in effect, there still are forbidden zones—but literature is no longer expected to make propaganda for the evolving political line. In practice, however, literary output continued to reflect the line of Teng Hsiao-p'ing, and by 1981 there was a retrenchment from the broadly liberal position of the previous year. The slogan remained the same but with a narrower view of just what served socialism. "Scar literature" was out of favor, and the dominant group among the rulers had come to see some value in the praise of virtue.[32] There had been ebbs and flows before, and the 1981 crackdown did not lead initially to a renewal of Maoist terror. But at least one author of scar literature was attacked by name: Pai Hua, the author of a screenplay, "Bitter Love," which is about a man who loves his country even if his country does not love him.[33] By the end of the year, writers were being nagged about their taste for "bourgeois liberalization." The retreat in literary policy was part of the more general retrenchment, the apparent failure of nerve of the Teng group after it had defeated its major enemies. Also, some of the crackdown was a reflection more of factional fighting than a general consensus among the rulers— although the rulers were no doubt worried about the "crisis of faith." Pai Hua was a soldier and the attack on him came from within the army, and by 1981 important elements of the military were disenchanted with Teng Hsiao-p'ing. The Teng group's response to the criticism finally came to be an outflanking movement. Writers were denounced (although usually not by name) as inveterate carriers of "bourgeois liberalization." People could still discuss current problems by means of fiction, but only if they gave the stories a happy ending. The policy may not have been reversed, but it certainly stagnated. Liberalization of literature remained embryonic, and no writer could be confident of being able freely to write anything he might want to.

## ECONOMIC POLICY

In the years after liberation, China followed the Soviet model of economic development. The regime encouraged the growth of heavy industry at the expense of light industry and of agriculture, and it controlled economic activity by means of planning. The Great Leap Forward substituted the mass line for centralized planning. In practice this meant that economic decisions were made by the local party committees. Emphasis was placed upon the development of agriculture and on the "localization" of heavy industry, as with the backyard steel furnaces. Technological rationality was disregarded since it was thought, enthusiasm and devotion could perform miracles, and too close a view of the limits of possibility would inhibit enthusiasm and devotion. "Moral" incentives replaced material rewards and for a very short period the regime mandated an extreme egalitarianism. While elements of the Great Leap Forward may have made sense in the abstract, they were applied in a disasterous manner and proved to be as inhumane as they were impractical. The Great Leap Forward brought China to economic collapse in three years.

The recovery of the early 1960s took place under the direction of a group centered on P'eng Chen, head of the Peking party committee and second to Teng Hsiao-p'ing on the Secretariat. The new policy, which the radicals later called the capitalist road, agreed with the Great Leap Forward's attention to agriculture and to decentralization but also urged the need for rational planning and material incentives. Allocation by plan was combined with a limited use of the market mechanism. This was all condemned during the Cultural Revolution, but in fact the basic structure of the economy remained what it had become in the early 1960s. The policy was retained because it more or less worked, while the radical policy did not. But the hegemonic position of Maoist ideology meant that the actual policy could not be legitimized, and those who applied it remained constantly vulnerable to Maoist attack. The overall consequence seems to have been economic stagnation, dressed up for foreign visitors as communal egalitarianism.

Unsatisfactory economic conditions contributed as much as anything else to the general unhappiness with radicalism, and the renunciation of

Maoist economics came early in the Hua Kuo-feng regime. The new policy, however, was not a liberalization; it was designed to restore central direction and planning. Given the social unrest during Mao's last days, the regime was eager to reimpose discipline upon the labor force,[34] There was more emphasis as well on the need for firms to show a profit, but this was a change in emphasis rather than in basic direction.[35] The Hua policy may at times have been even more unrealistic than the Gang's. It was revealed, for example, that in 1971 Yao Wen-yuan had suppressed a *People's Daily* editorial calling for the mechanization of agriculture by 1980: the wicked Yao had thought such a goal impossible.[36] Yao, of course, was right, and this should have been even more obvious in 1976 than in 1971.

The genuine change in policy began to take hold coincident with the return of persons once affiliated with P'eng Chen, especially Hu Ch'iao-mu. He had been purged during the Cultural Revolution, had collaborated with Teng in his 1975 Report Outline, and had been repurged with Teng a few months later. In July Hu Ch'iao-mu argued against Maoist economic voluntarism. Economics, he said, has its own objective laws, and these are disregarded even by a socialist state only to its own peril. Against the tendency of Hua Kuo-feng and Li Hsien-nien to encourage comprehensive planning at the provincial level, Hu argued the need for a national plan. At the same time, however, he asserted that firms and enterprises should have more individual autonomy. Firms should be able to arrange financing through banks and make contracts with other firms, and courts should enforce these contracts.[37]

Hu favored indirect control of the economy, with less control by administrative fiat. It is interesting to see how indirect Hu himself had to be. The Maoists had sometimes claimed that to talk about objective economic laws violates the principle that politics takes command. In 1978 Hu therefore felt obliged to assert that to follow objective economic laws is precisely to put politics in command—a ploy he would have treated with contempt a couple of years later. This kind of timidity was vanishing. A few weeks after the publication of Hu's speech (which was several months after it had been delivered), the regime rehabilitated Sun Yeh-fang, an economist who during the capitalist road period had advocated allocation of resources by the market and not by plan. The only fault with Sun's ideas that one review could find was that they did not go far enough.[38]

The new policies received the most publicity for their application in Szechwan province, then ruled by Chao Tzu-yang. These policies allowed firms to invest profits more or less as they thought best and to set prices and wages so as to maximize profit. At the same time, the state would not bail out firms that made bad decisions. In some cases this went along with profit-sharing schemes with the workers, the profits being distributed as bonuses, and the election by the workers of certain managerial personnel.[39] The Szechwan experiment apparently had mixed results, but elements of it, in limited ways, have subsequently been adopted nationwide. Hsueh Mu-ch'iao, who was head of the State Statistical Office, until the Cultural Revolution said in 1980 that the market mechanism and enterprise autonomy were ways of getting around the bureaucratism inherent in state ownership. Hsueh thought China would do well to examine some of the ways capitalist countries insure the social accountability of business firms[40] (a recommendation that might surprise Ralph Nader).

Because of attacks from the democratic movement, the regime in 1979 and 1980 was under pressure to assert the socialism was indeed better than capitalism. Looking at the pronouncements about economic policy, however, one finds it difficult to say just what the excellence of socialism was or even what socialism might be. One writer asserted that socialism means there should be as much public ownership as objective conditions allow, but no more: public ownership is not a goal in itself.[41] In 1980 the bulk of public attention was in fact given the drawbacks of public ownership. Direct political control of economic activity was called a residue of feudalism that hinders economic development.[42] According to the new line there is, as the Gang said, a close connection between politics and the economy: political meddling damages the economy.[43]

The new policies brought no economic miracle, and by the end of 1980 there was a change of emphasis. The new watchword was "readjustment": the reform would go on, but it would take second place to readjustment. Autonomy was a good thing, but it had gotten out of hand, and there must be more adherence to the central plan. Those outside China may have exaggerated the scope of the reversal. The main target of the readjustment was not the new policies but overinvestment in heavy industry, which was attributed to the "overambition and unrealistic slogans and goals" put forth "in the first two years after the smashing of the 'Gang of Four,' " that is, when Hua Kuo-feng was still on top. A more particular target seems to have been the remnants of the Chou En-lai group, such as Li Hsien-nien and Yü Ch'iu-li, or, as the regime put it, "some comrades, including some leading comrades, in the economic departments."[44] In addition to the purely political motives—the desire to put antagonists in the wrong—the retrenchment was motivated by the dismal state of the economy, particularly, according to Hong Kong rumor, to a disastrous performance in the petroleum sector. But like the retrenchment in literature, the economic retreat seems also to be a sympton of a strange failure of nerve by the Teng group, a feeling that at its moment of triumph it was losing its grip on society.

## AGRICULTURE

At the end of 1980, the regime was worried about the rural as well as the urban economy. Drought had caused the harvests of 1980 to be lower than those of 1979. The regime seemed, however, rather less inclined to limit its liberalization of agriculture than of industry. One writer urged that controls should be relaxed even further, and that efforts should be made to convince the peasants that this relaxation was more than a tactical expedient.[45]

At the time of liberation, party policy had been land reform, the distribution of land to those who actually worked it. By the mid-1950s the regime was collectivizing the land, merging the fields of the various villages. In 1958 the Maoists created the communes, huge collective units sometimes containing as many as 10,000 households, with egalitarian (and low) distribution of food within the commune. The grandiose version of this system collapsed almost immediately, and the level of collectivization by the early 1960s reverted to the village or, in the new term, the production team (*sheng-ch'an-tui*). At that time Liu Shao-ch'i, P'eng Chen, and others wanted to set production quotas at the household level, but the Maoists were able to avoid this. Households were allowed private plots, however, and private ownership of chickens, ducks, and pigs; households could retain income from sideline production, such as the manufacture of brushes or sandals; and work in the collective sector would be rewarded according to how much the individual peasant put into it ("to each according to his work"). The standard code word for these practices was "the policy," with criticisms of radicalism couched as exhortations to "follow the policy."

The radicals found the policy to incorporate "bourgeois rights." A tolerated alternative to the official policy was the Tachai model. The precise content of this model was not fixed. It usually involved a higher level of collectivization than was the norm, the basic unit being not the team but the production brigade, the *sheng-ch'an ta-tui*. It also meant the use of moral rather than the material incentives; that is, a peasant considered to have a good political attitude would receive a higher income than one who was just as productive but whose attitude (or background) was not as good. The Maoists preferred the Tachai model to the official policy and tried to get it adopted wherever possible. Peasants could not, therefore, have much confidence in the stability of the policy, despite its official approbation.

Hua Kuo-feng had been a strong proponent of Tachai, and during his reign the basic commitment to collectivization remained what it had been. The major change from Gang times was that Hua gave more attention to the material preconditions for collectivization. According to Hua, full ownership of land by the commune would come about with the mechanization of agriculture; thus, by disrupting the four modernizations the Gang were sabotaging socialism. The regime continued to condemn the setting of quotas at the household as the work of the still evil Liu Shao-ch'i. In recent years, it was said, under pressure of the poverty resulting from the rule of the Gang, in certain places villages had divided the land up among the families, but this was undermining socialism.[46] More wholehearted approval of the policy began to be heard in the spring of 1978. Wan Li, boss of Anhwei province and a close associate of Teng Hsiao-p'ing, asserted that whatever the Gang may have thought, private plots, renumeration according to work, and the like, were fully and legitimately socialist, not capitalist concessions to peasant backwardness. Wan Li continued, however, explicitly to oppose making contracts with the household.[47] The party remained extremely sensitive to the old Maoist talk of the restoration of capitalism. A letter to the *People's Daily* said that private plots and capitalist tendencies should never be mentioned in the same breath, even as a joke.[48] As long as the policy remained associated with capitalism in the official mind, the peasants would believe (as the Maoists wanted them to) that the policy was pure expediency and that as the agricultural situation improved the concessions to peasant interests would be withdrawn.[49]

Wan Li's position—presumably that of the Teng group in 1978—was that the policy should not only be followed, but that it should be treated as legitimate. In 1979 the regime began to liberalize beyond the bounds of the policy, introducing the "responsibility system,"[50] an old euphemism for household quotas. The Szechwan experience also emphasized individual farming. Chao Tzu-yang argued that it was unrealistic to expect a rapid modernization of argiculture, and that the only way under current conditions to improve production would be to allow greater individual initiative and responsibility, in particular, to allow private farming on poor land (on land that would not be farmed willingly unless those working it could dispose of the product by themselves).[51] In 1980 household quotas were openly defended, and the commune system itself was criticized. It was held to be false to assert (with Mao) that the larger a unit and the higher its level of collectivization, the more advanced it was.[52] Tachai was repudiated as a fake,[53] the repudiation being both a cause and a consequence of the purge of Ch'en Yung-kuei.

It would be an exaggeration to say that China was reverting to the conditions following land reform. The household might be held responsible for production on a certain piece of land, but the land itself remained under collective ownership and could not be bought or sold. Nor was there universal enthusiasm for individual farming. In July 1980 a *People's Daily* commentator maintained that peasants could indeed get rich (this no longer being thought a bad thing) through collective farming. We no longer want "empty collectivism," and the peasants must be allowed their "little freedoms," but collectivism must be encouraged wherever possible.[54] Another editorial admitted small peasant holdings were not the same thing as socialism. China could, however, afford to set household quotas in order to boost production because the collective base was so strong that there was no danger of the restoration of capitalism.[55]

Another popular theme of 1980 was similar to one of the Gang's: China's problems derive from the prevalence of a "petty producer" (peasant) mentality, a legacy of feudalism. The peasant background and consequent peasant slovenliness, it was said, of many party cadres inclines them to paternalism, authoritarianism, and a desire for special privileges.[56] A peasant hearing this sort of analysis might be slightly apprehensive about the future of the liberal policies; one way to eliminate the petty producer mentality might be to eliminate the petty producers by, say, introducing collectivism on such a massive scale that peasants are reduced to a rural proletariat. This, however, did not seem to be the mainstream position in the campaign against feudal residues. Some writers, for example, distinguished two kinds of private production. Subsistence farming leads to feudal narrowness, but individual farming linked to the market encourages self-reliance and is progressive—and allegedly is, as indispensable under socialism as under capitalism.[57] The general position was that while household quotas and individual production are not the communist ideal and are not to be introduced everywhere, their objective necessity is something every communist must recognize. Failure to do so is a sign, precisely, of petty producer fanaticism, a desire to perpetuate the "false socialism of universal poverty."[58] The general tendency was for more and more household farming. In 1982 the communes themselves were deprived of any administrative functions, although they remained as economic units.

## UNFASHIONABLE INTERESTS

A liberalizing regime may indulge certain interests previously deprived in order to gain advantages for itself. A liberal regime, on the other hand, defines its policies by the general play of interests in society. Policies and priorities may be set at the convenience of those who hold power, but those who hold power are responsible to the will of the people. In China the initiative for change remains clearly with the rulers. This section examines demands that may have wide social support but that the regime chooses not to indulge. These include the demands of rusticated youth, particularly those sent to the countryside before 1977; demands for greater toleration for religion; and popular opposition to the regime's population control policy. Were the regime to change in a more democratic direction, there would probably be more pressure for change in these policies. The regime's policy toward religion and population control are also interesting for the light they shed on the nature of the liberalization. On both of these issues, I suspect, the regime is carrying out policies that the ruling groups of advanced or post liberal societies do not really disapprove of, or at least do not become greatly upset about. Secular liberal intellectuals favor religious toleration in principle but have a hard time taking religious belief itself seriously; and while they may welcome religious support for their own policies, religiously motivated political activity for causes they do not favor is seen as a return to witch burning. State enforcement of population control is, of course, seen now as simply the normal course of things, and not oppression at all.

### Rusticated Youth

The rustication policy began during the Great Leap Forward.[59] In part it reflected of the populist prejudices of the party leadership. More pragmatically it brought educated personnel out of the cities, which could not absorb it, and into the backward areas where it was needed. During the Cultural Revolution, forced rustication was used to close down the Red Guard movement. That generation was told they would become peasants for the rest of their lives, and many concluded that rustication was simply disguised labor reform. The influx of mainland youth into Hong Kong since the late 1960s comes from rusticated young people from the farms in that area. Rusticated youths attempted when possible to sneak back to the cities. This return increased after Mao's death and again around the time of the third plenum. Since those who did return could not get ration cards, they could not legally support themselves, and their families found it difficult to feed them. They became a major factor in the general tendency toward disorder.[60]

Hua Kuo-feng supported the Maoist policies. Youths attending a Tachai conference he sponsored in December 1976 wrote him a letter afterward, promising to study the "Ten Great Relations," Hua's "extremely important report," and Yeh Chien-ying's "important report." They professed gratitude for the concern that Hua and Yeh had shown for them and pledged to return to the countryside to make it a "glorious pleasure garden."[61] In other words, things were to continue as they had been.

The Teng regime attempted to ensure that youths sent to the countryside had work appropriate to their education rather than simply serving as unskilled day laborers.[62] New cohorts of youths ceased being sent down to the farms, at least in the numbers they previously had been.

Those already in the countryside, however, were supposed to stay. Parents were instructed not to demoralize their children by dwelling upon how much they missed them, or how much they were needed at home, or how hard life in the villages must be. The parents were also told not to run around to different offices trying to get their children's lot improved. When officials had been disgraced during the Cultural Revolution, their families would be sent into rural exile. Newly rehabilitated cadres were explicitly instructed that they were not to try to get their children to return to the cities,[63] although many cadres did so anyway. In the spring of 1981, it was reported that youths who had previously been sent to far-off Sinkiang from Shanghai and then had returned to Shanghai but were unable to find work there were being shipped back to the border region.[64]

The Teng group seems to have a certain hardheartedness toward the more troublesome segments of the educated youth. It may have less enthusiasm for the rustication policy than did the Maoists, but it may also have less sympathy for the problems of the youths themselves.[65] The Teng group sometimes seems to assume that most young people have been corrupted by the Gang of Four (and, indeed, many have certainly become more open in their failure to recognize the authority of the party), and even those who have escaped corruption are seen as frivolous, shallow, callow.[66] That age group had been used as a symbol by the Gang in their battle against the "old cadres," and for some of the young the benefits of this were more than symbolic. The old cadres in their triumph were not inclined to indulge the follies of childhood. By 1980 the old cadres themselves were no longer in the best of odor. The term "old cadres" refers not only to a general category but also to a specific tendency—the bureaucrats survived the Cultural Revolution under the protection of Chou En-lai. These were not the persons closest to Teng and by 1980 were under attack as the petroleum gang or as examples of peasant stupidity. The official line then called for the rejuvenation and professionalization of the party. The coupling of professionalization with rejuvenation, however, was small comfort for the rusticated youth—because they had been in the countryside, they had lost the opportunity for advanced education. At the same time, this category, because of the recruitment practices of the Gang, constitutes a large segment of the party at the lower levels. There are even worries about the professionalized youth; worries that putting younger persons in responsible positions would bring in Gang elements have a "certain amount of reason," and there must be a careful scrutiny of those promoted. The real worry is perhaps less about direct affiliation with the Gang than that the younger generation has been influenced by the democratic movement.

## Religion

In 1980 the regime complained of a crisis of faith. One response to this crisis in society may be the apparent upsurge of religious activity made possible by the regime's more liberal policy. There is certainly more religious toleration than there had been during the Cultural Revolution—that is, there is more than none—and popular religion in particular seems to be flourishing. The regime is not happy about this and expresses dismay, for example, when large numbers of people flock to the shrine of the White Snake Lady (*pai she niang-niang*) to be cured of their diseases.[67]

The regime has consistently claimed to support freedom of belief and has just as consistently opposed religion itself. Religion is the opiate of the masses. It makes people think of heaven and of life after death instead of the real world of struggle and strife. Chinese popular religion is said to underpin feudalism, while Christianity supports imperialist aggression. Religion may at times have provided a motive for the peasants' rebellion, but this only illustrates the limitations of peasants as a class. The regime purports to find striking analogies between religion and the Maoism of the Gang of Four.[68] The policy reflecting this attitude has in the past not been as liberal and as tolerant as the regime makes out.[69] Believers have been harrassed, religious organizations have been forced to place themselves under political control, and groups not amenable to political control (such as certain Taoist sects) have been suppressed. Religious leaders who resisted state encroachment have been jailed. In 1957 the Catholic church in China was forced into a de facto schism from Rome. Religious activity was openly persecuted during the Cultural Revolution, to the general applause of organized Christianity in the West.[70] Virtually all traces of both Buddhism and Christianity as living religions were wiped out, although, of course, the spores were only dormant.[71]

By 1980 religious policy was reverting to what it had been in the 1950s. As Chao P'u-ch'eng, a perennial survivor inside the Chinese Buddhist Association put it, "The illogical activities of sabotaging the religious policy have been repudiated."[72] There were even hints that toleration might go beyond the rather bleak pre-Cultural Revolution situation. A historian praised Thomas Jefferson's ideas on religious liberty but mildly criticized Jefferson for qualifying this liberty by holding that religious freedom could not justify the disruption of the state.[73] This, of course, is how the Chinese communists have always qualified their own commitment to freedom of belief, and they have been very free in deciding just what does disrupt the state. A Protestant delegate to the 1980 session of the National People's Congress complained that most churches remained closed and most believers met in private homes. Some of the authorities say this is illegal but, according to the delegate, "The constitution cannot be construed to mean there is freedom of belief inside the church but no freedom of belief at home."[74] This does not describe great religious toleration but it is significant that a religious spokesman could articulate his own interests without sycophantic adulation of those in power and could even openly defend the underground church.

But what the regime gives it can also take back. Relief from religious persecution leads to what the regime considers superstition. Most concretely the regime denounces practices such as seances, fortune telling, the casting of spells, all of which in the context of popular religion may have genuine religious meaning. The regime can also castigate any religious activity it finds inconvenient as superstition or subversion. Probably because of the religious revival, the regime feels the need to "intensify the atheist education of young people."[75] Nor are all cases of refraining from overt persecution genuine instances of liberalization. The revival of Catholicism, for example, was marked by the ordination of new bishops not approved by the Vatican, while some of the older bishops of the state-approved church are said to be married.[76] This "revival" was soon followed by renewed persecution of priests and believers who had refused to conform. The regime's 1982 constitution forbids foreign interference in Chinese religion; concretely, this refers to the Vatican. Orthodox Catholicism is in effect outlawed. Late in 1980 the regime complained that "cadres" were refusing to implement the official policy of religious toleration. "Leftists" inside the party "slandered" the policy, saying the party was "burning incense to conjure devils." Not without reason, religious people have "doubts" about the policy. But these doubts have more foundation than the opinions of leftists. Thus religion is to be distinguished from "feudal superstition practices," and the latter will get you five years in jail.[77]

The stereotype persists that China is and always has been a nation of materialistic agnostics.[78] The evidence indicates, however, that there is a social demand for religion greater than the regime is disposed to indulge. The jibe that the party's policy of toleration, such that it is, is "burning incense to conjure devils" indirectly shows the limits to liberalization. As the regime's policies become depoliticized, they will tend less and less to shape the society and more and more to reflect the society as it is. Given the party's revoutionary pretensions together with the inevitable dissatisfaction with any status quo, this probably cannot be done smoothly. In the meantime the regime worries about a crisis of faith. Some may find faith in religion, but the regime wants faith in itself. But when it comes to the regime, people are now alleged to "see through" everything and to believe nothing. The regime attests, I think, to needs and desires it admits it cannot satisfy.

## Population Control

Particularly since Mao's death, the regime has been outspokenly in favor of population control. The minimum age for marriage is set high (although in the past this was not strictly enforced in rural areas, and couples are now encouraged—where possible, virtually forced—to have only one child. Women in their third pregnancy (and increasingly in their second) are bullied into abortions by officialdom and by officially controlled "public opinion," and the same methods are used to encourage sterilization of men and women.[79] In China food staples are rationed, and a family's ration will not be increased for the third and younger children. Population control may be a commonplace for people in rich countries but, as Hua Kuo-feng points out, in rural China it is a "great affair, a radical transformation of custom and habit (i-feng i-su ta-shih)."[80]

Some reasons for resisting population control are perhaps not very compelling to Western educated urbanities. The Chinese dote on children and like to have some of each sex in each family (a traditional ideal is three boys and two girls). A family with all boys will keep trying until a girl is born and, especially, a family with all girls will keep trying until it has a boy. The family line is transmitted through the males, since, when a girl marries, she normally becomes a member of her husband's family. China is not yet a welfare state, and children are expected to support their aged parents. It is important for a peasant couple to have at least one grown son by the time they are too old to work—especially important, of course, for that grown son's widowed mother.

Mao Tse-tung was not an enthusiast for population control and was inclined to think China's huge population a good thing. He sometimes hinted that China's large population meant it did not have to worry about a nuclear war. A more important consideration, no doubt, was Marxist theory, which holds that labor creates value and that each new little mouth brings along with it two little hands. During the hundred flowers period, the demographer Ma Yin-chu, president of Peking University (who celebrated his hundredth birthday in 1981)[81] opposed this Marxist doctrine and advocated an active birth control policy (but opposed abortion as murder). Because he would not give in to political pressure to change his opinions, Ma himself was disgraced,  but his views became the tacit policy.

Under the Gang (and Chou En-lai), the official function of birth control was said not to be for limiting population but for protecting the health of women. But population control measures were enforced as rigorously as any measures in those days. According to a short story by a former Red Guard who later moved to Hong Kong, couples from class enemy backgrounds were required to be sterilized after two children, and work units were assigned quotas for how many employees could have children each year. In the story a worker whose wife is just giving birth to their second daughter and who desperately wants a son is forced to have a vasectomy. The "bare-foot doctor" who performs the operation accidently ties the urinary canal instead. Fortunately the poor man gets to a real doctor before he dies, but because he tells what had happened to him to a friend he meets on the bus he is "struggled" (criticized in small-group sessions) for attempting to sabotage the planned parenthood program.[82] In later years the political distinctions have probably been abandoned, and one suspects there is a less tolerant official attitude toward medical incompetence. But the essence of the Hua-Teng policy is the same as that of the Gang.

Hua Kuo-feng says birth control must be promoted by propaganda and not be forced upon people. For party and youth league members, however, the one child per couple goal is "not an optional (jen-i) policy."[83] The fuss made about the policy shows the difficulty of enforcing it, but is is one policy from which no public dissent is allowed. The closest approach to public disagreement seems to be discussion of the psychological problems of the only child.[84] Little if any concern is voiced about the effect of population control on the stability of family life or, for that matter, for the troubles in store later for a big and aging population.

Some may find this discussion unnatural. Even if population control is unpopular, it might be argued, it is not really a matter of choice. Opposition to it is ignorant and selfish and is properly suppressed and ignored. Population controllers often sigh and point with envy to China, which has the kind of government that can do what they want done. It is not, however, self-evident that population control is really necessary for human happiness. One writer argues: "there are not now, and there have never been, any empirical data showing that population growth or size or density have a negative effect upon the standard of living, the level of population, or any other important measure of human welfare."[85] Even if this overstates the case, it still seems a little perverse to use a statistical method in which the birth of a cow is an addition to wealth and the birth of a child a diminution.[86] A large and growing population means, after all, that people are alive who would otherwise be dead since population grows by means of a declining death-rate, not a growing birth-rate and that taken by itself would seem to be an improvement. Hostility to population growth is probably not the automatic attitude of any reasonable person but is, rather, conditional upon mindset and ideology.

The wisdom and morality of the policy, however, are beside the point as far as this study is concerned. It is sufficient to note that the rulers are not responding to a social demand but are pushing an unpopular policy regardless of what those affected by it might think. It is another indication that the official liberalization is a tool of the rulers, limited by what the rulers see as contributing to the wealth and power of the state.

## DEPOLITICIZATION: A FEW SUMMARY THOUGHTS

According to a student of Soviet politics, "The ideal of mature Stalinism was to politicize all spheres of social and even private endeavor and to depoliticize the political process."[87] Maoism entailed a similar drive to bring all life under the dominion of politics but with no tendency to reduce politics to administration. Administration was as politicized as everything else. The concept of politics was narrow, however. It did not imply an ongoing process of choice among different public policies but merely the struggle to see who would exercise arbitrary domination over whom. In these circumstances, the attempt to depoliticize does not mean to become apolitical. Depoliticization is itself a political program and part of the political demands of at least one type of Chinese dissident. Depoliticization is, inherent, for example, in the critique of the regime in the stories by Chen Jo-hsi.[88]

This hostility to politics also pervades the recent work of the mainland writer Wang Meng, a possible candidate for the much-speculated-about "Chinese Solzhenitsyn," that is, a writer of genuine talent and independence who affirms traditional and universal human values in the face of totalitarianism. Wang Meng, a more Apollonian temperament than his putative Russian analog (a reflection perhaps, of the different cultures), usually takes as his theme the inner life of tired disenchanted bureaucrats. In 1956, as a very young man, he published a controversial story, "The Young Newcomer in the Organization Department."[89] tracing the degeneration of revolutionary enthusiasm into bureaucratic sclerosis. After the harrowing of the hundred flowers periods Wang endured 20 years of obscurity and persecution, most of it in exile in Sinkiang.[90] His recent stories do not rail against the regime; the regime and its ways are simply taken for granted as background. Neither does he make concessions to its sensibilities, such as the ritual genuflections to the memory of Chou En-lai, which are apparently common in more overtly political "dissident" works.[91]

Wang's earlier story was about the loss of revolutionary idealism. His later work seems to suggest that the idealism itself was vain.[92] One story is set at the Chinese New Year or "spring festival" of 1980. An old bureaucrat is riding home on the train for the holidays. He can go home that year because his 80-year-old father is no longer classified as a landlord, a class enemy. The story consists of the protagonist's mental ruminations—his shame for his past compromises, his disappointment with the tawdry reality of today, and his dismay at the rudeness of the passengers and the conductors. His life has been nothing but self-examinations, and his work has involved empty sloganeering and small performance. He reflects that at least the railroad he is on has been built since 1949 (but the reader is inclined to ponder that, given a generation of peace, Chiang Kai-shek or even the emperor would have done as much). Also, some things are no longer measured by politics—the spring festival is no longer "revolutionized," and there is hope that life will get better.

> The February wind carries the hope of warmth, the news of spring. . . .
> It is still winter? Of course. But it is winter which is already making contact with spring, the bridge from winter to spring. The wind is a proof: the wind is already less cold.[93]

"The Butterfly" is a less optimistic story.[94] The protagonist, Chang Ssu-yuan, is a party functionary and a soldier in the revolution. After liberation he marries Hai-yun, an enfatuated school girl. Totally dedicated to the party and the people, Ssu-yuan neglects his wife and child. One evening Hai-yun phones him at work: the baby has a fever. But Ssu-yuan has meetings to attend. When he gets home after two in the morning the baby is dead. Unable to think of anything proper to say, Ssu-yuan gives his wife a little lecture: "This very second, American planes are bombing Pyongyang, thousands of Korean children are being killed by napalm . . ." Hai-yun leaves to study at a university. Home on vacation she becomes pregnant again and Ssu-yuan, the eternal oaf, urges her to have an abortion. She refuses and comes to resent him even more. She drifts into a love affair with another student, but Ssu-yuan becomes really scandalized only when she is criticized as a rightist in 1957. He decides Hai-yun is an incorrigible bourgois intellectual.

But Hai-yun has had enough of Ssu-yuan and she divorces him. Ssu-yuan tries to stay close to his new son by giving him presents, candy, and the like, but the child is always wary of him and finally rejects him. During the Cultural Revolution, the son, now a Red Guard, publicly denounces his father, slapping him on the ears. Ssu-yuan, it appears, is a capitalist roader. His second wife, a shallow, flashy woman, divorces him to save her own skin. Hai-yun is also mistreated by Red Guards and hangs herself.

In 1971 Ssu-yuan is released from prison and moves to the mountain village where his son has been sent. He learns that it was not as he suspected, that Hai-yun had embittered the boy against him, but that his son had come to his opinion himself. He more or less becomes reconciled with his son and also makes friends with Ch'iu-wen, a doctor whose husband has been in labor reform camp since 1957. While in the countryside Ssu-yuan, now simply "old Chang," finds peace of mind and begins to recover his humanity. After a couple of years, he is rehabilitated and goes back to Peking, rising ultimately to become a vice-minister. He hears that Ch'iu-wen's husband has finally died and he proposes to her but he is refused. She (and her son) prefer the village. Meanwhile, Ssu-yuan loses himself in his work. "It seemed many people were watching him, supporting him, hoping great things of him. Tomorrow the pressure of work would be even greater."[95]

That this kind of story could be published with official approval is a measure of how far liberalization had gone. It is not a dissident story, but its theme seems to be profoundly subversive. According to the regime's official critics, Ssu-yuan is a good man whose early idealism has been corrupted by power and privilege. This does not seem to be the case. If he is corrupted by anything, it is by work, and it is only from a certain point of view that he has been corrupted. Ssu-yuan is not lazy, cowardly, stupid, venal, selfish, or deliberately cruel. He is, in fact, a decent man through-out: it would have ruined him to have remained married to Hai-yun after she had been declared a rightist, but it is not he who asks for the divorce. He is a good cadre, and precisely because of this he is not much of a human being. In the village he learns how to be happy, but he does not learn it for long. Away from the village, he immediately reverts to the stereotyped communist. He writes to Ch'iu-wen and to his son:

> The second letter was written in the spring of '76, when he had to go along with the campaign against Deng Xiaoping. In that political climate he wrote fearfully, using the language of editorials. "We must trust that Chairman Mao's revolutionary line will win the final victory."[96]

It is this performance, I think, that convinces Ch'iu-wen she should stay single. Ssu-yuan's early idealism has not been corrupted: it contains all the later corruption within itself. Ssu-yuan has become exactly what the system demands that he be. The system is corrupt and inhumane.

It is also meaningless. The central metaphor and the title are taken from Chuang-tzu's familiar parable. Chuang-tzu dreamed he was a butterfly; when he woke up, he did not know whether he was a man who had dreamed he was a butterfly or a butterfly dreaming that he was a man.[97] When Ssu-yuan first comes to the village, he is as free as the butterfly. Later he becomes dimly aware that the real butterfly world is the blind busyness of Peking—but he keeps this realization at bay by working harder.

One theme of the story is, no doubt, that the communist system in China produces people like Ssu-yuan. But people like him are hardly confined to China, and Wang Meng would probably not be as sanguine as some in the democratic movement that a change of the system will take care of all problems. For the democratic movement as for the regime itself, life is earnest, life is real, and the democratic movement would probably reject Wang Meng's Taoist antipoliticism as much as the regime would. But both the regime and its critics know that Wang Meng identifies an actual state of affairs: a prevalent sense of meaninglessness among the educated and cynicism and disenchantment especially among the young (such as Ssu-yuan's son). This kind of alienation is sometimes held to be characteristic of democratic systems.[98] China and probably the Soviet Union as well tend to show that the phenomenon exists in totalitarian (or "mobilization") systems too, even though the disenchantment can find public expression only when the regime liberalizes. But that it is expressed gives the rulers a constant temptation to repress—precisely because the problem, while in part a product of totalitarian (or maybe even modern) politics, is not really amenable to political solutions, and the best the regime can do is to make everyone shut up about it. But this only feeds the crisis of legitimacy. This is perhaps the real headache of the regime, beyond all questions of "readjustment" and the "liberation of thought."

## NOTES

1. George Konrad and Ivan Szelanyi, *The Intellectuals on the Road to Class Power* (New York: Harcourt Brace Jovanovich, 1979).

2. *Kuang-ming Jih-pao*, December 7, 1976 (hereafter cited as *KM*).

3. *Jen-min Jih-pao* January 11 and 13, 1977; ibid., March 16, 1977 (hereafter cited as *PD*). A book on the mutual relationships of the study of earthquakes and of archaeology, published as late as October 1977, however, still urges the benefits of dialectical materialism to scientific discovery. Meng Fan-hsing et al., *Ti-chen yü Ti-chen K'oa-ku* (Peking: Wen-wu Ch'u-pan She, 1977).

4. *PD*, March 13 and 22, 1978.

5. *KM*, May 23, 1978; ibid., July 16, 1978.

6. *PD*, May 6, 1978; *KM*, July 23, 1978.

7. *KM*, May 7, 1977.

8. *PD*, November 17, 1978. On the occasion of the late chairman's birthday, someone caused to have printed in the *People's Daily* a brief essay of his endorsement of the 1957 purge. Mao Tse-tung, "On Uninterrupted Revolution," ibid., December 26, 1978.

9. Ibid., November 29, 1979.

10. *KM*, January 18, 1980.

11. *PD*, October 31, 1979.

12. *KM*, May 23, 1977.

13. *PD*, October 28, 1977.

14. Ibid., October 19, 1977; ibid., November 13, 1977.

15. *KM*, September 5, 1978.

16. See, respectively, *PD*, April 20, 1977; ibid., January 15, 1977; *KM*, March 20, 1977; and *PD*, March 31, 1977.

17. *PD*, May 5, 1977.

18. Mao Tun, "Some Shallow Opinions on the Study of Lu Hsun," ibid., October 19, 1977.

19. Hu Feng, the most important of the Chinese literary dissidents, was rehabilitated without publicity. He was apparently released from jail in December 1979, but this did not become known until almost a year later. Agence France Presse, November 14, 1980 in Foreign Broadcast Information Service, *Daily Report, People Republic of China*, November 17, 1980, pp. L9–L10 (hereafter cited as *FBIS/PRC*). In December 1978 Chou Yang (freshly rehabilitated himself) urged writers to write the truth: Hu Feng's slogan, one Chou Yang had denounced when Hu Feng used it. *PD*, February 24, 1979.

20. Huang Chen, "Welcoming a New High Tide in the Building of a Socialist Culture," *KM*, May 21, 1978.

21. Ibid., June 17, 1978.

22. Liu Hsi-sheng, "Discussing a Few Questions about the Way Short Stories Should be Written," ibid., March 30, 1979.

23. For example, Tsu Wei, "Oh, Fathers and Brothers!" *PD*, November 8, 1980, a kind of nonfiction short story about the horrors done in a supposedly model county in Hupei in 1977.

24. Ibid., February 24, 1979.

25. *KM*, July 11, 1979.

26. Wen Shan, " 'To Encourage Sounds of Praise—How Can That Do Us Any Good?' " *PD*, August 13, 1979. The title is a quotation from a 1961 speech by the late foreign minister Ch'en I.

27. Shao Yen-hsiang, "Eliminate the Influence of Feudal Residues," ibid., November 12, 1980.

28. *Hung Ch'i* 14 (July 16, 1980): 18.

29. *Chung-kuo Chien-she* 10 (October 1980): 21–24. This should be understood mainly, of course, as an attempt to score points against Taiwan, whose regime has not reciprocated by allowing the publication of other than underground mainland fiction.

30. *KM*, April 23, 1980.

31. *Hung Ch'i* 14 (July 16, 1980): 18.

32. Chu Chung-i, "The Thrust of Document No. 7," *Tung-hsiang* 30 (March 16, 1980); in *FBIS/PRC*, March 19, 1981, pp. U1–U3.

33. For excerpts, see *Inside Mainland China*, June 1981, pp. 14–19.

34. See *PD*, November 24, 1976 and the speech by Ch'en Tso-lin, ibid., December 19, 1976.

35. Ibid., August 27, 1977.

36. Ibid., December 23, 1976.

37. Hu Ch'iao-mu, "Work According to Economic Laws; Speed up the Realization of the Four Modernizations," ibid., October 6, 1978. The speech was delivered "during July."

38. Ibid., November 23, 1978; Ma Jia-ju (Ma Chia-chü), "A Pioneering Work on Economic Reform—Notes on Sun Yefang's *Theoretical Questions of the Socialist Economy*," *Social Sciences in China* 1 (March 1980): 216–27.

39. Ren Tao (Jen T'ao), "Investigation Report: Enterprises in Sichuan Province Acquire Greater Independence," *Social Sciences in China* 1 (March 1980): 201–15.

40. Hsueh Mu-chiao, "Some Opinions on the Reform of the Economic System," *PD*, June 10, 1980.

41. Li Hung-lin, "What Kind of Socialism Do We Uphold?" ibid., May 9, 1980.

42. Wang Chao, "A Critique of the Centralized System of the Sung Dynasty," *KM* October 21, 1980.

43. Lin Wei, "Uphold Historical Materialism in the Relation between Economics and Politics," ibid., May 15, 1980.

44. *PD*, January 1, 1981. Retrenchment was discussed at a work conference in late December, and the pronouncements by Ch'en Yun, Chao Tzu-yang, Teng Hisao-p'ing, and Li Hsien-nien, the last being a self-criticism, were circulated for study within the party. There

is a summary of these in *Inside Mainland China*, April 1981, pp. 14–20, adapted from the February 1981 issue of *Cheng Ming*.

45. Chin Wen, "Agricultural Policy Must Consist of Relaxation and of Stabilization on the Basis of Relaxation," *KM*, December 15, 1980.

46. *PD*, May 1, 1977; ibid., June 9, 1977.

47. Ibid., March 17, 1978.

48. Ibid., August 24, 1978.

49. Ibid., January 27, 1979.

50. Ibid., September 6, 1979.

51. Chao Tzu-yang, "Study the New Situation, Fully Implement the Direction of Readjustment," *Hung Ch'i* 1 (January 1, 1980): 15–20.

52. *PD*, May 12, 1980; *KM*, June 21, 1980; ibid., February 2, 1980; *PD*, June 13, 1980.

53. *PD*, July 12, 1980.

54. Ibid., July 31, 1980.

55. Ibid., November 1, 1980.

56. Hsueh Mu-feng, "How to Struggle Against Bureaucratism," ibid., April 28, 1980.

57. *KM*, November 28, 1980. The writer fails to point out that in traditional China peasants were also tied into a complex market system. G. William Skinner, "Marketing and Social Structure in Rural China," pt. 1, *Journal of Asian Studies* 24 (November 1964): 3–43: Evelyn Sakashida Rawski, *Agricultural Change and the Peasant Economy of South China* (Cambridge, Mass.: Harvard University Press, 1972).

58. Chin, "Relaxation and Stabilization."

59. For a good general study, see Thomas P. Bernstein, *Up to the Mountains and Down to the Villages: The Transfer of Youth from Urban to Rural China* (New Haven: Yale University Press, 1977).

60. Thomas B. Gold, "Back to the City: The Return of Shanghai's Educated Youth," *China Quarterly* 84 (December 1980): 755–70.

61. *PD*, January 4, 1977.

62. *KM*, July 13, 1978.

63. *PD*, April 22, 1979.

64. Agence France Presse, March 22, 1981; *FBIS/PRC*, March 24, 1981, p. O6.

65. In the early 1970s, a father wrote to Mao to complain of the hard life of his son down on the farm. Mao responded and thereafter the treatment of rusticated youth improved. After Mao died the father was denounced as an agent of the Gang of Four. See B. Michael Frolic, *Mao's People: Sixteen Portraits of Life in Revolutionary China* (Cambridge, Mass.: Harvard University Press, 1980), pp. 45–47.

66. *KM*, January 30, 1977.

67. *PD*, June 3, 1979.

68. Jen Hsu-yu, "Study Religion, Criticize Theology," *KM*, September 27, 1977; on the last point, see also *PD*, January 27, 1981.

69. For material on religious policy prior to the Cultural Revolution, see Tu Mo, *Chung-kuo Ta-lu T'ien-chu-chiao Chen-hsiang* [True Picture of the Catholic Church in Mainland China] (Hong Kong: Chiu-chen Hsueh-she, 1966); Holmes Welch, *Buddhism Under Mao* (Cambridge, Mass.: Harvard University Press, 1972).

70. See *Christianity and the New China* (South Pasadena, Calif.: Ecclesia, 1976); and, with a few honorable exceptions, the articles by the churchy types in James D. Whitehead, Yu-ming Shaw, and N. J. Girardot, eds., *China and Christianity: Historical and Future Encounters*, (Notre Dame: Center for Pastoral and Social Ministry, 1979).

71. John Strong and Sara Strong, "A Post-Cultural Revolution Look at Chinese Buddhism," *China Quarterly* 54 (April/June 1973): 301–30; E. H. Johnson, "Christian Voices from the Church in China: April, 1975," *China Notes* 13 (Summer 1975): 26–30.

72. Chao P'u-ch'u, "The Revived Glory of Chinese Buddhism," *Chung-kuo Chien-she* (October 1980): 48.

73. Liu Tso-ch'ang, "Comments on Thomas Jefferson's Democratic Thought," *Li-shih Yen-chiu* 4 (August 15, 1980): 151.

74. *PD*, September 9, 1980. The suggested policy has not been adopted.

75. Lei Chen-ch'ang, "Strengthen the Atheist Education of Young People," *KM*, August 25, 1980.

76. *China News Analysis* 1186 (August 1, 1980). The state constitution adopted at the end of 1982 forbids religious groups from having connections with foreign powers. The provision is directed against Chinese Catholics who wish to maintain or reestablish ties with Rome.

77. *KM*, November 30, 1980.

78. For example, David Bonavia, *The Chinese* (New York: Lippincott and Crowell, 1980), pp. 40–41.

79. In traditional China abortion (like female infanticide, which was practiced by the extreme poor) was considered a form of wrongful homicide. See the discussion in Lu Hsun, *A Brief History of Chinese Fiction* (Peking: Foreign Languages Press, 1964), pp. 282–83. The regime is not proud of encouraging abortion, and until a few years ago abortions were rare despite official encouragement. William L. Parish and Martin King Whyte, *Village and Family in Contemporary China* (Chicago: University of Chicago Press, 1978).

80. *PD*, September 15, 1980.

81. *KM*, February 1, 1981.

82. Tung Tung, "One Baby for You, One Baby for Me," *American Spectator* 14 (January 1981): 15–17. The time of the story is August or September 1976; it is after the T'ang-shan earthquake but before the purge of the Gang of Four.

83. *PD*, November 4, 1980.

84. Ibid., April 6, 1980.

85. Julian L. Simon, "Global Confrontation, 1980: A Hard Look at the Global 2000 Report," *The Public Interest* 62 (Winter 1981): 18.

86. Peter Bauer and Basil S. Yaney, "The Third World and the West: An Economic Perspective," in *The Third World: Premises of US Policy* (San Francisco: Institute for Contemporary Studies, 1978), p. 107.

87. Seweryn Bialer, *Stalin's Successors: Leadership, Stability, and Change in the Soviet Union* (New York: Cambridge University Press, 1980), p. 15.

88. Chen Jo-hsi, *The Execution of Mayor Yin* (Bloomington: Indiana University Press, 1978).

89. Wang Meng, "The Younger Newcomer in the Organization Department," *Jen-min Wen-hsueh* 9 (September 1956): 29–43.

90. *KM*, March 5, 1980.

91. Bonavia, *The Chinese*, pp. 237–38.

92. In the 1981 crackdown, Wang escaped serious criticism. He was praised for his refusal to present one-sided, simplified characterizations in his stories. Liu Men-chieh, "Preliminary Discussion of the Mainstream of Literary Development in 1980," *Hung Ch'i* 3 (February 1, 1981): 34. Another critic, however, was irritated by what he took to be Wang Meng's overuse of the stream of consciousness technique. Feng Wu, "On Some Problems of Literary Creativity," *PD*, February 11, 1981.

93. Wang Meng, "The Voice of Spring," *Jen-min Wen-hsueh* 5 (May 1980): 10–16, quote at p. 14.

94. I am using the English translation. Wang Meng, "The Butterfly," *Chinese Literature* (January 1981): 3–55.

95. Quotes from ibid., pp. 12, 55.

96. Ibid., p. 50.

97. Arthur Waley, *Three Ways of Thought in Ancient China* (Garden City, N.Y.: Doubleday Anchor, n.d.), p. 32.

98. David E. Apter, *The Politics of Modernization* (Chicago: University of Chicago Press, 1965), p. 31.

# 7

# Liberalization and Popular Protest: The Democratic Movement

Totalitarian systems contain a tension between the leader and the party. Mao, unlike Stalin, sometimes attempted to resolve this tension in his own favor by direct appeals to the people (although, of course, he was also willing to use the police and the army). Although different in content, the hundred flowers campaign and the Cultural Revolution are similar in that they represent public opinion mobilized by one group within the regime (centered on Mao) against the party bureaucracy. The democratic movement, too, was in part a result of the mobilization of the people by one faction of the rulers against enemy factions.

But while none of the mass movements have been completely spontaneous, neither have any been completely fake. The rulers attempted to mobilize mass discontent for their own ends, but in each case there was genuine discontent and while the rulers may have had their purposes, so too did the ruled have theirs.

The democratic movement bloomed most luxuriantly in the winter of 1978-79, when China was more than normally open to the outside. There are abundant data on the movement, although they wait to be completely digested.[1] This chapter treats only one aspect of the movement—the relationship between popular protest and the politics among the rulers. In the short term, the extent to which popular protest will be effective or even heard will be up to the discretion and interests of the rulers. Over the long run, the rulers may be increasingly faced with a choice between reverting to terror (which would be destabilizing to their internal relationships) and repression, or to making concessions to popular sentiment.

## BACKGROUND TO THE POST-MAO PROTEST

Radical popular dissent in communist China has been directed against the party's monopoly of power and its suppression of democracy. At least until recently, this strain of dissent has not been liberal, although it has been democratic in one of the senses of that by now bloated word. It is somewhat similar to the left-wing opposition to Lenin after the Russian Revolution and also has some affinity with radical Maoism. In 1956 the student dissident Lin Hsi-ling complained that the party had become a new ruling class. Without more democracy the revolution will die.[2] This was similar in content if not purpose to the 1966 Maoist claim that the party had been taken over by "persons on the capitalist road" who needed to be overthrown by the popular masses. From the point of view of Liu Shap-ch'i, the greatest person in power on the capitalist road, the Red Guard movement was an antiparty counterrevolution. Some Red Guards, taking Maoism at its word, carried the Maoist critique beyond what the official radicals were then willing to tolerate. In 1968 the Hunan Provincial Proletarian Alliance argued that the state machinery (run by Chou En-lai, the boss of China's red bourgeoisie) perpetuated class domination. This state machinery must be smashed by revolutionary action and replaced by direct democracy, as in the Paris commune.[3] The Li I-che protestors of 1973 and 1974 are a chastened version of this form of dissent. They identify the repressive machinery of the state with the activities of the official radicals themselves and call for rule by law as well as for democracy. The T'ien-an-men demonstrators in April 1976 denounced the current system as feudal and demanded the four modernizations.

This last incident, however, seems to represent a confluence of the radical line of dissent with another line. The demonstrators emphasized less how the rulers suppress democracy than how the official radicalism inhibits modernization. The esteem for Chou En-lai that provided the occasion for the demonstration is common among highly educated young Chinese (who wish they could be just like Chou) but was not shared by the more radical dissidents.

In China there has been a second strain of protest, one rather less concerned with the idea of mass democracy. This line was directed not so much against the lack of participation in politics as against the politiciza-tion of life—something the Provincial Proletarian Alliance, for example, had no problem with at all. This strand would emphasize themes such as the legitimacy of finding satisfaction in private life and the value of indulging individual tastes and differences. It also favored education without constant political indoctrination and, in work, the setting of criteria for performance (and promotion) on professional rather than political grounds. This line was the initial target of the Cultural Revolution and received its most articulate exposition from Teng T'o and Wu Han before the Cultural Revolution; it was echoed, perhaps hypocritically, by those around Lin Piao in their 1971 desperation.[4] This is the general position taken, I think, by Wang Meng in "The Butterfly."

These two "lines" among the discontented parallel the Red and Expert division within the regime (it may be useful to use those terms as a convenient shorthand, with the initial letters capitalized to indicate that the terms are a useful jargon but are not always to be taken literally). In the official dogma, Red and Expert are supposed to form a dialectical unity, although in practice to emphasize one has meant to neglect the other. Too sharp a line, however, should not be drawn between the lines in their dissident manifestation; since the Cultural Revolution the two lines of dissent have been growing together. The Li I-che poster was a Red recognition that there is much in the Expert view that makes sense; the T'ien-an-men demonstrations were Expert in inspiration, but with a recognition that Red methods might be needed to achieve the Expert end.

Some distinctions do remain, however. There may be social differences between the two types of dissidents. The Reds would tend to include, one suspects, those who by ability, temperament, or opportunity do not do as well in formal schooling as they would like to. Red dissent was nourished among former Red Guards who felt sold out by the establishment radicals. The Experts on the whole may in the early 1970s have led a more comfortable life, but their position was always insecure. They would be the victims of any new radical upsurge and the establishment radicals could always hope to mobilize Red resentment against him.

The official liberalization discussed in the last two chapters, particularly the policies associated with Teng Hsiao-p'ing, is an indulging of Expert discontent. The democratic movement, however, seems to be more of a Red phenomenon. The most prominent spokesman for that movement, Wei Ching-sheng, was not an intellectual of the type canonized by the Teng line but an electrician (although he claims he could have been a party bureaucrat if he had wanted to). He was also, to put it unkindly, a former Red Guard thug (although a member of a faction hostile to those supported by the Gang of Four).[5] A critique of the democratic movement from the inside complains that the educational level of the movement was not high. The participants were mostly young workers with secondary school educations. Few of the activists were college students or higher-level intellectuals; these had been bought off by the regime.[6] It may not simply have been a matter of having been bought off, however. The Expert dissidents might have ambivalent feelings about their Red sometime allies. They would not be entirely unpersuaded when Teng Hsiao-p'ing would depict the democratic movement activists as nothing but a bunch of Red Guards, people, in the 1981 locution, whose only fear was that there be no chaos under heaven.[7]

Once again, then, a rejection of the democratic movement is not in itself a rejection of liberalization. It may instead be a choice for a particular kind of liberalization. Yet it should also be stressed that the feelings of the Experts for the Reds would not be rejection, but ambivalence. The same kind of ambivalence may have been felt inside the party itself. If the depoliticization entailed in Teng's line is carried to the point at which the spontaneous expression of social interests and opinions is allowed, this would imply democratization as well as depoliticization. A Hong Kong coterie that seems to reflect the opinions both of the Expert dissident line and of the Teng faction noted in 1979 that democratic centralism is not democracy. It is a technique for achieving unity and discipline inside the party, not for allowing popular control of leaders. The latter requires not democratic centralism but general elections.[8] In the last half of 1980, democracy had become a slogan of Teng himself, and his followers were making some astonishing proposals for the democratization of the polity. The Red and Expert lines of dissent are distinct in origin and different in emphasis, but in practice they have come to be mixed together. Teng Hsiao-p'ing for his own ends nourished them both. Because he associated himself for a time with the democratic movement, its fate is not entirely irrelevant to his.

## POPULAR ACTIVISM UNDER HUA KUO-FENG

The demonstrations in Peking, Shanghai, and elsewhere in late 1976 may have been no more spontaneous than those the Gang used to sponsor, but they were probably more sincerely felt. The rulers must have taken pleasure in their unwanted popularity, while dissidents became bolder about testing the limits of the permitted. The increasing openness of China to foreigners also encouraged the voicing of complaints.

A wall poster in Canton in early 1977 complained of Chinese economic backwardness relative to Japan—a theme that would become an official commonplace in the months to come but was still daring at the time: "is the Chinese socialist system inferior to the Japanese system?"[9] A "young intellectual" from Shanghai, hearing that President Carter had "met the leader of the Soviet human rights movement and discussed the question of human rights in the White House," wrote to tell the uninterested U.S. president about the political prisons in Shanghai, the hardships of rustication, and the indignities of political tyranny.[10] The major break with past practice here, aside from complaining to foreigners, was the grounding of the complaints in terms of human rights, a reflection of the United

States' use of the concept at that time. Despite official U.S. indifference to the human condition in China, the popularization of the concept of human rights by the United States was a major factor in the shaping of the subsequent democratic movement.

By 1978 the protest movements had become linked with the machinations of the Teng group, or at least it would so appear from the themes stressed. Around the time of the anniversaries of the death of Chou En-lai and the April 5 riots, wall posters proclaimed that incident to be truly revolutionary and denounced the "wind faction," which disagreed. Wu Te and Ch'en Hsi-lien were attacked by name.[11] A wall poster published on the anniversary of Teng's second rehabilitation effusively praised that leader and not so subtly demanded that Hua tell the truth about the T'ien-an-men incident.[12] In sum, the dissent of the earlier part of 1978 looks a bit pat: the criticisms were no doubt genuine, but they also fit in neatly with the interests of Teng. By winter the organic connection between Teng and the dissidents had become looser. Hua Kuo-feng was criticized directly, perhaps for the first time since the Cultural Revolution, by one poster writer because Hua had had the bad taste to write the calligraphy for the cover of the official edition of the T'ien-an-men poems. The writer, a contributor to the anthology, thought that honor should more appropriately go to Teng Hsiao-p'ing.[13] The culture minister, Huang Chen, was criticized for his advocacy of censorship.[14] Hua and Huang were not Teng's men, but neither were they then Teng's targets of choice. Someone signing himself Wu Wen ("no culture") said Mao was senile in his last years, and Mao's nomination of Hua as his successor was typical of a feudal fascist dictatorship.[15] Teng's people would come to say this sort of thing eventually, but not for another two years or so.

"If the masses feel some anger," Teng said, "we must let them express it." He did not, however, approve of attacking Mao by name.[16] So he told U. S. reporters, and the interview became known in China immediately. One response was a poster criticizing Teng's lack of candor: "You can clamp down silence again upon the people, but that won't solve anything."[17] Some put up posters defending Mao, but this theme did not catch on.[18]

On November 27 "thousands of people" marched in Peking in what a participant said was the first spontaneous demonstration ever held in People's China[19] (but what, then, about the April 5, 1976 demonstrations?). At the end of December, rusticated youths and other former residents began returning to Peking and Shanghai, and for a time spontaneous demonstrations became common despite halfhearted attempts to repress them. In the meantime the themes of protest became more subversive. Wei Ching-sheng's essay, "Democracy: The Fifth Modernization", appeared in early December.[20] This in itself was fairly innocuous—until it became evident that Wei meant what he said. Around the same time, a Chinese human rights group sent yet another appeal to Jimmy Carter, asking him to "pay attention to the state of human rights in China." The poster reproducing this appeal was torn down but was replaced immediately by a second poster with a preface added, noting that the constitution permitted people to express themselves through big character posters.[21] The theme of the official press remained: trust the masses. The movement, however, had gone beyond official control.

## THE PEKING SPRING

At the turn of the year (but, surprisingly, not on New Year's Day itself) the regime gave a hedged endorsement of the demonstrations and of the democratic movement generally. The demonstrations, according to the *People's Daily*, do not violate democratic centralism. We must tolerate criticism of the Party Center and of leading cadres. We need peace and unity, to be sure, but not feudal despotism. Some comrades fear chaos. They are like Lord She, who loved dragons: they love democracy until they actually see it, and then they go into a panic. Such comrades "do not understand what democratic centralism is. They think democracy means that I give you democracy and let you speak out as long as what you say does not go beyond the limits of what I want to hear." "Only if the masses can express all sorts of opinions can the leadership implement correct centralism." Of course, not all of these opinions will be correct. "This is unavoidable and also nothing to be afraid of. If we let people speak the sky won't fall." The masses can have only a partial view of the situation, and some are corrupt people who act in bad faith. But we (the party) want an atmosphere that encourages talk and criticism.[22] Around this time the Li I-che dissidents were released from prison.[23] It was almost as if the regime had come over to their point of view—but only almost. The regime's attitude toward democracy remained elitist. The people could express opinions, but the leadership would evaluate them. There was then no suggestion that the people might choose their own leadership. The small comment about bad people was a reminder that if pushed the regime could still revert to rough methods.

The protest movement was fed by the influx of peasants coming to "*shang fang*" to "petition the superior" for redress of grievances. These peasants seem to have been mostly city dwellers long exiled to the countryside. They now demanded food, clothing, and equal treatment. Foreign reports tell of horrors: people in rags, women trying to sell their babies because they could not feed them, and the like. It may not be overly cynical to wonder whether some of the petitioners might have been dramatizing for effect. But it is certainly true that their lives were hard, and they no doubt had objective grounds for their belief in official indifference. Several of the petitioners were reported to have died of exposure in the cold Peking winter. The human rights activists in Peking made common cause with the peasants, although some of the peasants reportedly thought the city kids were spoiled and shallow, with nothing really to compalin about. The ostentatious displays of poverty for the edification of foreigners (for foreign reporters were given advance notice of the demonstrations: the media event seems to be worldwide now) were an embarrassment and an irritation to the regime. In some cities, especially Shanghai and Hangchow, the return led to the disruption of the railroads and to rioting in the streets.[24]

The peasants concentrated on demands for better treatment, not for changes in the political structure of the regime. These, however, became the main interest of the human rights groups, now organized as the Human Rights Alliance. Their "Chinese Human Rights Declaration" called for freedom of speech and thought, constitutional safeguards for liberty, a "national referendum to . . . elect state leaders," public accountability by the state, access to foreigners, freedom of job choice, and a demand that the state "ensure basic food rations for peasants and get rid of beggars." The rustication policies should be liberalized and the secret police abolished. "This league appeals to the governments of all countries of the world, to human rights organizations, and to the public for support."[25] The document has a general bias toward human rights as they affect educated youths in danger of rustication. It is less sophisticated politically than the Li I-che poster, perhaps because the freer atmosphere allowed sloppier reasoning and greater self-indulgence. But even with its bias it is a measure of the sorts of things ordinary thoughtful people found objectionable in China, and it is a testimony to the spontaneous appeal of liberal ideas even among persons indoctrinated against them for their entire lives.

The regime lost its early enthusiasm for the democracy movement. In February a Shanghai paper said that liberty does not mean that people are allowed to shoot their mouths off in front of foreigners,[26] but it was not until March that the national press began to say this sort of thing. The regime was acting behind the scenes, however. In the middle of January, it shot three former Red Guards for crimes committed during the Cultural Revolution.[27] The timing suggests this was killing the chicken to scare the monkey. A couple of days later, the first arrest connected with the democratic movement took place, that of Fu Yueh-hua. She was eventually convicted of slander, of falsely accusing her boss of raping her and of making her accusation public after the police had ignored her. Her friends say that the accusation against her boss was true, but the slander charge in any case was a pretext. Her real crime was that she had helped organize the peasant demonstrations in Peking.[28]

The regime could not satisfy the demands of the democratic movement, and therefore, as long as the repression was weak and sporadic, the movement was encouraged to intensify its critique. The most mature elaboration of the more radical ideas of the movement is found in the writings of Wei Ching-sheng, editor of *Exploration (T'an-so)*, an underground magazine that began to appear in January 1979. Wei was then an electrician at the Peking zoo. During the Cultural Revolution, he had belonged to United Action (*Lien Tung*), a relatively conservative Red Guard organization composed of children of communist officials. He became radicalized, he says, by the poverty he saw during his Red Guard wanderings and later during his service in the army.[29] In December 1978 he wrote a poster demanding democracy, the fifth modernization, and after the turn of the year, he began developing some of the implications of this demand.

The fullest exposition of his ideas is perhaps "More About the Fifth Modernization," which appeared in March.[30] It is divided into sections on human rights, democracy, and equality. Human rights, Wei says, are not absolute and unlimited but are contingent upon historical development. Their content changes over time. They develop in the course of struggle against nature and struggle within society. "Political activities are activities to fight for and to repress human rights." In order that this struggle may be properly carried out, there must be equality, by which Wei seems to mean an equal chance with the other fighters in struggles or the equal enjoyment of freedoms of speech, assembly, belief, habitation, and the like. He rejects the notion of equality of result. If I have the freedom to eat an apple, you should have the same freedom, but that does not mean you should have to eat an apple if you do not want to. Equality (*p'ing-teng*) is not the same as leveling (*p'ing-chün*). Democracy is the form of government that allows the struggle to go on. It is thus not good in itself, but a means to the goals of liberty and human rights. The Marxist concept of democracy focuses only on popular control of social activity. By failing to treat people equally—by failing to take into account that people's desires differ—it becomes a "democratic dictatorship" (*min-chu tu-ts'ai*—the regime uses the less harsh synonym, *min-chu chuan-cheng*, to describe itself). Democracy is a political system, not an economic system. Marxism wants to control everything. Taking advantage of human sloth and cowardice, it promises the limitless satisfaction of all desires. It is based not on objective reality but on the fallacy that "a society in which all hopes and desires can be attained" is possible. It is a confidence trick. "As a result of the dictatorial rule of Marxism and Mao Tse-tungism" there is no political liberty in China. People have no influence on government. Dictatorial methods and idealistic delusions, however, cannot provide the basis for managing a modern society. If the people are powerless, enslaved, and exploited, even with economic growth their lives will be without meaning, and this will hinder social development. A democratic political system is a precondition for successful modernization.

This essay is turgid and maddeningly abstract. Its ideas may not be completely coherent. Wei has a historicist and relativist conception of human rights (and why, then, call them rights?) but also the notion that in history our rights become more complete. This implies, however, that Wei has some ahistorical or superhistorical standard by which he judges the condition of rights at any one time. By equality Wei does not mean that people are all alike, but that each person's opinions and desires should have the same political weight as those of anyone else. It is hard to see, however, where he gets this value judgment. This kind of equality needs to be grounded in some system of morality, such as the natural law that Wei rejects. Otherwise, some people may be my equal, but there is no reason for me to recognize their interests if I have them in my power. For that matter, the very idea of human rights would seem to refer to rights enjoyed by all persons simply by virtue of their being human. It is hard to see how this kind of right can be other than universal, if not absolute, or how it can be contingent upon historical development. Wei's confusion of rights with power may be facilitated by the Chinese language, but it is a confusion shared also by such undisputed masters of English style as Thomas Hobbes.

Wei's work may transcend the Red-Expert distinction drawn earlier. I think, however, that it is legitimate to place it on a trajectory from earlier instances of Red dissent. Wei's position shares with Maoism its relativism, its rejection of objective value, and its emphasis on struggle. Wei does repudiate the total politicization that is a part of Maoism, but in one way this does not seem to be of much purpose. Human rights are seen as by-products of struggle and are grounded in nothing but desire and the power to attain that desire. Wei is less consistent here than the Maoists: he puts arbitrary limitations both on the struggle and on politics; it is arbitrary because he gives the limitations no rational moral grounding. Wei criticizes Marxism for postulating an end to history, a time when all desires will be totally satisfied. This may be an element in orthodox Marxist ideology, but it is not a part of radical Maoism. For Mao, as for Wei, the struggle goes on forever:

> With the arrival of communism will there be no more struggle? I don't believe it. With the arrival of communism there will still be struggle between the old and the new, between the correct and the mistaken. Tens of thousands of years hence mistakes will still be unsatisfactory and will be unable to stand.[31]

This is not to suggest that Wei is in any literal sense a Maoist. Indeed, his relativism, antinomianism, and vision of total social openness are also characteristic of radical liberalism.[32] This may show some affinity between radical liberalism and totalitarianism, or totalitarianism as a perversion of liberalism. But Wei's position may be contrasted with that of Wang Meng in "The Butterfly." For Wang a moderation of the regime would require that it leave the people alone, that it cease to oppress them with politics. Our rights, if Wang used that kind of language, would be to do what we want without harming others or violating our duties and without the comrades officiously bossing us around. For Wei our rights are creatures of the political struggle. Once again, however, the line should not be made too sharply. Wei explicitly recognizes that politics is not everything; the Expert line of liberalization, to have any vitality and to be more than apathy and impotent contempt by the educated toward their indulgent rulers, must allow for some kind of open political participation.

Around the middle of March, the press began to comment that while democracy is no doubt a very fine thing, there is also the need for "revolutionary order." There is no "abstract democracy"; democracy always has a class nature.[33] Around this time Teng Hsiao-p'ing demanded that Wei Ching-sheng be arrested for selling military secrets to foreigners.[34] Wei had in fact discussed Chinese military operations in Vietnam with foreign reporters.[35] It is doubtful, however, that this was a major element in China's poor showing there; and Wei would be guilty, if anything, of arrogance and poor judgement, not treason. Just prior to his arrest, Wei returned Teng's compliment with a denunciation of his own: the public used to have great hope in Teng, but now he has become a dictator.[36] Teng also spelled out four "basic principles" governing the exercise of free speech. There is freedom only for those who uphold socialism, proletarian dictatorship, the leadership of the party, and Marxism-Leninism, that is, the thought of Mao Tse-tung.[37] The regime began systematically tearing down all wall posters except those on the so-called democracy wall on Hsi-tan road. The regime promised to be "merciless toward error" (but not toward persons fallen into error) and explained the continuing need for dictatorship. The liberation of thought was redefined to mean Teng's four principles.[38] The April 5 incident, on its third anniversary, was said to have been a demand for *socialist* democracy, and people were warned not to put too much emphasis on its spontaneity.[39] Socialist democracy, in turn, was not to be confused with anarchy, and law and democracy do not mean *bourgeois* law and democracy.[40] The regime worried about youths seduced by foreign ways and about those who fancied capitalism better than socialism.[41] The *People's Daily* published a review of a "new left" textbook on the U.S. government. The author is too much of a petty bourgeois to know what the real problems are, but his book does show that even U.S. citizens realize that their much-vaunted democracy is nothing but a hollow sham.[42] China's democracy, no doubt, is the real thing. The Peking spring had frozen over just as the real spring had begun to thaw.

## THE RULERS' AMBIVALENCE

The crackdown, however, was not followed by the repression, the servile self-incriminations, and the turn to radicalism that followed the hundred flowers campaign 22 years earlier. Nor was the crackdown entirely a matter of Teng Hsiao-p'ing's turning against those who had served him after they were no longer useful. For tactical reasons Teng led the crackdown, but later evidence indicates that he feared it would go too far. Teng, like Wei Ching-sheng, seems to have had at least an inchoate program for major structural reforms in the regime, and until the end of 1980 or so he may have considered the democratic movement among the least of many evils. Teng's main complaint against the movement would seem to have been that the extremism of its demands reflected on his own position, making him vulnerable to leftist attacks within the party.

Teng, or his supporters, were in the meantime developing an ideological program to justify structural reform, a program with its own affinities with the tradition of Red dissent. This can be reconstructed from scattered contemporary newspaper essays, but its clearest exposition is given by "Chi Hsin," the pen name of a communist writing group in Hong Kong that has given voice to the ideas of the liberalizers in general and of the Teng group in particular.

Shortly after the summer 1979 session of the National People's Congress, at which Hua Kuo-feng announced that there were no more exploiting classes in China even though class struggle still continued, Chi Hsin published an analysis of the current contradictions. According to Mao Tse-tung, Liu Shao-ch'i, Chou En-lai, Lin Piao, and Hua Kuo-feng (a most peculiar lumping together of names), the main contradiction is between the bourgeoisie and the proletariat. In fact, however, Mao came closer to the truth when he worried about the "possible emergence of a privileged class within the party." The reason Mao could mobilize so many people at the start of the Cultural Revolution was not because he had high prestige but because he had identified a real problem: people resented the privilege enjoyed by those with power. These were not really "capitalist roaders," however. The cadres who are coming to constitute a privileged class are not those who want to develop the economy; they are those who, for spurious leftist reasons, hinder development. Rather than being capitalists, "they would be better described as people in power who follow a feudal autocratic road." The contradiction between the rulers and the ruled is a "relatively major one" and "may develop into an antagonistic class contradiction." Fortunately, the regime is now developing a legal system and this, by curbing the cadres' arrogation of special privilege, will moderate the potential antagonism.[43]

This is a more systematic and blunt presentation than can be found in the mainland press—one of the functions of the Hong Kong communist press in those years was to be blunt and systematic about what could only be hinted on the mainland. It is perhaps an extreme statement of the Teng program. In the retrenchment of 1981, the regime once again explicitly repudiated the idea that bureaucratic privilege, however bad it may be, is or can be a question of class struggle. The party is not a "privileged stratum," and it is impossible that it should give rise to a bureaucratic class.[44] When the Teng group is not on the defensive, however, it seems spontaneously to tend to identify "feudalism" rather than capitalism as China's biggest worry, and feudalism has become a code word for closed bureaucratic rule. Feudalism manifests itself today as extreme leftism, which is used to justify the arbitrary power and privilege of those in authority.

In emphasizing differences between rulers and ruled, the Teng program is in the tradition of the radical Red Guards, of Li I-che, of, for that matter, the Gang of Four in early 1975. While the Gang purported to prevent the emergence of a new ruling class by the exercise of dictatorship, the Teng program relies on law. The program has obvious democratic implications as well. If the relationship between rulers and ruled might become antagonistic, it would seem proper to prevent this by finding ways whereby the people might hold their rulers responsible.

At the end of July, the *People's Daily* complained that a "cold wind in spring" had threatened to destroy the hundred flowers.[45] The democratic movement had provided the occasion for a revival of the influence of the leftists defeated before the third plenum. By the end of summer, those who denounced the democratic movement were themselves once again being denounced.

The leftists raised the witty slogan, *wu hu luan hua*. This means literally that five barbarian tribes bring chaos to China. It can also mean five people named Hu bring chaos to China, or five people named Hu confound Hua Kuo-feng.[46] The major Hu they had in mind was Hu Yao-pang, Teng's most reliable supporter and, behind the scenes, the strongest supporter of liberal reforms.

This leftist revival was defeated during the summer, although it remains hard to chronicle exactly what went on. Toward the end of May, the tone in comment about the democratic movement began to shift. The *People's Daily* reverted to a more moderate version of the line taken at the turn of the year: comrades should not worry too much that criticism of Lin Piao and the Gang will damage revolutionary things.[47] Chao Tzu-yang admitted that some "in society" violated Teng's four principles, but this was no reason to blame the third plenum for all of China's problems.[48] The general attitude toward the democratic movement, however, remained harsh. As late as June 7, one writer could still link the movement with Lin Piao and the Gang and continue, with the effrontery that dialectics makes so easy, to argue that the April 5 riots may have been fine as a rehearsal for the overthrow of the Gang, but now that "our country's history has already turned a new page" troublemakers are going against the tide of history.[49]

Teng found his weapon in Chang Chih-hsin, a party functionary from Liaoning who had been imprisoned and tortured under Lin Piao and finally shot (after having been mutilated) by the Gang of Four. She had been physically attractive, apparently a nice person as well as a courageous one, and the mother of small children: the regime was able to milk the injustice done her for all it was worth. Unlike the people in the democratic movement, she always observed party discipline without falling into blind obedience or yielding to incorrect principle. Her whole life was devoted to the party. As an unspoken bonus, three of the major leftists on the Politburo were at least indirectly responsible for her murder: Hua Kuo-feng, Wang Tung-hsing, and Ch'en Hsi-lien.[50]

The campaign to mourn Chang Chih-hsin, however, probably did not cause a shift in the balance against the left but was, rather, a sign that the balance had already shifted. It may also have given temporary help to the democratic movement, showing, by analogy, that the regime did not want any more such injustices. By the end of June, the left was on the defensive. Hua Kuo-feng's speech to the National People's Congress is an attempt to salvage what could be salvaged of the leftist position—a situation Hua should have been becoming used to. Hua has strong, if indirect words, about the democratic movement. According to him, while the Gang did encourage autocracy, bureaucratism, special privilege, and "patriarchalism," all current targets of the Teng group, their special faults were anarchism and factionalism. Hua is very worried about the "anarchist thought tide." No one is allowed to "damage the interests of the state in the name of personal so-called 'freedom.'" Socialist democracy has no use for anarchy, and sabotage. In discussing the Teng policy on material incentives, Hua says that the ultimate goal is distribution by need, not work, "as I don't think any of you at this meeting doubt." In context the last addition has a somewhat snide tone to it. In one respect, however, Hua is even more moderate than Teng. He elaborates the new party line: there is no more exploitation in China and the socialist workers, peasants, and intellectuals are masters of the country. Their interests are not exactly the same, but there is no antagonism among them. There are no antagonistic classes in China. Class struggle still exists, but it is no longer the major problem.[51] If, as seems likely, the Hong Kong communists were giving an extreme statement of the Teng view, there is a curious reversal here. Now the Maoists advocate the extinction of class struggle, while their former victims have taken up the Maoist theme that the relation between rulers and ruled can be a class antagonism. According to the Hong Kong communists, the left turned against the concept of class struggle because they feared they would be its next victims.

This setback to the left was followed by a more relaxed attitude toward the concept of democracy, if not to the participants in the democratic movement. One article explained that, despite appearances to the contrary, the current talk of dictatorship did not mean that the regime was tightening up because the third plenum had liberalized too much. Rather, democracy is the same thing as proletarian dictatorship. "Obviously, if we really want to uphold proletarian dictatorship we must truly implement people's democracy" and stop treating all demands by the people as if they were demands for capitalism.[52] Human rights is an anachronistic concept that once served a progressive function, but if the regime does not further human rights, it should protect civil rights (kung-min ch'üan), which were defined by the constitution and the laws.[53] Although the natures of bourgeois and proletarian democracy are entirely different, the latter must still encompass elements of the former. In fact, both China and the world at large have had very little experience of proletarian democracy, and it is, therefore, hard to know just what it is. Both modernization of the economy and popular participation in politics will be required to overcome bureaucratism.[54] Whatever some comrades may think, democracy is not just a matter of style but also of the structure of the state. The law must protect democracy.[55] The hundred flowers campaign is not just a policy for art and science but a basic direction of the state. Without political democracy there can be no hundred flowers campaign.[56] The regime now echoed Wei Ching-sheng: "as everyone now understands," only with political democracy will the four modernizations be possible.[57]

Just what the content of this democracy would be remained unclear. Around August there was a renewal of wall poster activity, the themes focusing upon a denunciation of the repression of a few months earlier and on the need to avoid new cases like that of Chang Chih-hsin. Some of the protestors were in personal contact with Hu Yao-pang.[58] The early fall series of protest was neither as lively nor as extensive as that of spring.

The Hong Kong communists continued to support both the liberalization and the democratic movement, and this should probably be taken to reflect one set of views within the party—those of, say, Hu Yao-pang, Chao Tzu-yang, and Ch'en Yun. But there was obviously opposition within the party as well, not merely from the left—by the fall of 1979 the left had been pretty much cowed—but increasingly from elements of the old moderate tendency, from people the Hong Kong communists were beginning to call the restoration faction. Their base was within the economic ministries, and their main representative was probably Li Hsien-nien (although for a time in 1980 Yeh Chien-ying seemed to act as their symbol). In inner party councils, Li was articulate about the need for "peace and unity." "A socialist state absolutely does not permit anyone to use socialist democracy to undertake plots and sabotage activities to overthrow proletarian dictatorship and the socialist system." That goes for that "despicable and extremely ugly counter revolutionary element" Wei Ching-sheng.[59]

In November the *People's Daily* printed a dialogue on freedom: it is proper to debate political issues, although liberty does not mean "bourgeois liberalization." There should not only be the freedom to speak but also the freedom to remain silent. Counterrevolutionary speech is bad, but the law punishes actions, not words.[60] In practice the line was becoming repressive again. Wei Ching-sheng was given a long prison term, and, later, Fu Yueh-hua a shorter one. Democracy wall was finally closed down.[61] The Central Committee's fifth plenum, meeting in February 1980, decided that the "four big freedoms," big blooming, big contending, big debates, big character posters would be eliminated from the constitution of the People's Republic.[62] These had been Maoist additions to the normal (and normally meaningless) guarantees of free speech and free press. It was explained that while these big freedoms may sound good in the abstract, historical analysis shows they had been tools of leftist tyranny, used to ruin the lives of decent people and to subvert democracy.[63] This, of course, is true for the Maoist period. Historical analysis of the role of wall posters since then, however, might show the regime's own interpretation to be rather abstract.

By 1980 the constellation of political forces in China had changed. At Mao's death power was shared by the establishment radicals, the police left, the State Council bureaucracy, and the military. By 1980 the establishment radicals had been eliminated as had, for all practical purposes, the police left. The dominant political force was an entirely new one, the "practice" or "reform" tendency around Teng Hsiao-p'ing. It had been in this group's interest to push for more and more drastic changes in the system. These changes, however, unleashed social forces that the others in the regime would have preferred to have remained quiet and began to drive the army and the old bureaucrats increasingly into opposition to Teng. The social forces Teng had released were not strong enough for him to rely upon, even if he could have continued to control them, and he therefore began instead to coopt the position of his opposition by taking a hard line against liberalization himself. The reforms were not reversed but were certainly stalled. The hard line, looked at piece by piece, appears as a series of tactical concessions, yet put together there is the possibility that these tactical concessions could kill reform entirely.

## THE CRISIS OF FAITH

The democratic movement was suppressed but not exterminated, and the kind of protest it represents is probably now a permanent part of the Chinese background. Minor demonstrations have continued since the spring of 1979. The police in Nanking attempted prematurely to enforce the Central Committee decision banning wall posters (that is, before the constitution had actually been amended), and student protestors were at least able to force a debate between their spokesmen and those of the police.[64] Protests occurred in Changsha when school authorities attempted to void a student government election won by a candidate who claimed not to be a Marxist.[65] In the spring of 1981, the official criticism of the writer Pai Hua occasioned unrest in Peking.

The regime's two minds about the democratic movement may also be a new constant. Sometimes regime spokesmen treat the attitudes of the movement as a relatively minor problem; at other times they seem genuinely to fear the movement. In early 1980 the regime accused those in the movement of being gangsters and of forming links with "foreign countries and Taiwan." These "ultra-individualists" complain about everything and spread rumors. They fear modernization; they fear there will be no chaos. "To say nothing not contributing to peace and unity, to say nothing not good for the four modernizations, that should be the principle we live by."[66] Almost a year later, Teng Hsiao-p'ing was still calling for an effective ban on underground publications.[67] In early 1980 Hu Yao-pang told in an unpublished speech of the proliferation of secret organizations among the discontented.[68] A year later the concern about underground activity became overt. All those who "raising the banner of 'freedom' and 'democracy', premeditatingly carry out counterrevolutionary agitation, join together in linkages, convene secret meetings, publish illegal periodicals, and plot to cause chaos should be dealt with by the penal organs and punished according to law."[69] Some of the opposition is taking forms not merely illegal by the regime's not always very reasonable laws, but criminal and terroristic by any standards: the planting of bombs in buildings and the attempted hijacking of airplanes.

The rulers' continuing ambivalence is reflected in some confusion in how the regime, particularly the Teng group, classifies the movement. Usually it treats it as a rightist current in society, a deviation balancing the more serious leftism of the whatever or restoration factions within the party.

At other times, however, it is treated as an extreme left line. Teng Hsiao-p'ing, for example, has said, "a small handful of people are just now using the methods of the Great Cultural Revolution to incite and cause trouble, and some people are even calling for something like carrying out a second Great Cultural Revolution."[70] Teng here would be (implicitly, of course) agreeing with the placing of the movement in the tradition of Red dissent. By 1981 the connection with the left may have been becoming functional rather than merely genetic: there were hints that at least some persons in the movement might again be making common cause with the establishment left. A bureaucratic opponent of the Teng Hsiao-p'ing line explicitly compares the democratic movement with Chiang Ch'ing and Chang Ch'un-ch'iao—who now, he alleges, are from their prison cells calling for a two-party system and free elections.[71]

While the regime may fear active subversion, a more chronic worry is its perception of a loss of social morale, the "crisis of faith." It might claim that Marxism is the only thing that has ever done China any good,[72] but the youth of the country in large numbers no longer believe it. The major concern of their elders is not doctrinal unorthodoxy (they seem on the whole to take that in stride) but a mood of apathy and cynicism. One student was quoted: "From primary school through high school not only did I gain no knowledge: more importantly, I gained no ideals and no faith. I feel spiritually empty and life has no interest."[73] Writers in one of the illegal publications Teng is so concerned about place their contemporaries in several categories: conformists who go along with those in power but "never help a comrade" and are distant from the masses; dropouts who lose themselves in private pleasure "and even religious ritual"; the frustrated, who work hard but have no goals and eventually turn into dropouts; outright delinquents; and (a group that no doubt includes the writers) "the enlightened and persecuted," who "have grasped the truth about society and the material world, but society rejects that truth."[74] A public opinion survey, perhaps the first one published in People's China, finds that substantial numbers of young people "lack appreciation for the excellence of the socialist system." They are hedonistic and fatalistic, cynical about politics, "bourgeois" in thought, and deficient in personal moral standards.[75]

The regime tends mostly to blame the crisis of faith on a confusion of the "false Marxism" of Lin Piao and the Gang with real Marxism. This confusion is exacerbated by corruption and incompetence among party cadres, particularly those belonging to factions under attack at the time. The activities of Lin and the Gang are plausible causes of general disenchantment with the official ideology, but Teng's own cat-and-mouse game of liberalization, with its fluctuating policy determined by the needs of the power struggle, may have done less than Teng might have hoped to restore the magic.

Some around Teng took a more constructive attitude toward the crisis. One writer began by blaming the crisis on the "leftist errors" the regime had committed "ever since the founding of the state" (it was more usual to date the bad times to 1957.) Also, however, our understanding of Marxist theory has not kept up with changes in the world. We might remember that the thought of Mao, for example, was supposed not to be a dogma but the adaptation of Marxism-Leninism to existing realities. The realities of the past will not be those of the future: history does not repeat itself (the *I Ching* [Classic of Changes], is cited as authority for this last generalization). Marxism now needs a new development to fit the objective needs of society. Seen in this light, the crisis of faith is nothing other than the liberation of the thought of the Chinese people, their perception of the irrelevance of the old ideology to the new reality.[76]

This attitude accords well with Teng's idea that practice is the standard of truth, but it could also lead to structural reforms more radical than Teng might care for and certainly more radical than others in the leadership group were prepared to accept. A more common reaction was the repression of dissent (however mild that repression might be compared with what had occurred earlier) coupled with exhortations to return to the old ways of thought. The crisis of faith sets off the inconsistencies of Teng's official liberalization program.

The main purpose of the public rehabilitation of Liu Shao-ch'i in 1980 was no doubt to discredit Mao and the Cultural Revolution. Liu also served as a symbol against the democratic movement, however. He was presented as the teacher and exemplar of communist morality and selfless dedication, someone young grumblers and sulkers might pay attention to with profit.[77] In the spring of 1981, the official press began to appeal for the cultivation of a "spiritual-civilization," stressing the need for collective spirit and respect for the common good, and for the return of good, old-fashioned patriotism.[78]

Exhortation is a notoriously ineffective way of changing people's attitudes. The logic of Teng's position and the exigencies of the power struggle served further to weaken the effect of the exhortation. One reformist slogan, for example, is to look to the future: *hsiang ch' ien k'an.* This term, to the happy discovery of those who oppose the reforms and to Teng Hsiao-p'ing's irritation, is pronounced exactly the same as "look to money," allowing the opposition to make a neat point about the deficient communist morality of Teng's economics.[79] More seriously, as part of the power struggle Teng found it expedient to tolerate ridicule of the Maoist bromides, exposing their inhuman side. In the assault on the petroleum gang in 1980, for example, there was much mockery of the old Maoist slogan, originally popularized by Lin Piao, "One, fear no hardship; two, fear no death."[80] Part of the same campaign was celebrating those who exposed the personal corruption of cadres in the economic systems. It looks a little strange, then, that the official press must explain a few months later that money is not everything; that selflessness is nothing to sneer at and one should not unduly fear hardship; and that not all officials are incompetent and corrupt.

Much of what the regime demands in the way of "spiritual civilization" is in itself unexceptionable. There is nothing wrong with courtesy, patriotism, and a willingness to sacrifice for the good of others. The problem is with the manipulation of such demands. One cannot convincingly mock slogans when they are used by one's enemies and then expect them to be taken seriously when one uses them oneself. That is precisely to precipitate a crisis of faith. The regime professes itself hurt that even when it is sincere in its relaxations people think it is merely trying to "tempt the snake out of his hole."[81]

Even to speak of a crisis of *faith* exposes an inconsistency in the Teng program. One had thought that Marxism was *scientific* socialism, obviating any need for faith. It is strange, then, when one of Teng's more hardline supporters says whether there is success or failure there is need for firm faith in communism[82] (so much for practice as the standard of truth).

The crisis of faith is not simply the result of the suppression of the democratic movement. Similar complaints of youthful apathy and cynicism were made at the time of the hundred flowers campaign and both before and after the Cultural Revolution. It is a perennial problem and, for that matter, a worldwide problem. China, after all, is hardly the only country with delinquents, dropouts, or heartless seekers after personal pleasure. The *specific* elements of the current crisis, however, do come from that suppression and to the propensity of the reformers to arouse expectations they will not fulfill.

The problem of Teng and those around him is complicated. Their program breaks with what they had been doing most of their lives, and even they may find some of its implications disturbing. Those they still share power with certainly do, and there the reforms impinge not only on their opinions but also on their interests. Should Teng push a certain line of reform too far, he could find himself alone and vulnerable. It is safer for him to hesitate and equivocate. There is a loss of nerve among the rulers coupled with a crisis of faith among the people. The rulers want the benefits of reform, but they fear the consequences for themselves and perhaps even for the general order.

Were the regime no longer to consider itself a moral arbiter, the crisis of faith would be much less of a crisis. In traditional China the state thought itself to have a pedagogical function, but there it imposed no values of its own but instead reflected those of the dominant interests in society, values accepted at least in the abstract by all "respectable" people even outside the dominant strata. The Maoist totalitarian regime attempted to reshape society's values and, therefore, felt the need to busy itself as much as it could with the whole of everyone's life, defining adherence to itself and its whims as the moral end of man. Part of the depoliticization was the exposure of the nastiness of many of these demands. Depoliticization should also, in principle, relieve the regime of the burden of concerning itself so much with the inner life of the ordinary person.

But as the government gets off of people's backs and out of their souls, it inevitably loses some of its control. People will be able to do things their rulers would rather they not do, and the previously silent and discontented public will voice complaints their rulers would rather not hear. In the terms used in this chapter, it is impossible, beyond a certain point to liberalize in the Expert line without liberalizing in the Red line as well: if the regime is no longer going to shape society, it is going to have to listen to society. In the face of new demands and pressures, the regime may liberalize further, risking at best a threat to its monopoly of power and initiative and at worst a collapse of public order. Or it may seek to reimpose control, in the process reasserting claims it has previously called sham. The regime truly does need a moral foundation, but under its current construction it will have trouble establishing one.

## NOTES

1. See Kjeld Erik Brodsguard, "The Democracy Movement in China, 1976–1979: Opposition Movements, Wall Poster Campaigns, and Underground Journals," *Asian Survey* 21 (July 1981): 747–74; more generally, see Roger Garside, *Coming Alive: China After Mao* (New York: McGraw-Hill, 1981).

2. Dennis J. Doolin, *Communist China: The Politics of Student Opposition* (Stanford: Hoover Institution Press, 1964).

3. Klaus Mehnert, *Peking and the New Left* (Berkeley: University of California Press, 1970).

4. Peter R. Moody, Jr., *Opposition and Dissent in Contemporary China* (Stanford: Hoover Institution Press, 1977), pp. 167–84, 218–21.

5. See the summarized autobiography of Wei in Garside, *Coming Alive*, pp. 263–78.

6. Agence France Presse, May 28, 1979; Foreign Broadcast Information Service, *Daily Report, People's Republic of China*, May 29, 1979, pp. L2–L3 (hereafter cited as *FBIS/PRC*); see also Brodsguard, "Democracy Movement," p. 774.

7. *Jen-min Jih-pao* [People's Daily], April 24, 1981 (hereafter cited as *PD*) speaks of youthful sympathy for the Cultural Revolution.

8. Qi Xin (Chi Hsin) et al., *China's New Democracy* (Hong Kong: Cosmos Books, 1979), pp. 8–9.

9. *New York Times*, February 2, 1977.

10. *Far Eastern Economic Review* 96, (April 8, 1977): 28.

11. See the reports in *FBIS/PRC* for the following dates: January 9, 1978, p. E1; January 11, 1978, pp. E6–E7; January 12, 1978, p. E1; April 5, 1978, pp. E1–E3; April 6, 1978, p. E1;

April 7, 1978, p. E1; April 10, 1978, pp. E1–E3, April 11, 1978, p. E1; April 14, 1978, p. E1. Taiwan reports protest at the time, apparently inspired by the left, directed against Teng. See ibid., January 25, 1978, p. E17.

12. Ibid., July 21, 1978, p. E1.

13. Agence France Presse, November 25, 1978; *FBIS/PRC*, November 21, 1978, p. E2.

14. Agence France Presse, November 25, 1978; *FBIS/PRC*, November 27, 1978, p. E1.

15. Agence France Presse, November 25 and 27, 1978; *FBIS/PRC*, November 27, 1978, p. E1; ibid., November 28, 1978. p. E1.

16. Agence France Presse, November 29, 1978; *FBIS/PRC*, November 30, 1978, p. E1.

17. Agence France Presse, November 29, 1978; *FBIS/PRC*, November 30, 1978, p. E1.

18. Kyodo, December 1, 1978 in *FBIS/PRC*, December 1, 1978, p. E4.

19. Agence France Presse, November 27, 1978; *FBIS/PRC*, November 28, 1978, p. E5.

20. Agence France Presse, December 6, 1978.

21. Agence France Presse, December 9 and 10, 1978; *FBIS/PRC*, December 8, 1978, pp. A1–A2; ibid., December 11, 1978, pp. E1–E2.

22. *PD*, January 3, 1979. The New Year's Day editorial stressed the need to concentrate upon production and not waste time and energy on politics.

23. Agence France Presse, January 14, 1979; *FBIS/PRC*, January 16, 1979, pp. E4–E5.

24. See the various reports from foreign and Chinese papers in *FBIS/PRC* for the following dates: January 15, 1979, pp. E1–E3; January 21, 1979, p. E2; January 22, 1979, pp. E1–E2; January 30, 1979, pp. E9–E10; February 12, 1979, pp. G1–G3; February 13, 1979, pp. N1–N2.

25. Excerpts from the document are translated in Garside, *Coming Alive*, pp. 431–34.

26. *Wen Hui Pao*, February 2, 1979.

27. Agence France Presse, February 1, 1979; *FBIS/PRC*, February 2, 1979, p. E1.

28. New China News Agency, January 6, 1980 in *FBIS/PRC*, January 9, 1980, pp. L10–L14. Human Rights Law Group, "What Is the Fu Yueh-hua Incident About?" *Chung-kuo Jen-ch'üan*, no. 2, reprinted in *Chung-kuo-jen Yueh-k'an*, vol. 1, no. 5, pp. 36–37.

29. Garside, *Coming Alive*, pp. 272–77.

30. Wei Ching-sheng, "More About the Fifth Modernization," *T'an-so* 3 (March 1979). This was reprinted in the Hong Kong journal, *Yellow River*, and the version I am using was reprinted from that in the Taipei *Lien-ho Pao*. Unfortunately, I have only undated clippings.

31. *Chung-yang Jih-pao*, August 10, 1972. This has not been published openly, perhaps precisely because, from the viewpoint of the official ideology, it is unorthodox.

32. Karl R. Popper, *The Open Society and Its Enemies*, 2 vol., 3rd ed. (London: Routledge and Paul, 1957); Ralf Dahrendorf, *Essays in the Theory of Sociology* (Stanford: Stanford University Press, 1968); Roberto Mongibeira Unger, *Knowledge and Politics* (New York: Free Press 1975), p. 76.

33. Hua Hsiang, "Democratic Spirit and Revolutionary Order," *Kuang-ming Jih-pao*, March 18, 1979 (hereafter cited as *KM*).

34. Agence France Presse, March 21, 1979; *FBIS/PRC*, March 21, 1979, p. L1.

35. Garside, *Coming Alive*, p. 280.

36. Yih-tang Lin, comp., *What They Say: A Collection of Current Chinese Underground Publications*, (Taipei: Institute of Current China Studies, n.d.), pp. 138–50.

37. *KM*, May 11, 1979.

38. *PD*, March 21, 1979; *KM*, April 1, 1979; *PD*, May 3, 1979.

39. *PD*, April 5, 1979.

40. Ibid., April 28, 1979; *PD*, April 27, 1979.

41. *KM*, April 19, 1979; *PD*, April 11, 1979.

42. *PD*, April 15, 1979; the review is of Michael Parenti, *Democracy for the Few*, 2nd ed. (New York: St. Martins, 1978).

43. Chi Hsin, "The Class Situation and Principal Contradiction in Mainland China: An Important Theoretical Issue at the Second Session of the Fifth NPC," *Ch'i-shih Nien-tai*, August 1979 in *FBIS/PRC*, August 13, 1979, pp. U1–U6. I shall make the methodological assumption that this article represents the views of persons on the mainland that they were not able openly to express there, rather than being simply the personal opinions of the Hong Kong writers. In its other writings, the Chi Hsin group shows a similar concern about bureaucracy but also keeps very close to the mainland line—remaining, say, no more than three months ahead of it. Thus they published a book on Teng shortly after his rehabilitation in which they continue to maintain that he made errors in his policy prior to the Cultural Revolution, albeit in good faith. Ch'i Hsin, *Teng Hsiao-ping: A Political Biography* (Hong Kong: Cosmos Books, 1978). For an exposition on the bureaucratic class in the official press, disguised as a critique of the past, see Li Shao-chün, "China's Ancient Feudal Despotism," *KM*, August 14, 1979.

44. *PD*, March 9, 1981.

45. Ibid., July 31, 1979.

46. *Cheng Ming* 20 (June 1, 1979) in *FBIS/PRC*, June 8, 1979, p. U1. The "five" should perhaps not be taken literally. I have seen only three of the Hus identified: Hu Yao-pang, Hu Ch'iao-mu, and the editor of the *People's Daily*, Hu Chi-wei.

47. *PD*, May 21, 1979.

48. Ibid., May 25, 1979.

49. Ibid., June 7, 1979.

50. Ibid., May 26, 1979; *KM*, June 12, 1979.

51. *PD*, June 26, 1979.

52. Ibid., June 22, 1979.

53. Ibid., June 19, 1979.

54. Ibid., June 9, 1979.

55. Ibid., July 5, 1979.

56. *KM*, September 15, 1979.

57. Li Shao-chün, "China's Ancient Feudal Despotism."

58. Agence France Presse, August 1, 1979; *FBIS/PRC*, August 2, 1979, pp. L29–L30.

59. *Chung-kung Wen-t'i Tzu-liao* 8 (November 19, 1979): 10.

60. *PD*, November 14, 1979.

61. Agence France Presse, December 2, 1979; *FBIS/PRC*, December 3, 1979, p. L1.

62. *PD*, March 1, 1980.

63. *KM*, April 2, 1980.

64. *Chung-kung Wen-t'i Tzu-liao* 49 (September 9, 1980): 22–29.

65. *Cheng Ming* 38 (December 1980) in *FBIS/PRC*, December 9, 1980, p. U2. Since one of the students involved in the protest was married to a U.S. citizen, the incident received a certain amount of publicity abroad.

66. *PD*, January 29, 1980; ibid., February 1, 1980. Among the general public, the four modernizations seem to be losing their patina and, while I have not made a word count, I think the use of the slogan in official propaganda has declined.

67. *Inside Mainland China*, July 1981, p. 7.

68. *China News Analysis* 1190 (September 16, 1980).

69. Yeh Tzu, "Is There Absolute Freedom of Speech?" *Hung Ch'i* 8 (April 1, 1981): 35. The answer is no.

70. *Inside Mainland China*, July 1981, p. 7.

71. *Cheng Ming* (April 1, 1981) in *FBIS/PRC*, April 10, 1981, p. W1. Wang Jen-chung, "Unify Thought, Earnestly Rectify Party Style," *Hung Ch'i* 5 (March 1, 1982):2.

72. *PD*, January 21, 1980.

73. Ibid., June 22, 1980. In the opinion of the person reporting this quote, "Most of them begin to learn to be bad by smoking."

74. *Inside Mainland China*, May 1981, p. 14; from the journal *Responsibility*.

75. Huang Chih-chin, "How, After All, Should We Understand the Young of the Present Generation?" *PD*, February 24, 1981.

76. Li Hung-lin, "What Does the 'Crisis of Faith' Show?" ibid., November 11, 1980.

77. See Teng Li-ch'un, "The Voice of Truth Cannot Be Smothered," ibid., June 24 and 25, 1980. Li-ch'un constitutes the left wing of Hsiao-p'ing's brains trust.

78. Ibid., February 4, 1981; *KM*, February 18 and 22, 1981; ibid., February 18, 1981; *PD*, March 19, 1981. This last article, a criticism of Pai Hua's "Bitter Love," lists many great figures in Chinese history: philosophers, poets, soldiers, statesmen, and the like. The choice of great communists and especially the order in which they are listed is interesting: Li Ta-chao, Ch'ü Ch'iu-pai, Mao Tse-tung, Chou En-lai, Liu Shao-ch'i, Chu Te, Tung Pi-wu, Ch'en I, Ho Lung, P'eng Te-huai.

79. *KM*, February 11, 1981.

80. Ibid., August 26, 1980.

81. *PD*, July 29, 1980.

82. Teng Li-ch'un, "Voice of Truth," June 25.

# 8

# Reform and
# Restoration

The immediate result of the democratic movement was to weaken Teng Hsiao-p'ing, since it gave the leftists a convincing case against him. Teng's people were able to ride out the criticism, however, and the attacks on them may even have encouraged their political creativity. The left had been decisively defeated by the fall of 1979: they were back to the position they had been in at the start of the year. For the next three years, they continued to suffer the death of a thousand cuts. The big leftists on the Politburo other than Hua Kuo-feng were formally removed from office in the spring of 1980. Hua lost his post as head of government in September of that year. In July 1981 he was demoted from party chairman to the lowest ranking of the vice-chairmen of the Central Committee and was criticized by name in a revised interpretation of party history. In September 1982 he was removed from the Politburo. But really by August 1979 the old left had ceased to be potent in Chinese politics.

This did not mean, however, that Teng could have everything his own way. As the Maoist dictum has it, one divides into two. Coalitions tend to weaken in proportion to the weakening of their enemies. In its fight against the left, the Teng group took positions that might promise or threaten major structural reform of the regime. This brought Teng increasingly into conflict with what is sometimes called the "restoration" faction, composed of old cadres, many of the top ones once close to Chou En-lai, whose base is in the economic ministries. These old cadres, prior to the death of Mao, would have figured as rational modernizers. They are not particularly identified with the left, but neither did they suffer unduly in the Cultural Revolution and have no interest in the systematic discrediting of the past. Their ideal would be a return to the way things were before the Cultural Revolution, or at least before the big radical explosions that began in 1957, without worrying too much about why things had gone wrong since then.

By 1980 the main conflict in China was between Teng's reformers and the restorationists. By early fall the restorationists seemed on the brink of collapse, while Teng's group was beginning to elaborate an exciting, far-reaching program of change. Then Teng seems to have pulled back. While some of the restorationists were removed from their positions or were demoted, their line remained in large part the public line of the regime. The Chinese economy was in bad shape, and while Teng attempted to put the blame on the policies of the restorationists, the regime at the same time appeared to be revising Teng's policies as well. A new leftist opposition seemed to be growing with the military, and there were even hints that elements of the democratic movement might be attempting to make common cause with the remnants of the official left. The reformers themselves may have become frightened of the implications of their own program. It had become clear that the liberalization of Chinese politics would not be a simple and straightforward process.

## THE DEFEAT OF THE WHATEVER FACTION

In 1979 the "police left," as it has been called before, acquired the public cognomen, the "whatever faction." Teng's group was then popularly known as the practice faction, although in 1980 the term "reform faction" became more common. The term "whatever faction" did not appear in the official press until August, but it was used by Hong Kong journalists as early as December 1978; Ch'en Yun may have applied it to the leftists at the third plenum.[1] The specific reference is to an editorial published in February 1977. In January of that year, it will be recalled, the party had made a tentative decision to rehabilitate Teng Hsiao-p'ing, but the rehabilitation did not take place until July. Around February the balance of power seems to have shifted back to those opposed to the rehabilitation. The editorial in question calls for the study of Mao's "Ten Great Relations" and Hua's December 1976 speech on agriculture—an interesting artifact in the abortive cult of Hua, in that it puts one of his pronouncements on the same level as one of Mao's. The editorial concludes: "Whatever decisions Chairman Mao has made, those we must firmly uphold; whatever Chairman Mao has directed, that we must from beginning to end without any exceptions respect."[2] One of Mao's decisions, of course, was that Teng be fired. The wider implication of the term "whatever faction" was that its members gave unthinking adherence to anything associated with Mao.

The democratic movement allowed the whateverists, as they were called, to recover sufficiently from their defeat at the third plenum to attack Teng at a work conference in April. According to a cryptic inside report, the whateverists had a "social base" among the lower ranks of party functionaries, many of whom would have been recruited under the Gang. Teng is alleged to have still had the support of the local military commanders. The gap between Teng and the economic bureaucrats was beginning to develop, but the bureaucrats were probably not yet prepared for an unambiguous victory for the left at Teng's expense. The focus of the leftist attack was on the five Hus who disrupt China, but Teng's main spokesmen at the conference seem to have been Chao Tzu-yang, seconded by Wan Li, rather than Hu Yao-pang.[3]

The publicity given the injustice done to Chang Chih-hsin is the outward sign that the whateverist attack had failed. The counterattack then began. One part of this was the assault on those who thought literature ought to praise virtue. The other model of leftist excess was the "affair of the melons." Agricultural policy allowed peasants to grow fruits and vegetables for sale on the free market to supplement their income from grain, but the Maoists considered too much attention to this sideline production to be capitalist. The party committee of a commune in Hopei had ordered the destruction of a village's melon patch. The official rebuke to the party committee was intended to show that those persisting along leftist lines would come to grief.[4] In early August the *People's Daily* reprinted an item from the local Canton paper asserting the leftist errors were worse than rightist ones and, without mentioning names, attacking the whatever faction (*fan-shih p'ai*).[5] In September *Red Flag* magazine apologized for not having participated in the campaign to affirm that practice is the standard of truth.[6]

At the end of September, Yeh Chien-ying read an imporant speech, a temporary consensus of the views of the Teng group and the restoration faction. It was later revealed that the principal author of the speech was Hu Yao-pang, but Yeh, the man who read it, was the symbolic representative of the restorationists. The speech is a systematic repudiation of radical Maoism and, something rare, perhaps unprecedented for a ruling Leninist party, an admission that the party had made basic mistakes in line. It is also an attempt in each case not to go too far.

For Lin Piao and, sometimes, for the Gang, Mao was a universal genius whose every word was truth. The whateverists, despite their nickname did not really agree with this, but they did have a stake in the continued veneration of Mao. In his speech Yeh is kinder to the thought of Mao than he is to Mao as an individual, and he puts the thought of Mao in its place. According to Yeh, Marxism is universal, while Mao's thought is Chinese. The thought of Mao Tse-tung, which the party takes as its guiding principle in accord with Teng Hsiao-p'ing's four principles, "naturally" is not merely the work of Mao as an individual, but also of Mao's comrades-in-arms (Yeh mentions Chou En-lai and Chu Te; he might, with more truth, have also credited Liu Shao-ch'i and Ch'en Po-ta), and for that matter of the party as a whole. Yeh thus dissociates the ideology itself from any imperfections of the man it was named for.

Like Hua Kuo-feng a few months earlier, Yeh repudiates Mao's emphasis on class struggle and continuous revolution. China is now a socialist society. It contains no hostile classes, although influences from the old society remain, and there is not yet the material base for full communism. But China is no longer as poor and blank as Mao once said it was. There is now a "relatively large number of socialist intellectual rank and file" (tui-wu). Also, Yeh stresses, China now has the A-bomb, the H-bomb, and ballistic missiles. In three short years, the country has recovered from an extended disaster.

In 1956 Mao quite properly, Yeh says, pronounced that the basic work of revolution was complete (although it was in fact Liu Shao-ch'i who said this). Mao also encouraged the blooming of the hundred flowers campaign. Then everything went sour. In 1957 the party overreacted to criticism from the right. In the Great Leap Forward, it fell into "blind commandism," issuing orders without regard to reality. In a somewhat selective review of what actually went on, Yeh says that in 1962 Mao made a self-criticism, renouncing leftist excesses. Chou En-lai, meanwhile, never fell into leftist error; he always recognized the need for a rational program of modernization. (This continued praise for Chou En-lai and the dating of all the troubles to 1957 are marks of the restoration faction, and they remained the official line of the regime as a whole; insofar as we can reconstruct the pristine interpretation of the reform faction, it would seem to want to argue that the party had made mistakes ever since the "founding of the state.")

The Cultural Revolution, which began in 1966, was intended to combat revisionism but was "usurped" by plotters like Lin Piao and the Gang, who wanted to fight a civil war. Because of China's long feudal history, its socialist system is bound to have imperfections. The party must humbly receive the opinions of the masses.

It is necessary, Yeh says, to continue the struggle against the extreme left line of Lin Piao and the Gang. This line manifests itself in subjectivism, in overemphasis on the role of ideology rather than economics, on the role of geniuses (that is, Mao), and on class struggle. In politics the left line held that a bourgeoisie developed inside the party (the denial of this, also still the official party line, is another mark of the restoration faction). The leftists wanted to set up a fascist dictatorship. They opposed the modernization of the economy and allowed no cultural freedom. They wanted to carry out revolution by kicking out the party committee.

At this point the following colloquy takes place:

> *Yeh Chien-ying*: Under these extremely complex and difficult conditions, Comrade Chou En-lai carried out a long-term, bitter, unrelenting struggle against Lin Piao and the "Gang of Four." Comrade Teng Hsiao-p'ing, Comrade Hua Kuo-feng, and other old comrades played a great role from beginning to end in the struggle against the "Gang of Four."
>
> *Hua Kuo-feng*: Comrades, here I must point out that our Comrade Yeh Chien-ying played a great role in the struggle against Lin Piao and the "Gang of Four." He put out especially great effort at the time of the smashing of the "Gang of Four."[7]

There is a catty touch to all this comradeship. Leninist practice requires that comrades be named in order of party rank, but Yeh transposes Hua and Teng. Both Yeh and Hua may be hinting that the other did not really do very much in the fight against Lin Piao. Teng, for that matter, is not credited with having fought Lin either, but he was in jail at the time and there was not much he could have done.

This speech perhaps goes farther in condemning the leftist line than Yeh personally thought prudent. According to a Taiwan source, Yeh had said at the meeting that resulted in this speech: "It's all right to recognize that the party has issued mistaken decisions. It's all right to restore the good name of Liu Shao-ch'i, to affirm him, to rate him very high. But we must not negate Chairman Mao's past history. We should not pursue the matter to its source, or dig our own cornerstone."[8] Teng's Hong Kong coterie criticized Yeh for failing to note that the cult of Mao orginated long before the Cultural Revolution and for not making enough of an issue of cadre privileges.[9] The Teng position in 1980 did not agree things were as rosy as Yeh asserted; rather than saying the Cultural Revolution had been usurped or perverted, the Teng line was that it was wrong from its conception. The Teng group flirted with the old Gang theme that the party or a segment of it was in danger of developing into a new exploiting class, but it never unequivocally asserted this and later rejected it. Yeh explicitly and decisively condemns the entire notion.

As with previous meetings since the fall of the Gang, the personnel changes announced at the fourth plenum were all promotions, with no explicit demotions[10] (see Table 8.1). The "new" members of the Central Committee were mostly old cadre purged during the Cultural Revolution, particularly cadres once allied with P'eng Chen. P'eng himself became a member of the Politburo, and Chao Tzu-yang continued his steady climb.

## TABLE 8.1:    Political Promotions, September 1979

| Name | Former Affiliation |
| --- | --- |
| To Politburo: | |
| Chao Tzu-yang | |
| (from alternate member) | T'ao Chu |
| P'eng Chen | P'eng Chen |
| To Central Committee: | |
| Wang Hsiung-t'ao | ? |
| Liu Lan-p'o | Liu Shao-ch'i, Teng Hsiao-p'ing |
| An Tzu-wen | P'eng Chen |
| Li Ch'ang | Chou En-lai? |
| Yang Shang-k'un | P'eng Chen |
| Chou Yang | P'eng Chen |
| Lu Ting-i | P'eng Chen |
| Hung Hsueh-chih | P'eng Te-huai |

## THE FACTIONAL STRUGGLE IN 1980

A few weeks before Yeh's speech Teng's Hong Kong spokesmen commented:

> It appears that, apart from the "whatever faction" and the "practice faction," there is a "restoration faction." The "whatever faction" regards every word of Mao Zedong as the criterion [of truth]; the "practice faction" regards the results of practice as the standard; and the "restoration faction" takes restoration of the political and economic order of the 1950s as the principle.[11]

The heart of the restoration faction was old party members, moderate relative to the Maoists, who had survived the Cultural Revolution. They tended to work in the big economic bureaucracies. Their time of glory was the early 1950s, when China followed the Soviet model of development, and their patron saint was Chou En-lai. Yeh was the most prestigious of the restorationists, but the more important ones were Li Hsien-nien and Yü Ch'iu-li. At Mao's death the presence of the restorationists in the ruling group dampened Hua's leftism, and they and the military gave Hua a base other than the Gang of Four. By 1979 and 1980, however, these people were inhibiting the purge of the left and were also inhibiting further liberalization. The fight against the restorationists may have caused Teng's people to develop proposals for reform more basic and radical than they otherwise would have; the same fight, however, prevented the full implementation of the reforms.

The restorationist viewpoint seemed particularly strong as China entered the new year and was even articulated by Teng Hsiao-ping. The regime greeted the new decade in a distracted and melancholy mood. There have been three years of progress, the theme ran, but the poison of Lin Piao and the Gang remains. We have too passive an attitude about our defects. Comrades are confused by the ideological diversity of the present time, by the attack on the whateverists, and by the idea of practice as the standard. Some comrades think bureaucratism has grown so much that it can never be eliminated. New China cannot be built in a day. A journey of ten thousand miles . . . (the Chinese in fact do sometimes use this cliché). This talk about beginning a journey of ten thousand miles was going on after the regime had been in power for 30 years. The line was particularly harsh against the democratic movement, then mostly dormant, with Hsi-tan wall off limits. An abstract democracy cannot exist; there can only be democracy in the context of modernization. Freedom is the recognition of necessity, not the following of your heart's desire. Democratic forms (elections, civil liberties) are subordinate to democratic content (that is, the power of the party). Economic progress depends upon peace and unity, not on factionalism and anarchy—the Gang's approach to organization. Some wonder how there can be class struggle if there are no exploiting classes. The answer is that class struggle is an objective fact. We will have no softness toward criminals. Nor will we tolerate praise of capitalism, especially from young punks who do not even know what capitalism is. Some say we play a cat-and-mouse game, that we loosen and then we tighten up. "May we ask: when have we ever said we would tolerate the activities of counterrevolutionary elements, of all kinds of saboteur elements? When have we ever said we would eliminate proletarian dictatorship?"[12]

The various pronouncements above are taken from the official press. These press statements, however, are paraphrases or direct quotations from an unpublished speech by Teng Hsiao-p'ing delivered on January 16. Teng made some additional points that did not then surface publicly. He very cautiously hinted at further reevaluations of Mao. Mao's thought should be restored to its original state. Yeh's speech in September was good as far as it went, but Teng indicates history will need even more rewriting. "If it is written too meticulously," however, "I am afraid it will not be appropriate."[13] In this curious statement, Teng tells the restorationists that he will not be too hard on the late chairman while simultaneously telling the reformers that any treatment of party history that is not hard on Mao is an expedient whitewash.

Toward the end of his speech, Teng hints at a party purge. One of the causes of dissident movement was that "some of our party members are not qualified." Many of the younger members were recruited during the leftist period and are no good, but also many older members who used to do good work are no longer suitable either.[14] In the version of the speech that presumably formally circulated within the party, Teng shows himself interested in recruiting technical experts into the party. A Hong Kong journal claims that in the actual speech Teng called on Yeh Chien-ying to set a good example and be the first to retire.[15] Teng soon hit upon a marginally more subtle way of handling the purge. Throughout 1980 he confided (if that is the word) to foreign reporters his intention to resign as vice-premier, suggesting implicitly and explicitly that the other elder politicians ought to retire as well.

The Eleventh Central Committee held its fifth plenum in February. It was an inconclusive meeting.[16] It formally and completely rehabilitated Liu Shao-ch'i, a move favored by the reformers but not seriously opposed by the restorationists. The rehabilitation was one more way of discrediting Mao. Liu's solemn funeral (he had actually died in 1969) was delayed for more than two months after plenum, and when it was held Yeh Chien-ying sent flowers but did not attend.[17] The plenum also urged, following a suggestion by Teng Hsiao-p'ing in January, that the state constitution be amended to eliminate the freedom to put up wall posters, something that would no doubt make the restorationists happy but would not particularly bother the reformers either.

The reformers do seem to have done well in terms of personnel and organizational changes see (Table 8.2). For the first time since the fall of the Gang, there was a formal, announced purge of the Politburo, with the removal of the whateverists, the "little Gang of Four" of Wang Tung-hsing, Chi Teng-k'uei, Wu Te, and Ch'en Hsi-lien. They were not subject to further public vilification (although Wang's activities during the Cultural Revolution were occasion for uncomplimentary comment during the trial of the Gang at the end of the year), but their removal left Hua isolated. The Secretariat was reestablished, headed by Teng's crony Hu Yao-pang. Hu formally replaced Hua as party chairman in the summer of 1981, but his appointment as general secretary already gave him effective control over the new party apparatus. Hu, along with Teng's other counterheir, Chao Tzu-yang (who was to replace Hua as head of government), was appointed to the Politburo standing committee. The secretariat was dominated by Teng's people, although they did not control it exclusively.

What did *not* happen may also be significant. The Japanese say that originally Ch'en Mu-hua (restorationist) and Keng Piao (?) were to be put on the Secretariat but then were not. Keng Piao was said to be too ready to enjoy a good time, while Ch'en Mu-hua had acquired a reputation for selfish arrogance.[18] P'eng Chen (reformist) was also supposedly to have become a member of the Secretariat but as a major spokesman for the regime's legal reforms was said to have botched the trial of Wei Ching-

## TABLE 8.2:   Personnel Changes, February 1981

| Name | General Function | Political Affiliation |
|---|---|---|
| Purged: | | |
| Wang Tung-hsing | Police, propaganda, military | Left |
| Chi Teng-k'uei | Police? | Left |
| Wu Te | Local party | Left |
| Ch'en Hsi-lien | Military | Left |
| Promoted to Politburo Standing Committee: | | |
| Hu Yao-pang | Party administration | Reform |
| Chao Tzu-yang | Local party | Reform |
| Secretariat:* | | |
| Wan Li | Party administration | Reform |
| Wang Jen-chung | Party administration | ? |
| Fang I | Economic management | Restoration |
| Ku Mu | Economic management | Restoration |
| Sung Jen-ch'iung | Party administration | Reform? |
| Yü Ch'iu-li | Economic management | Restoration |
| Yang Te-chih | Military | ? |
| Hu Ch'iao-mu | Theoretician | Reform |
| Yao I-lin | Economic Management | Reform |
| P'eng Ch'ung | Local party | ? |

*Note that Hu Yao-pang was secretary general.

sheng.[19] P'eng had been second to Teng on the old Secretariat. To bring P'eng back into favor might be a nice slap at the Maoists, but Teng would not necessarily want his old bridge partner to have real power.

Another victory for the reformers was the adoption of a resolution on standards for political life within the party, for some reason not published until two weeks after the close of the plenum.[20] Superficially the standards are ordinary enough, except, perhaps for the one saying that inner party democracy means that "in general" there should be more candidates than vacancies in party elections. The import of the others is that party members should be red and expert (with the effective stress on expert), honest and incorruptible. This last received major press play[21] and is probably a code: a theme of the political struggle became the allegation that the restorationists, because of their feudal mentality, were given to corruption and abuse of their privileges. A *People's Daily* editorial found an easy way to summarize the standards: the successors to the old guard must uphold the line of the third plenum.[22] It would have been even easier to say they must support Teng Hsiao-p'ing.

One reformist theme was that the restorationists were feudal. The second strain in the developing attack was that they had mishandled the economy. The latter theme may have been true: the economic difficulties were real enough, at any rate and by the end of the year the troubles were helping to cool Teng's enthusiasm for reform. Hu Yao-pang began the open criticism of past economic management in March. Hu told a meeting of scientists that the purge of the Gang had led to an "excessively optimistic outlook." We must all lower our sights.[23]

In May the *Kuang-ming Daily* spoke of hidden opposition to the current direction. After 1957 the party's "outstanding personages" (meaning Mao) grew proud and fell victim to the flattery of ambitious schemers. Feudal thought thus entered the party. Cadres became rigid and dogmatic. It is certainly still necessary to oppose the democratic movement, that is, what the paper calls ideological indisicipline, anarchism, and liberalism, but this is really a secondary problem. The main fight is against rigidity and dogmatism.[24] The Hong Kong journal *Cheng Ming* further specified that this hidden opposition, overly rigid in its thought, consists of those "who control real power in economic work and have real strength."[25]

The attack on feudalism included continued sniping at the cult of the individual. In late 1979 Wang Jo-shui, one of the more liberal of the party theoreticians around Teng, attacked Mao directly in a secret speech, asserting that the Cultural Revolution had been caused by Mao and that the Cultural Revolution was an unlimited disaster. Mao cannot be separated from the Gang of Four.[26] In the summer of 1980, Hu Yao-pang told Yugoslav reporters that Mao had many merits but must also be blamed for errors in his later years, particularly the Cultural Revolution.[27] A few weeks later, Teng himself rattled on in the same vein to Oriana Fallacci. Around this time all references to the Cultural Revolution ceased: the name of that series of events became instead the "so-called 'Cultural Revolution.'" The Hu-Teng position on Mao became the official one in the reevaluation of party history in 1981, but it was probably intended at the time as an intermediate stage. According to rumor the Teng group hoped ultimately for the following evaluation: before 1957 Mao achieved merit; from 1957 through 1965 he made mistakes; from 1966 until his death he committed crimes.

Overall, however, criticism of Mao was no longer big news by the summer of 1980. Yet the official press remained puzzlingly mealymouthed on the issue, as were official policy directives. Marxism stresses the role of the great man, but "some in our ranks" go too far. There should be less propaganda about individuals. We should build no more memorial halls, and some now built should be shut down. We should not exaggerate the achievements of old revolutionaries, we should not overuse the statues and quotes of Mao, and we should no longer make fusses about rehabilitations.[28] One reason for this vagueness is probably that Mao was not the only old revolutionary under criticism. The Teng people may have been hoping to extend the critique to other sacred cows, particularly to Chou

En-lai; the argument would have been that Chou was too subservient to the Maoists.[29]

The criticism of past economic performance focused upon the petroleum sector, perhaps because overestimates of China's oil resources were partly responsible for the earlier grandiose projects to build up industry and import foreign technology. Around July the Hong Kong journals began to discuss a petroleum faction or, if liberty of translation be allowed, a petroleum gang. The journals admitted, however, that this was merely a code word for cadres in economic planning and management work generally.[30] The earlier unofficial adverse comment was directed against the Ta-ch'ing oil field, the industrial equivalent to Ta-chai. The issue became public, however, with the exposure of the Po-hai incident right before the opening of the National People's Congress. Po-hai No. 2, an oil rig in the Po-hai gulf, had sunk the previous November with great loss of life. The Petroleum Ministry allegedly failed to investigate the accident until July 1980. This treatment of the disaster was said to show the ministry's bureaucratic rigidity and its lack of concern for human life. The petroleum minister was dismissed, and K'ang Shih-en, head of the State Economic Commission, received a public reprimand. The incident became the occasion for gibes at Maoist slogans about fearing neither hardship nor death.[31] Purges in China begin with the small fry and work their way up. The intermediate target here would be Yü Ch'iu-li, head of state planning and a former petroleum minister himself. The ultimate target would have been Li Hsien-nien.

All during this period, the undercutting of Hua Kuo-feng continued. The open criticism of K'ang Sheng, which began in July, probably had Hua as its real target.[32] In early August several articles critical of eunuchs in traditional China appeared. Eunuchs used to usurp the power of the emperor. They flattered and intrigued and sometimes even took military power. They caused the intensification of class struggle.[33] According to interpretations from Hong Kong and Taiwan, these were slaps at Hua. Hua's connection with eunuchs would be that he had once controlled the police (in traditional China eunuchs performed the functions assumed in modern autocracies by the political police) and had been a pet of Mao. At the National People's Congress, Hua himself pronounced his replacement as premier by Chao Tzu-yang as "appropriate, reliable."[34] The leftist Ch'en Yung-kuei was dismissed as vice-premier, and Teng and the other older vice-premiers retired (see Table 8.3). The left was now eliminated from the major organ of the state as well as from the party, although restoration influence remained strong. The major restorationist, Li Hsien-nien, retired along with his antagonists, Teng Hsiao-p'ing and Ch'en Yun. Li, however, was no longer putting his own people into the other positions. The symbolic head of the restorationists, Yeh Chien-ying, met no public

## TABLE 8.3:    Vice-Premiers of the State Council, August 1980

| Name | General Function | Affiliation |
| --- | --- | --- |
| Promoted: | | |
| Chao Tzu-yang (to premier) | General leadership | Reform |
| Yang Ching-jen | Minority work | ? |
| Chang Ai-p'ing | Military | ? |
| Huang Hua | Foreign affairs | ? |
| No Change: | | |
| Hü Ch'iu-li | Economic management | Restoration |
| Keng Piao | Military, foreign affairs | ? |
| Fang I | Economic management | Restoration |
| Wang Chen | Agriculture | Restoration |
| Ku Mu | Economic management | Restoration |
| K'ang Shih-en | Economic management | Restoration |
| Po I-po | Economic management | Reform |
| Yao I-lin | Party administration | Reform |
| Ch'en Mu-hua | Economic management | Restoration |
| Demoted: | | |
| Hua Kuo-feng | General leadership | Left |
| Retired: | | |
| Teng Hsiao-p'ing | General leadership | Reform |
| Li Hsien-nien | Economic management | Restoration |
| Hsu Hsiang-ch'ien | Military | ? |
| Ch'en Yun | Economic management | Reform |
| Purged: | | |
| Ch'en Yung-kuei | Model Peasant | Left |
| Ch'en Hsi-lien | Military | Left |
| Chi Teng-k'uei | Police? | Left |

setback at all (according to an unkind Hong Kong rumor, he was holding on to his positions with senile tenacity), but his influence was largely diminished. The general result of the reorganization was inconclusive, however, and Teng had an incentive to push for further reform.

## THE KENG-SHEN REFORMS

The 1980 session of the National People's Congress was the most open and most democratic-spirited one ever held in People's China. The watchwords of the time were reform and democracy and in the air were proposals for reforms that would, if carried out, have greatly enlarged the scope of democracy in China. The proposals came to be known collectively as the *keng-shen* reforms (most of 1980 being the year *keng-shen* in the traditional 60-year calendar cycle). The term "*keng-shen* reforms" was apparently first used by a party theoretician Liao Kai-lung at an "academic seminar" held jointly by several party schools in October. The term did not come into public use in 1981, indicating, no doubt, the tentative and controversial nature of the entire program. Liao in his turn attributed the inspiration for the reforms to a speech by Teng Hsiao-p'ing delivered to the Politburo in August, just before the opening of the National People's Congress.[35] Democracy was more a slogan of the Red tradition of dissent than the Expert, but in the year *keng-shen* segments of the party were groping toward a democracy consistent with the Expert bias toward depoliticization. The program emphasized not so much mass action and participation as limited government and an institutionalized system of checks and balances.

Teng's August speech, like many he gives, was not published on the mainland, although the press in the fall of 1980 was full of allusions to it and unattributed quotations from it.[36] The speech was rather less radical than the reform program as a whole, but it can probably be taken as a skeleton of the program. Teng identifies four basic problems: power is overconcentrated; the top leadership hold too many concurrent posts; there is no clear separation of the functions of party and state; and younger and more professional cadres must be promoted more rapidly.[37] Teng goes into a discussion of the problem by promoting younger party members, one ulterior purpose probably being to get rid of the restorationists without bringing in Gang elements. Teng does not approve of the "rocket or helicopter" method of promotion (whereby persons with ability or connections may skip grades on their way to the top). Promotion should go one step at a time, although the talented should be able to use what Teng calls a "light ladder." By talent Teng means especially technical skills: he wants, in effect, a party of technocrats. He also, however, endorses popular election of the basic level leadership.[38]

Teng then turns to bureaucratism, which he holds to be a defect in the state and party system, and here at least he is more outspokenly bold than many other reformers in identifying the root of the trouble. Bureaucratism today, he explains (tacitly at odds with the ploy of tracing the problem to residues of feudalism), is not quite the same as in old China but is "closely related to the fact that we have long held that the socialist system and the planning management system must exercise a system of highly centralized control over economics, politics, culture, and society. . . . This could be said to be the general root of the disease of our particular bureaucratism."[39] The different sectors of society should have more autonomy. Bureaucratism also results from concentration of power in one person, and this *is* a residue of feudal patriarchalism. One-person rule allowed the Lin

Piao and Chiang Ch'ing counterrevolutionary cliques to take shape.[40] Mao was a great man, but he made mistakes, and these mistakes should be discussed. "We communists are thorough-going materialists and can only affirm what should be affirmed and negate what should be negated in a truth-seeking way."[41]

Teng says all these problems are "tinged with feudalism to a greater or lesser extent,"[42] but he does not disapprove of feudalism as much as some of his supporters do. Teng has a sensible fear that the use of feudalism as a stick to beat political enemies could lead to a wholesale denunciation of the Chinese past, and he does not want that.[43] Teng is also much more worried than most of his supporters at the time about "bourgeois and petty bourgeois ideology, extreme individualism, and anarchism." This hostility by Teng to the democratic movement has been consistent since at least the spring of 1979. He hates those who think capitalism is better than socialism, and he worries (with reason, it appears) that the reform program itself might encourage money grubbing and pornography. The way to counter this, he says, is to propagate a "lofty morality to the whole people and to all youths and juveniles."[44] The specific reforms Teng has in mind would weaken his enemies: to retire old cadres and to eliminate concurrent positions would be a civil way of getting rid of restorationists without a divisive party purge. But Teng's proposals would also have the potential for a more far-reaching liberalization, even though Teng continued to dislike the word and had misgivings about the reforms even while proposing them.

Lower down in the party, the enthusiasm was less ambiguous. Teng was afraid that the emphasis on feudalism would lead to a denigration of the cultural heritage. The reformers were not really interested in denouncing the past, however, and were certainly less openly hostile to what was beautiful and humane in Chinese culture than were the radical Maoists. In their more casual writings, the Maoists tended to couple "bourgeois" with "feudal" to characterize everything they did not like. The reformers of 1980 focused upon the alleged evils of feudalism in order tacitly to rehabilitate much that the Gang (and probably Teng as well) would consider bourgeois. Their goals resembled the "formal" democracy and "bourgeois" liberties the democratic movement had been denounced for wanting.

One writer pointed out (in an article urging the "old cadres" to make way for the new) that while bourgeois equality is a sham, at least the bourgeoisie never tolerated the autocracy inherent in lifetime tenure for the state's highest ruler. How much less should the proletariat![45] China has in fact advanced enough that a capitalist restoration is impossible. This threat was a figment of the "feudal fascist" imagination of Lin Piao and the Gang.[46] A plausible interpretation of this is that if a capitalist restoration is impossible, bourgeois ideology is nothing to fear. But a feudal restoration apparently does remain possible. At any rate, the Gang's thought is said to be nothing but feudalism masquerading as revolution.[47]

In August Teng broached a theme he stresses more strongly in his winter moods, the need for continued ideological training. One of his followers gently demurred. Some say the liberation of thought has gone too far, and we should make people study Marxism more than we do. But the danger then is dogmatism, and true Marxism is never dogmatic. Opposition to revisionism does not mean opposition to all revision. Without revision Marxism becomes dogmatic. The liberation of thought is a demand of Marxism itself.[48]

Teng worried about the moral effects of the reform. According to one writer, he could have spared himself the anxiety. No moral system, this writer asserts, can transcend historical development. China is not yet communist; it is only socialist. Therefore, we can only have socialist morality (for those unsympathetic to it, money grubbing and the pursuit of personal advantage), not communist morality. Those who think otherwise show themselves to be extreme leftists.[49] This argument was perhaps not calculated to reassure the more old-fashioned comrades that the reforms were a good thing. Here and in some other places, one suspects, the reformers might have done marginally less harm to themselves by showing more tact on inessentials. A major theme of the 1981 crackdown was an insistence on the inculcation of communist morality.

Most of the public statements in the fall of 1980 reiterated Teng's themes: the evils of lifetime tenure and one person rule and the desirability of rule of law. The most interesting aspect both of Teng's delineation of his program and of the public statements on reform was the defense of pluralism. A typical Leninist slogan calls for "monolithic leadership" by the party. One writer asserts, however, that this discourages variety and innovation. Civilizations show great diversity, and socialism cannot be expected to fall into any single pattern. There should be no monolith but, rather, diversity or pluralism.[50] A writer who sticks more closely to Teng's thought explains that the trouble with monolithic (*i yuan-hua*) leadership is that it easily becomes personalized (*i-jen-hua*) leadership. In 1956 "we" criticized Stalin, and Comrade Teng Hsiao-p'ing denounced the cult of the individual. Alas, after 1958 the cult of Mao grew and grew, resulting finally in the Cultural Revolution.[51] While monolithic leadership might be alright in principle, in practice it means overconcentration of power at the center and an attempt by the party to gain total control over everything. The party does not need monolithic leadership. It needs, rather, to endeavor to deserve the support of the people.[52]

The reformers proposed specific institutional changes to bring about the desired diversity. In particular the parliament, the National People's

Congress, should become an "organ with real authority," not just a rubber stamp for whatever faction happens to control the party. Delegates to the congress should really be elected rather than appointed.[53] The reformers were particularly taken with the United States' system of separation of powers, a system that effectively maintains bourgeois rule and prevents individual dictatorship. Franklin Roosevelt held his job for life, but the Twenty-second Amendment took care of that problem. Socialist democracy is better than bourgeois democracy, but China has a few things to learn. The separation of powers is worth investigating: it might be helpful in the fight against feudalism.[54]

In his "academic seminar" Liao Kai-lung proposed there be a bicameral National People's Congress, one house chosen on the basis of territory and the other by a system of functional representation. "Just as bourgeois parliaments safeguard the interests of the bourgeois, we must ensure the interests of the proletariat and of the people." The party should not have direct control over the legal system and should remove itself from the routine work of government, keeping only to the exercise of political leadership. Workers should elect union leadership, and unions should start to represent the interests of workers. Otherwise China will become just like Poland. Peasants also should establish their own independent organization. There should be less secrecy in government, and newspapers should report the news independently, although journalists and commentators "must be responsible to the party and to the people." The party should stop directly managing factories and firms, and there should be direct democracy at the local level. There should be checks and balances within the party organization itself. Liao says the next party congress will elect not one overall Central Committee but "three parallel central committees which will mutually supervise and impose constraints on one another. . . . Each of them will have clearly defined tasks and a jurisdiction of its own." "Some comrades" propose the abolition of the Politburo, substituting for it another three separate committees. An executive committee would be in charge of routine work under the eyes of the supervisory committee, this being a kind of genro-en composed of the "sturdier old comrades." This later became the Advisors' Committee, and the sturdier comrades were eager to stay off it. There would also be a discipline committee to handle violations of party rules.[55] Over all this seems to be a combination of U.S., Yugoslav, Soviet, Kuomintany, Ch'ing, and Meiji practice. By late 1982 a few of these reforms were put into effect, but it remains to be seen whether they will actually mean anything. Their original form held the potential for a radical break with Leninist norms.

There is a criticism of Leninism implicit in Teng's August speech: China's problem has been the tendency to define socialism in terms of centralization and bureaucratic control. There were also public hints of a criticism of Leninism:

> Why can a social organization, whether scientific, productive, or cultural, manifest its social existence only by subordination to a certain administrative department? Can it be that a society can be called socialist only if this kind of structure organizes itself? I am afraid Marx or Lenin never discussed this kind of socialism. It is a post-Lenin mutation.[56]

The rejection of Leninism here remains implicit, of course. An idealized, abstract Leninism is salvaged. But the passage does seem to imply that every existing Leninist polity has the defects identified.

The climax of the year *keng-shen* was the trial of the Gang of Four and of the survivors of the Lin Piao gang. This has ambiguous significance as far as liberalization is concerned. As noted earlier the analogy with the Moscow trials should not be pushed too far. Someone has remarked that the function of defense lawyers in communist states is plea bargaining, and this was certainly true of the Gang's trial. But the trial was not quite an orgy of self-incrimination. Most of the defendants admitted their guilt and then tried to make excuses. But Chang Ch'un-ch'iao maintained a dignified silence, while Chiang Ch'ing put up an articulate, shrill, and on its own terms persuasive defense. In one sense the trial could even be considered a logical extension of the reforms. If China really wants rule by law, people should be punished for committing crimes, not for losing power struggles, and whether or not they have committed crimes is something a court should decide.

The trial itself, however, is hardly evidence of the independence of the courts from politics; nor is it a shining example of a genuine rule of law. Justice may have been done, but it was certainly not seen to have been done. Issues of pretrial publicity and the like aside, there was an absence of the most elementary safeguards. Both the chief judge and the chief prosecutor had been victims of Lin Piao and the Gang, and prominent among the crimes of both cliques were the injuries they had done to the current big wig, Teng Hsiao-p'ing. It is inconceivable that any of the defendants could have been found not guilty. Chinese spokesmen are in fact quite defensive about the lynch-law atmosphere of the trial ("Legal systems vary in different countries," they explain), and one of them suggests an appropriate model for the trial might be those of the war criminals at Nuremberg and Tokyo.[57] In other words, it was a political show.

That there was (finally) a trial at all may be an improvement over the Maoist period—in the sense that Wei Ching-sheng's trial is an improvement over past practice. But one of the political functions of the trial was that it was an alternative to the reform program for Teng to discredit his enemies. Both the leftists and the restorationists were tied to the Maoist past. The *keng-shen* reformers repudiated that past and undercut the institutional strength of both groups. The trial, however, could serve to discredit Maoism without the bother of any structural reforms. Chiang Ch'ing, especially, could be counted upon to do just as she did. She said for the world to hear: "Arresting me and bringing me to trial is a defamation of Chairman Mao Zedong." "Defaming Chairman Mao through defaming me . . ." "I have implemented and defended Chairman Mao's proletarian line."[58] By the end of the year, Teng probably knew he did not have the political strength to have put through a formal declaration that Mao had committed crimes. As an alternative, however, the restorationists had to agree to the trial, a trial they would prefer to avoid as long as Chiang Ch'ing remained unintimidated. After Chiang Ch'ing had her say, the prosecutor could stand up and primly sniff: "This is a vicious slander and a vilification of Chairman Mao Zedong."[59] But the thoughts that had passed through everyone's head for four years had finally been vocalized, and the world was left to ponder who really knew the chairman's mind better: his wife or those who were persecuting her.

The trial coincided with a period not of reform but of retrenchment. The business with the petroleum gang came to an anticlimactic, if perhaps temporary, conclusion. In late December Teng called for a slowing of structural reform of the economy, blaming China's economic troubles on the improvidence of the Hua regime. Li Hsien-nien made a self-criticism, accepting blame for the policies Teng criticized.[60] At about the same time, a couple of restorationists lost some of their positions, not in an explicit purge but as part of the campaign to end the holding of concurrent jobs. K'ang Shih-en was replaced as head of the State Planning Commission by Lin Hu-chia, until then the boss of Peking (and under criticism for how he was doing), whose political affiliations are unclear but who is probably a restorationist more than a reformer. Ku Mu was replaced as head of the State Planning Commission by Han Kuang, probably a reformer.[61] The petroleum minister had been fired in August because of the Po-hai scandal. He was finally replaced in the spring of 1981—by K'ang Shih-en, who had been reprimanded for his own role in that scandal. According to the story, no one else was willing to take the job.[62] Perhaps as a sop to the restorationists, the party published an edition of the selected works of Chou En-lai.[63] Any plans there might have been to discredit Chou had been set aside for the time.

## TWO STEPS BACK

The political pattern since the trial of the Gang has been small but continual gains by the reformers, as they consolidate their control, but until 1983 there were few gains for reform. If the trial of the Gang is the informal repudiation of Maoism, its formal, if diluted repudiation came at the sixth plenum of the Eleventh Central Committee, held in June 1981. This meeting published an evaluation of Mao's historical role. The thoughts of Mao will always be the party's guiding light, but there will never again be a cult of the individual. The late chairman committed many grave errors, especially after 1957, but was guilty of no crimes. Just as Mao's earlier achievements were not his alone but were also the work of the party, so too should Mao not have to bear the entire blame for the errors. More important, really, than this by now familiar criticism of Mao was the open criticism of Hua Kuo-feng. Hua deserves credit for his role in the fight against the Gang of Four, but after the purge he persisted in the erroneous leftist line, with things not being made right until the third plenum (that is, until after Teng Hsiao-p'ing achieved supremacy).[64] Hua was removed as chairman of the Central Committee, becoming the lowest-ranking member of the Standing Committee. He was replaced by Teng's ally, Hu Yao-pang.

This renewed repudiation of Maoism and leftist errors, however, was followed by a new crackdown on literary dissent and a campaign (or activities—*huo-tung*: the third plenum had decreed there would be no more campaigns, *yun-tung*) against "bourgeois liberalization." In 1982 the reformers returned to the offensive and even began once again to talk of reform. Watered-down versions of some of the *keng-shen* reforms were enacted, although it was far from clear whether they would work in the way those who had first proposed them intended. The prestige of the party continued to decline, especially among the educated young. To counter this the party continued to call for the cultivation of a "socialist spiritual civilization," which most of the time seemed to mean nothing more than the same old dreary communist indoctrination. There is little to indicate that it was very effective against the crises of confidence and faith.

### Economic Reforms

The retrenchment first showed itself in economic policy. The 1980 pronouncements on the economy mentioned both reform and readjustment. In 1981 the line was that readjustment would take priority over reform. Economic difficulties included inflation resulting from the removal of artificial price controls. There were also major shortfalls in petroleum production. Strapped for money, China temporarily reneged on agreements with foreign firms and began once again to emphasize centralized planning and control, although firms that had been operating autonomously under the Chao Tzu-yang system continued to do so. In context not all of the readjustment was necessarily illiberal. The economist Hsueh Mu-ch'iao pointed out that state ownership had become in effect ownership by the various bureaucratic systems, each of which attempted to operate autonomously from the others. More rational centralized planning would break up these independent kingdoms and allow the market to work more efficiently.[65] Other readjustment policies, however, went against the market. One complaint was that after firms had been told to make profits, some factories began to produce what the public wanted, such as bicycles, rather than what the state wanted, such as military equipment or farm machinery. Perhaps because it lacked the money, rather than make it worthwhile for the firms to produce what the state wanted, the state found it simpler to issue commands.

The retrenchment spread beyond the economic sphere. There may be here one more illustration of the loose but organic connection that seems to exist, for good or ill, between economic and other forms of liberty. There may have been "organic" contradictions in the reform program in any case—a willingness to talk about democracy without the nerve to do anything about it. The restorationist opposition had not been completely beaten, and in 1981 a new source of leftist opposition to the reforms was growing in the army. Both the opposition to the reforms and the reformers' own failure of nerve were perhaps fed by growing evidence of social disorganization.

## The Army

Perhaps the earliest evidence of military discontent with the reforms can be traced to late 1978, when Hsu Shih-yu, according to some a former protector of Teng, began to show signs of unease. As commander of the Canton military region in 1979, Hsu no doubt had the prime responsibility for the punishment of Vietnam; China's less than impressive performance may not have helped Hsu's reputation for competence. There are vague indications of trouble even before that. We saw Hsu boast in 1978 of his intimacy with Mao and perhaps threaten Teng with a coup. In 1980 Hsu, like Yeh Chien-ying, failed to attend Liu Shao-ch'i's funeral. The strengthening of the regular central apparatus under Teng may have cut more deeply than Hsu (and, by extension, the other old regional commanders) would have liked into the autonomy he had come to enjoy. Rumors say Hsu was piqued when Teng failed to make him minister of defense.

The issue is not, however, limited to Hsu or confined to personalities. The PLA is concerned with China's stingy military budget and the low priority given by the regime to modernization of the military, especially its conventional capacity. The trial of the Chiang Ch'ing-Lin Piao cliques was supposed to have been followed by a trial of 60 of the lesser criminals, most of these being soldiers, and the army was afraid that this would be yet another blow to its prestige and influence. The economic reforms in the countryside make the army less attractive to peasant boys. Teng seemed to be ruthlessly attempting to concentrate military power into the hands of his own followers, both a consequence of existing military discontent and a cause for further discontent.

The army's unhappiness found expression in criticism of the Teng regime from the left. The earliest spokesman of military discontent was Huang K'o-chieng, P'eng Te-huai's old chief of staff and now a member of the Discipline Inspection Committee. The *People's Daily* printed a speech by Huang three months after it had been delivered. Huang bewailed the party's loss of prestige, attributing it in part to bad influences from the outside (especially in Kwangtung and Fukien, the two provinces most open to Western influence) and to bourgeois thought, which causes people to lead rotten lives. Some cadres also are guilty of irresponsible bureaucratism. Newspapers should publicize improper conduct by cadres. But the papers should deal not only with the question of *shih fei*, true or false, but also of *li hai*, will the publicity do good or do harm, that is, is it really expedient to publicize a given scandal.[66] (The reformers, no doubt, had not found it expedient to publicize Huang's speech when he had delivered it.)

Huang also published his evaluation of Mao. In outline it is much the same as that officially adopted by the party in July, although Huang perhaps emphasizes a little more of Mao's positive side while glossing over certain aspects of what the party was later to declare to be Mao's faults. Huang refers several times to the high opinion that "Comrade Hsiao-p'ing" has of "Chairman Mao," as Huang calls the dead leader throughout, rather than the now more common Comrade Mao Tse-tung. Mao gained immortal merit in the encirclement campaigns. He led the party to victory in the revolution. As Comrade Hsiao-p'ing says, without Chairman Mao the Chinese people might still be groping in the dark for a long time to come. In Huang's "personal opinion," Mao made two major mistakes in his later years: he was too impatient, and he was careless in seeking the sources of error. But all the bad things that happened, should not be blamed on Mao alone. For example, Huang says, Comrade Hsiao-p'ing says that all old cadres are responsible for some mistakes. Huang says that he himself is responsible for some, although not for the Cultural Revolution, since he had been purged at the time. But anyone who was able to speak out and did not do so bears some of the blame (a slap, probably, at Hua Kuo-feng and the restorationists and perhaps at some of Huang.'s colleagues in the army as well). "Some comrades say many extreme things about Chairman Mao." Some say he was not good at all. These people will "lead the country toward capitalism" (a reversion here to Gang talk). They have been led astray by "western individualist and liberal thought." Actually, only Marxism-Leninism, the thought of Mao, can save China: for what else is there? The three People's Principles of Sun Yat-sen and the Kuomintang were all right in their day, but they cannot save China now. Confucius certainly cannot either. The capitalism that some people worship so much is thoroughly corrupt. Well then, what about Marxism all by itself? But it is the thought of Mao that gives Marxism a Chinese content.[67] (The alternatives Huang lists have all been discussed in China.)

Huang is a man of courage and honor, not a rabid leftist. His use as a spokesman is probably intended to show that discontent is common throughout the army. The root cause may be that the reformers' policies threaten the army's institutional interests, but there is probably a principled side to the military leftism as well. It is a curious kind of leftism—a conservative leftism, if there can be such a thing. Huang defends the leftist line not because it is humane, effective, or liberating, but because it has been the regime's historical line. Mao in turn is defended as a symbol both of the left and of the regime. Huang's defense of Mao's thought comes down in the end to the assertion that it might not be much, but it is all that we have. This might persuade the old timers and intimidate the reformers; the argument may carry somewhat less conviction with society at large.

Teng Hsiao-p'ing has responded to military discontent by asserting his personal control over the PLA. At the sixth plenum, he took charge of the party's Military Affairs Commission, the regime's most important institution for dealing with security matters. At the giant fall maneuvers of 1981, Teng had himself photographed with Hu Yao-pang. Hu wore a Western coat and tie rather than the usual Mao suit, while Teng appeared in military uniform: *wu wang* and *wen want*, the military and civil kings, side by side. Military affairs is one area where Teng is not content to exercise his power *behind* the scenes.

Teng has also had trouble finding someone to help him control the army. The former minister of defense, Hsu Hsiang-ch'ien, was one of the old cadres who retired in August 1980. Many months later he was replaced by Keng Piao, perhaps the most civilianized of China's soldiers; he had previously spent most of his time in foreign affairs and international party liaison work. This appointment did not work out very well.

In late summer 1982, right before the convening of the twelfth party congress, the army paper, *Liberation Army Daily*, published an article subtly taking issue with Teng's program—so subtly that apparently even

Teng did not figure out what was going on for several weeks. Throughout the summer of 1982, the *Kuang-ming Daily*, the Peking newspaper that appeals mainly to intellectuals, had complained of recurrences of Maoist anti-intellectualism.[68] From further developments it would appear that the army was the source of this anti-intellectualism. The army distrusts intellectuals as the source of bourgeois liberalism and may also resent the civilian technocracy the Teng group is trying to recruit for positions of responsibility.

Around this time Teng had made two statements discussing socialist spiritual civilization. The first time he said spiritual civilization demands ideals, morality, and discipline. In the second statement he amended the list, adding "culture"—in effect, education. On August 8 the *Liberation Army Daily* cited Teng on spiritual civilization, citing only his first formulation. This was later construed to mean the army disapproved of Teng's policy favoring intellectuals and also considered Teng to be soft on bourgeois liberalization. The soldiers were told that culture is just as important as ideology and that to deny this shows lack of understanding of dialectical materialism.[69] The repudiation of the earlier military article was followed by a purge of the military regions and the army's General Political Department.[70] This military mutiny against the reform group took a long time to detect or at least to get itself taken seriously by those whose serious attention matters. Wei Kuo-ch'ing, the former head of the General Political Department, had been reelected to the Politburo during the period between his defiance in August and his purge in October.

The army's resistance to Teng may have brought misfortune to some of the resisters, but it may have improved the general political position of the army taken as a whole, causing Teng to appease some of its discontent. In November Keng Piao was replaced as minister of defense by Chang Ai-p'ing, a regular soldier.[71] Chang had been rather ignominiously dismissed as vice-premier of the State Council a few months earlier. He is known to be deeply interested in the technological modernization of the armed forces, and his appointment may mean that as compensation for suffering the purge the military will get a better deal on the budget. Even more surprising is the replacement of Wei Kuo-ch'ing by Yu Ch'iu-li of the restoration faction. Yu will certainly not oppose military modernization. Perhaps Teng figures Yu will do less harm indoctrinating soldiers than he will helping to manage the economy. In any case, the suppression of anti-Teng dissent in the military would appear to have come at a price of diluting Teng's control over that institution.

## Literature

The army led the attack on Pai Hua, the author of *Bitter Love*. The general attitude of the regime toward that writer was less harsh than that of the army,[72] but by the fall even Hu Yao-pang was finding it expedient to denounce subversive literature and even threaten obstreperous writers with charges of counterrevolution.[73] Hu Ch'iao-mu, the head of Teng Hsiao-p'ing's brain trust in the Chinese Academy of Social Sciences, made a self-criticism for his early failure to appreciate the perniciousness of *Bitter Love*.[74] While the military opposition may have reinforced the regime's determination to crack down, there may have been a determination to take a hard line even independently of the military. Probably in response to Teng's concern about illegal organizations and illegal publications, persons associated with the democratic movement who had escaped previous dragnets were rounded up in 1981. The regime once again arrested Wang Hsi-che, a member of the old Li I-che group and in the 1980 context probably not a dissident at all but only a strong supporter of the *keng-shen* reforms.[75] Pressures from the mainland led to the closing of a couple of the informative and critical communist publications in Hong Kong.

The regime meanwhile continued vociferously to proclaim that the policy had not changed a bit. There was at least no return to Maoist totalitarianism. The leftism of the regime as a whole, like that of the army, was conservative. The purpose was not, as under Mao, to promote continuous revolution, but to stifle audible criticism of the regime's pet attitudes. Even the criticism of the literary figures was civil when compared with Maoist norms. There was some attempt to focus the criticism on the works, not on the people, and there were no criticism campaigns. Pai Hua himself was trotted out to explain that he had not been penalized or abused or humiliated,[76] although this in itself is hardly evidence that he had not been mistreated. The regime's censors point out that works critical of Chinese socialism are not by that fact immune from being criticized themselves, and this is certainly true. The most offensive thing about the official criticisms is, precisely, that they are official, backed by political power.

The change in policy, the new pressure to "praise virtue," certainly must have a stifling effect. Some, like Wang Meng, try to put the best face on things. Wang says he is not upset by "criticism" (although the word he should really use is censorship) since it shows that someone is paying attention to what he says.[77] The more cynical assert that literary production has been reduced to "singing folk songs to entertain the party" (*ch'ang shan-ko kei tang t'ing*)—the title of an anthology of popular poetry that nicely, if unintentionally, captures the essence of the Leninist notion of the function of literature. Even so, without denying the extent of the repression, it seems fair to say that the Chinese literary scene in the early 1980s remained freer, more varied, and more lively than it had been, with the exception of very brief intervals, since the establishment of the People's Republic.

## Bourgeois Liberalization

The crackdown on literature represents the conjunction of military interests and those of at least the left wing of the restoration faction. The reformers tried to resist the crackdown but failed. Immediately after the sixth plenum, whose theme had been a repudiation of extreme leftism, Teng Hsiao-p'ing turned around and denounced "bourgeois liberalization," especially the tendency to disregard party leadership.[78] Teng probably intended this to be a tactical retreat. For the remainder of 1981, however, the reformers were completely on the defensive. Rumors even circulated at the end of the year that Teng had been the victim of a "bloodless coup." Hu Chi-wei, the editor of the *People's Daily*, one of the Hus who brought chaos to China or to Hua Kuo-feng, was reported by the Japanese to be under criticism for his role in the exposé of the petroleum gang in 1980.[79] Visible evidence of the strength of the opposition includes at least one partial defense of the Great Leap Forward[80] and a direct denunciation of the reformers' attack on the restorationists:

> For the past few years we have deepened the criticism of the extreme "left" line of Lin Piao and the "Gang of Four" and put great effort into liberating thought. This was completely correct, completely necessary. However, some comrades mistakenly believe that to criticize the old concepts of the exploiting class, to criticize old customs, and to set up a new style is also extreme "left"; and that to carry out bourgeois liberalization and restore feudal superstition and backward thought is to "liberate thought."[81]

In early 1982 Wang Jen-chung, like Chao Tzu-yang a member of the old T'ao Chu system and in the early 1980s head of the party's propaganda department, made a relatively direct attack on the idea of reform itself. Wang warns that unless things get better and party discipline improves the party will "change color," *pien se*, a Cultural Revolution term rarely heard since Mao's death. Wang gives some inside information on party decision-making procedures:

> Our Central Secretariat is empowered by the Politburo to handle and decide by itself a few concrete questions of routine work. . . . Most of the meetings of the Secretariat are convened by Comrade Yao-pang. Some important questions concern government work, and then Comrade Tzu-yang joins us. No matter what the opinions of Comrade Yao-pang or Tzu-yang might be, naturally everyone gives them great weight, but it has never been a question of what one man says, goes. Rather, the decision is made by collective discussion.

He also analyzes the causes of China's past problems:

> If the party's system of democratic centralism had been correctly
> upheld, stuff like the "Great Leap Forward" of the '50s, the "anti-rightist
> deviation" of the Lushan meeting, including the ten years of the "Great
> Cultural Revolution," all could have been avoided.[82]

Wang thus indicates that he is not only not overly awed by Comrades
Yao-pang and Tzu-yang but also that the party has no need for basic
reform: if it would only follow the set procedures it already has,
everything would be fine.

## THE REFORMS OF 1982?

Even as Wang spoke the reformist counterattack was under way.
Wang himself did not fare well. In the summer of 1982, he was removed as
propaganda director and later purged entirely, apparently implicated in
the army's "culture" flap.

Two sets of "activities" dominated 1982, one against economic crime
and one for structural reform. Both themes had been a part of the *keng-
shen* reforms and had then been directed against the restorationists. Thus
in those days corruption was said to be a result of bureaucratism, itself a
consequence of the feudal mentality. In December 1981 Chao Tzu-yang
still associated the proliferation of economic crime with bureaucratism.[83]
The following year, however, Li Hsien-nien took up the theme. Economic
crime became associated less with bureaucratism than with "corrupt
capitalist thought."[84] Economic crime thrives on the liberal economic
policies that encourage greed and speculation. The theme of economic
crime had been at least partly coopted by the restorationists.

The theme of reform, however, which had been in abeyance all
throughout 1981, was again introduced into public discourse. In March
Chao Tzu-yang called for both a continuation of economic reforms in
addition to readjustment and for structural reform of the state. The
proposals picked up threads of the *keng-shen* movement, although those
threads were somewhat frayed. The *keng-shen* emphasis had been on
institutional and legal controls over political power. The reforms of 1982
were still aimed toward weakening the restorationists, but their main
thrust was less to check abuses of power than to rationalize the system and
make it more efficient.

Chao Tzu-yang said there were too many bureaucrats and these
bureaucrats were too old. There should be a retirement system and also a
training system for ignorant cadres. There should be a proper division of

responsibilities between party and state, between the various agencies of the state, and between the center and the localities. As Teng Hsiao-p'ing had said earlier, the leading group in all state offices should be young, revolutionary, educated, and professional.[85] It was later intimated that such paragons would be found among persons belonging to the Communist Youth League prior to the Cultural Revolution—when Hu Yao-pang had been in charge of that organization.[86] Yet some proposals did tend toward greater democracy and control over power. Thus proposals to give the National People's Congress greater real power by strengthening the powers of its standing committee accord well with the *keng-shen* spirit.

The first concrete result of the reform was the reorganization of the State Council. The number of vice-premiers was reduced to two (although most of the dismissed vice-premiers became members of the new "State Council Committee").[87] The State Council was the stronghold of the restorationists, and the reorganization was at least a symbolic defeat for them. The remaining two vice-premiers were both reformers: Wan Li, who is close to Teng Hsiao-p'ing; and Yao I-lin, a friend of Ch'en Yun's (see Table 8.4).

The party congress held in September also introduced structural reforms. One, which probably has no necessary consequence one way or another for liberalization, is the abolition of the position of party chairman. Hu Yao-pang remained at the top of the official hierarchy, but became secretary general instead of chairman; the structure of the CPC came to resemble more closely that of other world communist parties. At a news conference Hu Ch'iao-mu explained that if there were both a secretary general and a chairman one would hold an empty title, and it

**TABLE 8.4:   Persons Dismissed as Vice-Premier, State Council, May 1982.**

| Name | Affiliation |
| --- | --- |
| Yu Ch'iu-li* | Restoration |
| Keng Piao* | ? |
| Fang I* | Restoration |
| Ku Mu* | Restoration |
| K'ang Shih-en* | Restoration |
| Ch'en Mu-hua* | Restoration |
| Po I-po* | Reform |
| Ch'i Peng-fei* | ? |
| Yang Ching-jen | Reform? |
| Chang Ai-p'ing | ? |

*Appointed to State Council Committee.

made no sense for one person to hold both offices.[88] Actually, secretary general is potentially a more powerful office than chairman (just considered in terms of the powers of the office, rather than the influence of the person who has to occupy it): the secretary general has formal authority over the party bureaucracy, whereas the former chairman did not. The Secretariat was dominated by reformers, although the restorationists were also represented (see Table 8.5).

The congress adopted a new party charter, one having as a major theme the *keng-shen* notion that the party should operate only within the sphere of law and that there should be a sharp division between the functions of the party and those of the state.[89] In spite of this, contrary to expectations, the party's Military Affairs Commission was not abolished. Teng Hsiao-p'ing continued as its chairman. Hu Ch'iao-mu explained that the overlapping of party and state functions here really did not matter much, since the future state Military Affairs Commission would probably consist of exactly the same people on the party Military Affairs Commission.[90] Despite appearance, this probably does not contradict his explanation concerning the abolition of the party chairmanship. It is likely that Teng Hsiao-p'ing wanted to have as many controls over the army as possible, and to have them all concentrated in his own person.

The congress adopted a modified *keng-shen* proposal, setting up an advisors committee. In 1980 this had been discussed as a kind of party upper house, a check on the powers of the Politburo. By 1982 it seems to have become a place the old restorationists could retire to while saving their faces—and if this was its purpose it was a flop. Yeh Chien-ying agreed there were too many old-timers still active in the party and that they should make way for the young people. He himself was perfectly willing to retire; unfortunately, so many comrades had begged and begged him to stay that he guessed he would just have to soldier on.[91] The

**TABLE 8.5:  Full Members, Secretariat, August 1982**

| Name | Affiliation |
| --- | --- |
| Hu Yao-pang | Reform |
| Wan Li | Reform |
| Hsi Chung-hsiung | Reform |
| Teng Li-ch'un | Reform |
| Yang Yung | ? |
| Yu Ch'iu-li | Restoration |
| Ku Mu | Restoration |
| Ch'en Pei-hsien | Reform |
| Hu Ch'i-li | Reform |
| Yao I-lin | Reform |

only old and active comrade to join the committee was Teng Hsiao-p'ing himself, who became its head. The other members were obviously too weak to have any influence over affairs or were in disgrace (Wu Te and Ch'en Hsi-lien, for example, were members of the committee). It once seemed such a committee might be an interesting innovation in Leninist organization; now it seems more likely to be nothing at all.

Hu Yao-pang discussed the need for rectification;[92] the reformers would obviously like a major purge of the party. Ch'en Yun said, in effect, that all persons who had joined the party during the Cultural Revolution and had been on the leftist side in those events should be denied further advancement.[93] Another official noted that 40 percent of the current membership joined during the Cultural Revolution and that while not all of them are bad, they do deserve special scrutiny.[94] The combined strength of the army and the restorationists probably delayed such a purge, but the major object of the purge would be to guard against a Maoist revival springing from below. The chances for liberalization would no doubt be enhanced if those committed to radical totalitarianism are denied the opportunity to make trouble—although one is also inclined to wonder whether much of the Cultural Revolution cohort might have been converted to some version of liberal democracy. Purges in recent years have been conducted with relative civility. Yet a massive enough purge, even one conducted by the reformers, could in the end negate all the reform and lead to a return to pure oppression. One would have more confidence in the possibility of long-term liberalization if institutions were developed that would control abuses of power regardless of who controls the institutions.

## THE TENG HSIAO-P'ING SYSTEM

The Gang is said to have maintained its influence through a Gang system, a factional network stretching through society. A theme of the post-Mao period has been the need to establish rule through law and institutions rather than through persons and factions. Despite all the brave talk, this had not been achieved after the twelfth congress. The continued, almost automatic search for remedies to problems by purges and ideological "education" shows more of a Confucian reliance on persons rather than a legalist trust in institutions. The fact that Teng Hsiao-p'ing, clearly the most powerful man in China, has eschewed the top position in either the state or party bureaucracies shows that the formal structure of power is not the real one.

Yet by accident or more probably by design, the factional structure of the regime after the twelfth congress contains a bias toward greater institutionalization. The factional structure and the way it is distributed through the institutions may inhibit the arbitrary exercise of power or its concentration in one locus.

The top places are all held by reformers, persons who, therefore, would not be by reflex hostile to all forms of liberalization, yet their personal affiliations are diverse. Teng's refusal to take the top positions in the institutional system probably serves to strengthen that system. Had he himself become secretary general, the party would have dominated the state. Had he become premier, the lines of authority after his overthrow, retirement, or death would have become thoroughly fouled.

The general secretary is Hu Yao-pang, and the premier is Chao Tzu-yang. Both are associated with Teng Hsiao-p'ing. Hu has been closer to Teng, and Hu and Chao have no particular relationship to each other. Neither does Chao have any particular relationship with his vice-premiers, both of whom used to outrank him in the party. Wan Li is close to Teng, while Yao I-Lin is probably closer to Ch'en Yun. Ch'en is perhaps Teng's major ally, but not a client or a follower. At one time Ch'en was the party's most outspoken proponent of moderation in economic policies. He now seems much more liberal than Teng on cultural matters and more relaxed about the dangers of dissent but at the same time has grown more cautious than before about economic reforms. Both vice-premiers are members of the Secretariat, but the premier is not. Were it not for the factional affiliations, the state would look institutionally weak. The crossing of factional affiliations, however, may mean that it will be difficult for any person or organization simultaneously to dominate all the centers of power and, when the inevitable power struggle comes, it makes it more probable that the institutions will function as their formal charters describe them.

Admittedly, this is pretty thin. The 1982 party constitution is praised as the best one the party has ever had. Some also note that the 1956 constitution was a good one, too; unfortunately it was ignored. The obvious question is why this one will not be ignored as well. "This worry is not entirely groundless."[95] The answer, for what it is worth, is that the party has learned from past errors. Similar worries are voiced about the new state constitution adopted in December 1982, which stresses the rule of law and strengthens the control of the National People's Congress over the bureaucracy. Will it be more than a scrap of paper? Yes it will because all power belongs to the people, and People's Democratic Dictatorship guarantees that the people will keep control. Sure. "We must believe" that we have learned from our tragic errors.[96] This would seem a matter less for faith than for hope. All power belongs to the people—but will the regime shed its fear of the people?

This study has stressed there is no necessary connection between the regime's official liberalization policies and any toleration of spontaneous political activity in society. The regime could depoliticize without having to democratize. Now, however, the evidence suggests a supplementary claim: this is true only to a point. The regime has reached a stage where depoliticization requires democratization, and the rulers may be either unable or unwilling further to democratize.

## NOTES

1. *Ching Pao*, December 29, 1978 in Foreign Broadcast Information Service, *Daily Report, People's Republic of China*, January 16, 1979, p. N2 (hereafter cited as *FBIS/PRC*).

2. *Jen-min Jih-pao* [People's Daily], February 7, 1977 (hereafter cited as *PD*). This is billed as a joint editorial of *People's Daily, Red Flag* and *Liberation Army Daily*. Although *Red Flag* was then controlled by Wang Tung-hsing, perhaps the most sincere whateverist, the editorial does not appear in that magazine until its March issue. This probably shows that the shift in the balance of power that resulted in the editorial did not take place until after the February issue of *Red Flag* (published that year on February 3) had already been set in type.

3. *Tunghsiang* 19 (June 16, 1979) in *FBIS/PRC*, June 28, 1979, pp. U2–U7.

4. *PD*, July 27, 1979.

5. Ibid., August 3, 1979.

6. *Hung Ch'i* 9 (September 2, 1979): 2–4. For a general outline of Chinese politics in 1979 from the Teng point of view, see Chi Hsin, "Around the Fourth Plenary Session of the CCP Central Committee," *Chi-shih Nien-tai*, November 1979 in *FBIS/PRC*, November 21, 1979. pp. U1–U20.

7. *PD*, September 30, 1979.

8. *Chung-kung Wen-t'i Tzu-liao* 28 (April 14, 1980): 9.

9. Chi Hsin, "Fourth Plenary Session."

10. *PD*, September 20, 1980. The "former affiliations" in Table 8.1 are taken from Peter R. Moody, Jr., *The Politics of the Eighth Central Committee of the Communist Party of China* (Hamden: Shoestring Press, 1973).

11. *PD*, February 1, 1980.

12. Ibid., January 21, 1980; ibid., February 21, 1980.

13. A text appeared in *Cheng Ming* 29 (March 1, 1980); see *FBIS/PRC*, special supplement, March 1980, p. 5.

14. *FBIS/PRC*, special supplement, March 1980, p. 24.

15. *Ching Pao* 3 (March 10, 1980) in *FBIS/PRC*, March 20, 1980, p. U1.

16. For the public report, see *PD*, March 1, 1980.

17. Ibid., June 18, 1980. Hsu Shih-yu also sent flowers but did not come himself.

18. Kyodo, March 15, 1980 in *FBIS/PRC*, March 17, 1980, p. L27.

19. *Cheng Ming* 40 (April 1, 1980) in *FBIS/PRC*, April 2, 1980, p. U2.

20. *PD*, March 15, 1980.

21. Ibid., March 8, 1980.

22. Ibid., March 10, 1980.

23. Ibid., March 25, 1980.

24. *Kuang-ming Jih-pao*, May 29, 1980.

25. *Cheng Ming* 43 (July 1, 1980) in *FBIS/PRC*, July 9, 1980, p. U4.

26. *Chung kung Wen-t'i Tzu-liao* 19 (February 4, 1980): 16–28.

27. *Tunghsiang* 22 (July 16, 1980) in *FBIS/PRC*, July 23, 1980, p. U3.

28. *PD*, July 4, 1980; ibid., August 12, 1980.

29. A Taiwan source reports criticism of Chou from delegates to the 1980 session of the National People's Congress. See *Chung-kung wen-t'i Tzu-liao* 45 (October 20, 1980): 11–13.

30. *Cheng Ming* 33 in *FBIS/PRC*, July 9, 1980, p. U4.

31. *PD*, August 26, 1980. For criticism of the slogans, see *Kuang-ming Jih-pao* of the same date.

32. For months previously K'ang had been criticized under the code name, "that advisor"; he had been the advisor of the Central Cultural Revolution Group. He was first attacked by name by Hu Yao-pang at the funeral of former Organization Department head An Tzu-wen. *PD*, July 13, 1980.

33. Wang Ssu-chih, "Feudal Autocracy and Eunuch Dictatorship," ibid., August 4, 1980; Li Shao-chün, "The Eunuch Dictatorship of Ancient China," *Kuang-ming Jih-pao*, August 5, 1980.

34. *PD*, September 15, 1980.

35. Liao Kai-lung, "The '1980 Reform' Program in China," *Ch'i-shih Nien-tai* 134 (March 1, 1981) in *FBIS/PRC*, March 16, 1981, pp. U1–U19.

36. For a text see *Chan Wang* 461 (April 16, 1981) in *FBIS/China* (the publication changed its name), April 26, 1981, pp. W1–W14.

37. *FBIS/China*, p. W1.

38. Ibid., pp. W2–W4.

39. Ibid., p. W5

40. Ibid., p. W7.

41. Ibid., p. W9. The last sentence became the theme of an anonymous *Red Flag* commentary directed against the cult of the individual, later revealed to have been written by Hu Yao-pang. *Hung Ch'i* 24 (December 16, 1980): 2–8.

42. *FBIS/China*, April 22, 1981, p. W9.

43. Ibid., p. W10.

44. Ibid., pp. W10–W11.

45. *PD*, October 28, 1980.

46. Ma Chia, "This Topic of 'Capitalist Restoration' Is Worth Studying," ibid., July 17, 1980.

47. Ibid., July 22, 1980.

48. Wang Jo-shui, "Marxism and the Liberation of Thought," Ibid., August 1, 1980. It may, of course, have been Teng who was demurring, since this was published prior to his speech on reform.

49. Cheng Wen-lin, "Communist Morality or Socialist Morality," *Kuang-ming Jih-pao*, September 18, 1980.

50. Hu P'ing, "On the Development of Diversity," *PD*, August 8, 1980. Hu explains he does not mean "bourgeois liberalization." Diversity is not a pretext for bringing back things discarded by history.

51. Feng Wen-pin, "On the Question of Socialist Democracy," ibid., November 24 and 26, 1980.

52. P'eng Hsiang-fu and Cheng Chung-ping, "On 'Monolithic Leadership,' " ibid., December 12, 1980.

53. Wen-pin, "Socialist Democracy," November 25.

54. Chang Sang-cho, "Theory and Practice of the Bourgeois Separation of Powers," *PD*, October 7, 1980.

55. Liao, " '1980 Reform,' " pp. U7–U15.

56. Pao T'ung, "A Few Opinions on Opposing Bureautcratism," *PD*, October 30, 1980. Although Teng Hsiao-p'ing had said much the same thing, the author (who is probably using a pseudonym) speaks in the first person, an indication of the controversial nature of his thesis.

57. *A Great Trial in Chinese History* (Oxford: Pergamon Press, 1981), pp. 143–44.

58. Ibid., p. 102.

59. Ibid., p. 104.

60. See *Inside Mainland China*, April 1981, p. 20.

61. *Wen Wei Pao* (Hong Kong), February 24, 1981; *FBIS/PRC*, February 28, 1981, p. U1.

62. *Cheng Ming*, June 1, 1981; *FBIS/China*, June 3, 1981, p. W1.

63. *PD*, December 28, 1980.

64. Ibid., July 1, 1981.

65. *China News Analysis* 1206 (May 8, 1981): 2.

66. Huang K'o-Ch'eng, "On the Question of Party Style," *PD*, February 28, 1981.

67. Huang K'o-Ch'eng, "On the Questions of the Evaluation of Chairman Mao and the Attitude toward the Thought of Mao Tse-tung," ibid., April 11, 1981.

68. For example, *Kuang-ming Jih-pao*, June 28, 1982; ibid., July 15 and 24, 1982; ibid., September 9, 1982.

69. Ibid., September 4, 1982; *PD*, November 14, 1982.

70. For a good treatment of this incident, see *China News Analysis* 1245 (November 5, 1982).

71. Keng's removal is probably not directly connected with the "culture" flap, since his disgrace came earlier than that of those more directly responsible for it. While Wei Kuo-ch'ing, who was directly involved in the defiance, had been reappointed to the Politburo in September, Keng had not. He may have harmed himself by his reputation for hedonism and by getting along all to well under the rule of the Gang and Hua Kuo-feng. See *Chung-yang Jih-pao*, October 22, 1982.

72. For a good discussion of the play, presented in dialogue form, see Yuan Fang ("a distant place"), "*Bitter Love* and the Patriotism of Intellectuals," *Hung Ch'i* 9 (May 1, 1981): 27–33. Pai Hua is called simply "the author."

73. Hu Yao-pang, "Speech at the Meeting Commemorating Lu Hsun's Hundredth Birthday," *Hung-ch'i* 19 (October 1, 1981): 2–6.

74. Hu Ch'iao-mu, "Several Questions on the Current Ideological Line," *Hung Ch'i* 23 (December 1, 1981): 2–22.

75. Agence France Presse, May 12, 1981. Fu Yueh-hua, on the other hand, was released from jail, having served her time. Agence France Presse, May 6, 1981.

76. *Wen Wei Pao* (Hong Kong), May 14, 1981; *FBIS/China*, May 14, 1981, p. W2.

77. *PD*, December 10, 1981.

78. Ibid., August 31, 1981; ibid., September 1 and 29, 1981.

79. Kyodo, December 9, 1981 in *FBIS/China*, December 9, 1981, p. K8.

80. *PD*, November 10, 1981.

81. Ibid., December 26, 1981.

82. Wang Jen-chung, "Unify Thought, Earnestly Rectify Party Style," *Hung Ch'i* 5 (March 1, 1982): 2, 4, 13, 16.

83. *PD*, December 14, 1981.

84. Ibid., January 25, 1982; *Kuang-ming Jih-pao*, February 9, 1982; *PD*, April 14, 1982.

85. *PD*, March 30, 1982; *PD*, March 9, 1982.

86. Ibid., December 22, 1982.

87. Ibid., June 14 and 20, 1982.

88. Ibid., September 14, 1982.

89. Sung Jen-ch'iung, "Use the New Party Charter to Educate Party Members; Make a Good Ideological Preparation for Party Rectification," ibid., December 14, 1982.

90. Ibid., September 14, 1982.

91. Ibid., September 7, 1982.

92. Ibid., September 8, 1982.

93. Ibid., September 7, 1982.

94. Sung Jen-ch'iung, "New Party Charter."

95. Ibid.

96. *PD*, December 11, 1982.

# 9

# The Liberalization of
# Chinese Politics

Has there been a liberalization of Chinese politics since the death of Mao? The easy but unsatisfactory answer is that it is hard to say. Liberalization refers to "structural" change, a permanent change in the manner of conducting politics, not a temporary relaxation or a loosening up in one policy area or another without systemic effects on other policy areas.

There are at least two ways in which a totalitarian regime can become more liberal. Those with political power can cease to concern themselves with aspects of life they had previously sought to control. They can begin to exercise power in a well-defined, routine fashion over a restricted sphere of activity, allowing matters outside that sphere to be done as those who do them please. Depoliticization itself can perhaps be further subdivided. It may be a "passive" depoliticization, in which those with power simply cease to bother with matters difficult or inefficient to control. Or they may develop institutional restraints on the scope of power and a mentality that puts certain matters in principle beyond the control of politics. Additionally or alternatively, those with power may democratize: they may allow persons subject to power some say in how power will be exercised over them. Depoliticization and democratization have been treated as if they were independent dimensions of liberalization, on the assumption that at least up to a point politics could change along one line without changing on the other. Thus Chinese politics seems to have undergone more an active depoliticization than it has a democratization.

Depoliticization and democratization correspond to the core demands of two separate indigenous lines of protest against the Maoist system: depoliticization is associated with what I have called the Experts and democratization with the Reds. The two dimensions are also logically distinct. The classical *Rechtstaat* is in the abstract a system in which political power is exercised in a responsible, nonarbitrary fashion, although without any democracy to speak of. On the other hand, the evolution of postliberal societies in the West and Japan may be demonstrating that properly functioning democratic institutions may coexist with an unlimited expansion of the scope and power of the state.

This, however, is rather abstract. Should the state continue to expand in scope and function, democratic forms will become empty. The people might still vote and their rulers might still change but without effect on the policy pursued. Similarly, it is questionable whether there has ever been a *Rechtstaat* with a completely nonarbitrary government. Beyond a certain point, empirically if not conceptually, it would seem that depoliticization must entail democratization, and the failure to democratize becomes a general limit on liberalization. There would seem to be more potential for liberalization in China than in the Soviet Union, say, precisely because the Teng program has genuinely democratic implications and because of Teng's unwillingness to democratize limits the extent of liberalization in China.

## THE EMPHASIS ON POWER STRUGGLE

A guiding assumption of this study has been that if liberalization occurs, it will be through the workings of the power struggle. Obviously the power struggle would not be the only reason for the change, but it will be the mechanism through which the change will be produced. The focus on power struggle shows how conflict for power shapes policy. But the power struggle is not a free for all, and the structure of policy also shapes the conduct of the power struggle. Liberalization would mean that future power struggles would involve limited stakes and would be carried out in a routinized manner. Here is a basic obstacle to liberalization: it can come about only through a struggle for power, but those ahead in the power struggle may not be willing to accept the limitations on power that liberalization implies, even if they got ahead by advocating just such liberalization.

At the apex of Chinese politics following Mao's death were several political forces. Most prominent were the establishment radicals—the Gang of Four. Probably allied with them, but keeping a distance, was the police left, nominally headed by Hua Kuo-feng. The army may have been potentially the strongest force, but it was politically incohesive, even amorphous. The rational modernizers—the economic bureaucracy—were probably in the weakest position. They had been hurt by the death of their patron, Chou En-lai, and by the purge of Teng Hsiao-p'ing. They were continuing to be savaged in the anti-Teng campaign.

The Gang's position was inherently weak. Its only real base of power was its relationship with Mao. Its ideological position was contradictory, even hypocritical. Members of the Gang desired the overthrow of the establishment, yet they were part of the establishment themselves and zealous in protecting their own power and privilege. They were demonstrably unpopular among educated public opinion. While they did have a vested interest in the status quo, however, this would cease as soon as the chairman died, at that point they had an interest in major changes in the system. They were thus not only weak but also dangerous: should they seize power they would endanger the other powers and a near miss by the Gang could bring the country again to chaos. They were obvious candidates for elimination.

The policy of the Hua coalition was conservative in an unprincipled sense. It seemed at first to stand for Maoism without the Gang of Four, for the continuation of the status quo and the reimposition of discipline. The coalition was compelled by circumstances, however, to change at least the tone of ideological discourse and to emphasize material improvement while loosening political controls. Some passive depoliticization began under Hua Kuo-feng. This coalition was not stable. The ins and outs of Teng Hsiao-p'ing s return are not known. Hua Kuo-feng certainly opposed it. Its prime sponsor was most likely the army, with less enthusiastic backing from the rational modernizers. Hua was then developing his own cult, and there was at least a chance he might become supreme leader in fact as well as name. Teng's return to power should probably be interpreted as an attempt by the non-Hua elements in the post-Gang coalition to broaden that coalition in order to dilute the influence of Hua.

To be sure of his own position, Teng had to develop a base independent of those who caused him to be returned to power. Further liberalization would enhance his appeal to educated public opinion, for whatever that appeal was worth. Teng, unlike the coalition that purged the Gang, had very little residual interest in Maoism. It would suit his purposes to discredit, within limits, the Maoist past. The renunciation of Maoism in itself meant more liberalization. The attack on Mao sharpened Teng's conflict with Hua, and this conflict in turn reinforced Teng's propensity to liberalize. Teng also attempted to recruit his own following. Those of high rank tended to be old party members who, like himself, had no interest in perpetuating Maoism and consequently (in the circumstances) an interest in discrediting it. The top echelon of the practice or reform faction was drawn from tendencies not a part of the original anti-Gang coalition. Ch'en Yun might be considered one of the rational modernizers around Chou En-lai, but he had also been ignored and in semidisgrace for about two decades. Hu Yao-pang was one of Teng's own old cronies. Chao Tzu-yang was a survivor of the old T'ao Chu group (although he, unlike most of those around Teng, had been returned to favor before Mao died). Hu Ch'iao-mu and many of the others were once affiliated with the old P'eng Chen combination: the pre-Cultural Revolution North China region, the Peking party committee, and the propaganda system. It is here that the ideological ancestry of the reform faction is found. It is not quite the standard Marxist-Leninist-Stalinist rational modernizing line of, say, Liu Shao-ch'i, Chou En-lai, or perhaps even Hua Kuo-feng, but rather a variation of the "Marxian Confucian" line elaborated by intellectuals around P'eng Chen in the wake of the collapse of the Great Leap Forward.[1]

Teng consolidated his position at the third plenum at the end of 1978. He did this in part by further broadening the struggle, encouraging the democratic movement and pushing the liberalization beyond mere depoliticization. The democratic movement, however, made demands beyond anything the ruling group was ready to grant. These demands gave the left an issue on which it could attempt a comeback. The final defeat of the old post-Gang left did not come until the fall of 1979. The repression of the democratic movement fed what promises to be a chronic crisis of legitimacy. The regime will neither satisfy nor completely suppress the demands being made upon it from society.

Although the left was defanged in 1979, Hua Kuo-feng continued to hold on to what offices he could while also continuing as the target of intermittent attacks. He also remained a potential rallying point for persons hostile to Teng. The defeat of the left precipitated a conflict between Teng and the non-Hua part of the old anti-Gang coalition—a conflict with those who restored him to power. Teng could meet this attack either by a hard line, which would coopt his opponents' position, or by a liberal line, which would discredit them, should he be able to pull it off. He in fact did both. During 1980 he repressed expressions of popular discontent. He, or persons around him, also proposed bold programs of democratic reform. The year ended with the trial of the radical Maoists, a trial that can be seen either as a move toward a true rule through law or, more realistically, as a way to discredit Maoism without the need to make further reforms. The factional fight continued, the reformers winning a series of tactical victories. Reform itself stalled, however, but gave signs of moving forward again in 1983.

## HAS THERE BEEN STRUCTURAL CHANGE?

The answer is that there has been a change from totalitarian politics, but that no new structure has formed yet. This section sets out some alternative general interpretations of what has taken place since 1976. The point is not so much to afix labels, since none of the labels really fit yet. The labels may, however, help to identify the nature of the change, each suggesting a somewhat different political configuration.

*There Has Been No Real Change.*    Some would assert that China is still totalitarian: it is certainly still a repressive dictatorship. Persons in liberal countries who are hostile to the Chinese regime often purport to see no change, and some Chinese dissidents seem to agree with them.

This view, however, fails either to take totalitarianism seriously or to take Maoist China seriously as a totalitarian system. China is repressive, but not all repression is totalitarian. Whether totalitarianism deserves to be called a model or not, it does have a fairly specific empirical referent. We may take either the checklist approach of Friedrich and Brzezinski or the more subtle approach of Hannah Arendt, the depiction of totalitarian rule as the working out of the proposition that not only is everything permitted but also that everything is possible,[2] the condition the Chinese call no law and no heaven. These depictions approximately fit specific historical systems, including Maoist China, that did not really take shape until after the descriptions had been elaborated. They do not fit China today.

Neither, however, do they fit the Soviet Union today. There may be another sense in which it is correct to say there has been no *basic* change in China. It may be that the system has become *merely* post-totalitarian. China may be evolving toward the kind of system that developed in the Soviet Union in Stalin's last years. The evolution in that country might have been reversed by the doctors' plot purges if the old tyrant had lived really to put them in motion; however that may be, he did not, and there is much continuity in the Soviet political structure from, say, 1950 on. What we are seeing in China may be simply a "natural" evolution within totalitarianism, not a basic change from totalitarianism.

*China is Authoritarian.*    Before discussing the post-totalitarian system, however, it may be appropriate to discuss whether China has become authoritarian: this would amount to a genuine structural change, although only liberalization in a very limited sense. In common usage authoritarian regimes are those that are neither liberal nor totalitarian. Common usage should perhaps add that neither are they traditional, although persons from a liberal heritage sometimes seem to have trouble recognizing a distinction between a traditional regime and any other "dictatorships." Robert Wesson asserts there is an evolution of at least communist totalitarianism toward an authoritarian form. Communist states are "gradually losing much or most of the specialness that sets them off from non-Western authoritarian regimes." They are becoming like standard third world dictatorships. In particular the communist state "necessarily reverts to something like the state it replaced, or what one might suppose the old regime to have been had there been no revolution."[3] Andropov's Soviet Union, then, is what the Tsar's Russia would be, if there were still a Tsar. In many ways China since 1976 is coming to resemble Taiwan. If it comes to that, dissent against Peking seems to ape at least one strain of the dissent against Taipei and comes from similar social strata.[4] Taiwan, in turn, might be what China would be had there been an evolution of the imperial system rather than a revolutionary break from it.

This kind of speculation can be as interesting as it as vain. Totalitarianism certainly does not obliterate national cultures, and as totalitarianism relents the culture reasserts itself. In the case of China, this is ground for optimism. It is probably too much to say, however, that old communist regimes resemble third world dictatorships: or, rather, third world dictatorships differ radically among themselves. Communist states in gross terms are certainly more stable than the typical third world regime. Among communist states only Poland has approached becoming a military dictatorship, a typical third world form.

Authoritarianism has been treated so far as a residual category: it is neither traditional, liberal, nor totalitarian. Some scholars treat it as a positive category in its own right. Juan Linz identifies an authoritarian regime as one that allows a limited pluralism. There may be a single party, but it is usually a congeries of the existing elites and does not worry overmuch about the grass roots. An authoritarian system has no real ideology but only a vague official "mentality" that almost anyone can adhere to in good faith since it is so lacking in content. The regime has only a limited capacity to mobilize the population and permits the autonomy of nonpolitical interests.[5] Teng's and even Hua's China could be perceived as evolving in an authoritarian direction. To say that practice is the standard of truth, for example, is to deprive Marxism-Leninism of much of its specific content. The regime now says this rather less often than before, but even in the ideological reaffirmations, the thoughts of Mao seem to be dissolving into one of Linz's mentalities. It is readily admitted that many of Mao's specific thoughts were out of date, and that not a few of them are perverse. But because Mao's thought is bound up with the regime itself, it should not be repudiated. "To deny the *historical position* of Chairman Mao and of the Thought of Mao Tse-tung is to deny the history of struggle of the Chinese people and of the Communist Party of China."[6] The man and his thought (which is not his alone, etc., etc., etc.) are idols before which good comrades will genuflect and then go on their way.

One question is whether Linz's authoritarian system differs in practice from the post-totalitarian system he suggests exists in the Soviet Union. A major difference would seem to be that in the authoritarian system there are social elites autonomous from the regime, while in the post-totalitarian regime the social structure is still a product of the political system.[7] In China as in other communist countries, intellectuals have more status than many of the politicians would like them to, but they have influence only insofar as they are tied into the power struggle among the political elite. Should the economic reforms continue in China, however, autonomous elites could evolve. China might become authoritarian if depoliticization continues while democratization is stifled.

For China to become authoritarian would be a liberalization of sorts, as any abatement of totalitarianism is a liberalization. It would also be a structural change, but one that might not promise much more liberalization. When the Reagan regime in the United States revived the old political science distinction between totalitarian and authoritarian regimes in order to criticize the Carter human rights policy, one contention was that authoritarian regimes have more of a potential to evolve into liberal ones. It would seem, however, that authoritarian regimes do not transform themselves into liberal regimes very often (and movement in the reverse direction is rather more common). Authoritarian regimes individually tend to be unstable, thus giving the impression that authoritarianism is a transitional form. But one authoritarian power structure most commonly simply gives way to another, and the basic form remains. An authoritarian China might be plagued by intrigue and perhaps palace coups and by a chronic crisis of legitimacy: for authority is precisely what a typical authoritarian regime lacks.

*China is Revisionist.*    Revisionism may be a rubric to distinguish the post-totalitarian system from other forms of authoritarianism. On the face of it, this seems unpromising. The term itself is usually one of abuse, and of abuse that has meaning only within an orthodox tradition of Marxism-Leninism (with orthodox here being as tendentious a term as revisionism). Nevertheless, Lowell Dittmer identifies the changes in China as "institutionalized revisionism." In an institutionalized revisionist system, people are mobilized according to their existing motives, and the regime does not bother any longer to transform those motives. The system seeks to avoid conflict inside the party and emphasizes "functional specialization and professionalization at the expense of political commitment." It seeks its primary social base among the educated and may encourage some cultural liberalism. "Perhaps the key ideological innovation is the abandonment of the dialectic."[8]

Much of this obviously fits post-Mao China. The announcement that China no longer contains antagonistic classes (even though class struggle continues) might be considered an abandonment of the dialectic (it certainly makes dictatorship harder to justify). Dittmer's revisionism, however, would seem to apply to any deradicalized communist system and thus might be too broad a term. It would seem to apply most directly to the East European countries, but it could also supply to the Soviet Union. According to one authority, the post-Stalin Soviet state is a stable bureaucratic oligarchy. Decisions are made by bargaining and compromise, with the party apparatus coordinating the activities of the other bureaucracies. Experts have a major role in making routine decisions, and the bureaucracies are at least minimally responsive to the aspirations of various social categories. In particular, there is a tendency toward expanding the scope of the welfare state.[9] This would seem to fit a rather harsh version of Dittmer's revisionism. A label that can apply to Brezhnev's and Andropov's Soviet Union, Dubcek's Czechoslovakia, and Teng's China may require some subheadings to be more fully useful.

The trouble is that while it is easy to distinguish the Soviet Union from Czechoslovakia it is not obvious where China should fit in. Dittmer's revisionism is derived in part from his reconstruction of the organizational line of Liu Shao-ch'i. Liu has been rehabilitated, and so has his general attitude. Should China come under the sway of the policy of the restorationist faction, it would probably become another post-totalitarian, deradicalized, revisionist state. It might be more liberal, or liberalized, than the Soviet Union, but less liberal than, say, Hungary.

But the restorationist line is not the only one active in China. Teng rehabilitated Liu, but he—or, more precisely, the reform faction, for Teng is careful to keep himself an inch or two above the battle—no longer completely follows the Liu line. The Hong Kong communists, it will be recalled, once spoke of the erroneous ideas held in common by Mao, Liu, Chou En-lai, Lin Piao, and Hua Kuo-feng. These names can be taken as symbolic of the various non-Teng, nonreform currents in the CPC tradition. Despite their differences, we are to understand they all are in the same family. The implication would be that the reform line transcends the old divisions and represents something new.

Mao, Liu, and the rest stressed the "class contradiction" between the proletariat and the bourgeoisie and argued about how acute this might be at any particular time. If one holds that the bourgeoisie has vanished or is no longer hostile, this might be considered an abandonment of the dialectic. "Revisionist" ideology in the Soviet Union and in much of Eastern Europe seems to rationalize a structure of functional bureaucratic interests coordinated by the party bureaucracy. Dissent in communist countries is generally directed against this bureaucratized state. So, at least verbally, is the reform program, and it seems somewhat gratuitous to dismiss as the abandonment of the dialectic an attempt to give voice to complaints people have against the actual structure of power. The Maoists and the Hong Kong communists explicitly and some mainland reformers implicitly introduced into Chinese discourse a new dialectic: the "class" contradiction is that between the rulers and the ruled, the bureaucracy and people. Related to this is the contention that the party itself has committed errors. Perhaps to their eventual regret, the Chinese rulers have demystified the role of the vanguard party. For the Soviet communists, problems have come about as the result of the weakness or wickedness of particular individuals such as Stalin or Khrushchev; but the party itself has, strictly speaking, never made a mistake. The Chinese take a more systemic approach (as, for that matter, they did as early as the first attacks on Stalin in 1956): the problem is with the system, and the system is the top-heavy structure of centralized bureaucratic dominance that seems to result from Leninism.

Admittedly, this line of reasoning exists only in germ in China. The official Chinese press has repudiated the notion of a class contradiction between the rulers and the ruled, even though the reform faction were clearly on the verge of enunciating it. The idea does not make much sense in Marxist terms. Politics reflects the class realities. States or political parties cannot create social classes. Many Chinese may find the embryonic reform notion uncomfortably Maoist. Yet the idea may resurface at a propitious time. This would mean a more radical break with Marxism than the regime has yet been willing to make, but this kind of break seems implicit in the reform program, and if the break is not made the program may slip into some more ordinary form of revisionism.

*Class Power of the Intellectuals.*    The Hungarian writers George Konrad and Ivan Szeleny propose that the post-Stalin state in Eastern Europe represents the class power of the intellectuals. This is another way of conceptualizing Dittmer's revisionism or perhaps the most liberal variety of it. "Under contemporary East European state socialism, for the first time in the history of mankind, the intelligentsia is in the process of forming a class." Intellectuals have developed interests distinct from those of other social groups. Under capitalism, we are told, technocracy does not benefit intellectuals who are not technocrats; so there is no intellectual class as such. Socialism, however, means a state-controlled culture, and from this comes an identity of interests of artists and technocrats. As the Communist party abandons revolution and attempts to deal with the machinery of the modern state and of big economic enterprises, it needs to make concessions to technocrats. "The stability of the post-Stalin era is founded on an alliance between the technocracy and the ruling elite." The state must allow cultural liberties, since the technocracy will feel insecure if creative intellectuals are suppressed. The state will also have to adopt something like the rule through law. The technocrats see their economic reforms being wiped out with each shift in the political balance and come to demand legal and constitutional guarantees for these reforms.[10]

An implication of the class power concept is that technocrats and intellectuals can be made happy without full democracy. Their demands for liberalization can be satisfied by giving favors to the intellectuals without necessarily satisfying other groups. This concept seems useful in understanding Teng's China. The Teng regime has tended to indulge intellectuals (although it has trouble with creative writers) and attempts, with what success it is hard to say, to play upon intellectuals' fears of turmoil among the less educated, thus inhibiting the further spread of democracy. Some intellectuals, for their part find the new order rather to their liking:

> When meeting foreign guests, the old Mao Zedong used to sink into a big soft sofa and beside his feet was placed a big spitoon. The rustic manner of former party chairman Hua Guofeng in his licking his thumb before he would turn the pages of his speech is even more incomparable. When Hu Yaobang jumped up, his manner, his gaze was just like that of a hawk ready to soar into the broad sky.[11]

While it is attractive to interpret the Teng reform program as an attempt at intellectual class power, the concept itself may be partly faulty. The domination of political life by the educated is certainly not unique to the post-Stalin communist state, and the concept of class power may not be an adequate description of the political structure of such states.

Most obviously, radicals are often intellectuals too. One hoary and not completely unconvincing critique of radicalism has it that Marxism is not the scientific expression of the class interests of the proletariat but a rationalization of the envy and greed for power of alienated intellectuals. Members of the Gang were themselves products of the effete intellectual decadence of treaty-port Shanghai.[12] The class power concept implies that the professional interests of intellectuals will be indulged, however, while radicalism seems to promise political control to specific intellectuals themselves. Under the class power concept, the literary critic can criticize as he pleases. Under radicalism the lucky critic can destroy his enemies and boss everyone else around.

More importantly, technocracy, such as it is, is not unique to communist states. In advanced industrialized countries, prestige, power, and perhaps even the more modest forms of wealth no longer derive from ownership of property but from affiliation with the large political and economic bureaucracies. Education gives access to these bureaucracies. The postliberal world has, to be sure, no formally official culture, and some purport to find a contradiction between the antinomian cultural system of the "new class" and the rational economic and social systems that generate that class.[13] This cultural antinomianism (which includes a healthy dose of antitechnocratic ideology), however, seems in practice to strike harder at traditional values than at the political or economic structure. The railing of the New Left against the Moloch establishment seems to have been completely without effect, but Moloch has made his own the cultural values of the New Left.[14] From one perspective the antinomian, antitechnocratic cultural system serves merely to reinforce the technocratic reality: it functions to corrode the moral, cultural, social, and personal obstacles to the technological society while being at the same time irrelevant to any understanding of the actual structures of power and control within that society.

The divorce of the cultural from the other systems in postliberal society may mean it has no real "new class" in any technical sense. More basically, however, it may be that the concept of class is of little help in understanding contemporary politics in countries in which the state itself is a major social force. As suggested above, the continuing popularity of class analysts may function to prevent an understanding of just what is going on. A Chinese comment on Herbert Marcuse is interesting here. Marcuse is said to present a better analysis of late capitalist society than do his non-Marxist competitors, but, alas, he is a bit of a pinko, an "extreme leftist." "It is not hard to see that many of Marcuse's ideas are very similar to slogans popular in China during the 'Cultural Revolution.' Today, when we are studying and criticizing the international extreme left thought tide, it is very significant that we should derive from this the necessary lessons."[15] The lessons are not spelled out, but at least one suggests itself. The ideologies of Mao and of Marcuse both throve in the societies they purported to criticize to their core. In historical perspective both are empty talk.

The postliberal instance shows that a certain amount of technocracy is compatible with formal democracy, and it may even be precisely the existence of formal democracy that has prevented the full triumph of technocracy in postliberal countries. Formal democracy, to the extent there is any, may limit class power in communist countries that are liberalizing. Also, while in postliberal countries technocracy may mean the erosion of democracy, it need not have the same implication in formerly totalitarian states, which are coming to technocracy from the opposite direction. The Hungarian writers say the overthrow of Dubček indicated that technocracy had gone as far as it could.[16] To appearances, at least, this limitation was imposed only by the Soviet army and is not necessarily inherent in the liberalization process itself. Events in Poland since the late 1970s give cause to wonder whether that country was an instance of intellectual class power. There may be in Poland a tension between the workers and the intellectuals analogous to that between the democratic movement in China and the reformers. But in Poland power had shifted in a democratic direction, and part of the background of the shift was an intellectual class power regime. Perhaps the intellectual class power regime is inherently unstable: it must go forward toward a more full democracy, or it must pull back. Beyond a certain point it seems impossible to indulge the intellectuals without indulging everyone else.

## THE CHINESE REFORM PROGRAM

The Chinese regime has certainly not liberalized as much as had the Polish or Dubçek regimes, much less the Yugoslav regime. The potential may be there, however. The impetus behind the Teng program, as behind the Hua or restoration programs, is no doubt technocratic rather than democratic. But technocracy will limit totalitarian control,[17] even if it results in only an attenuated sort of liberalization. China may easily become a posttotalitarian "revisionist" system; this may even be its most probable future. The Teng program would seem to promise something different. It seems to entail a more positive kind of depoliticization, one with genuinely democratic implications. Unlike the Maoist or general Red encouragement of mass activism, the program seemed to recognize the legitimacy of social diversity, to seek to build institutions to take account of this diversity, and by means of these institutions to limit the scope of political power over society and the person. It attempted to evolve a systemic explanation of past totalitarian errors, the explanation hinging either on leftism as a feudal residue or on the nature of the bureaucratic socialist state. This search for systemic errors, something the reformers have in common with the Maoists, in itself implies a willingness to make systemic changes.

To recognize the legitimacy of social diversity implies in modern conditions the legitimacy of some open social conflict. For the political regime to encourage spontaneity and to relax its controls over society is to expose itself to demands from society. Some form of democracy is implied, ultimately, in Teng's program. The contradiction is that every time democracy raises its head, Teng gives it a kick. The *keng-shen* reforms were articulated well after the suppression of the democratic movement and while official hostility to that movement continued. The reformers were cut off from what should have been their mass base, and some of their actions may even have alienated that base. The talk of democratic institutions coupled with hostility to democratic content is probably evidence of the reformers' failure of nerve: Lord She loved dragons. As long as the mass base is absent, the reforms will be empty talk.

One encouraging thing about the *keng-shen* reforms is that they stress institutional development. But to talk about institutional development is not to develop institutions. Institutions are established when to do so will serve concrete interests (after which concrete interests serve themselves by conforming to established institutions). A victorious group may set up institutions to perpetrate its power, or an institution may result as a compromise among competing groups. Here it is necessary to return to the power struggle to assess the chances for further liberal reform in china.

A complete victory by a united reform faction is unlikely to lead to the institutionalization of liberal reforms: a united ruling group would have relatively little use for institutionalized limitations on power. The reformers will probably not stay united, however, and conflict among them could lead to more liberalization. This is also true (one asserts with less confidence) for conflict among the reformers and other elements of the regime, especially if those elements imitate the reformers by appealing for popular support.

Competition with other elements could also lead to the abandonment of reform altogether and a turn to repression. Conflict can evaporate institutions as well as solidify them. Conflict in China lends itself more easily to proposals for liberalization than to its institutionalization. Conflict is intense, but it is not tied to well-defined social interests that can act autonomously from the regime. Ethnic multiplicity in the most liberal of all communist regimes, Yugoslovia, is said to limit liberalization there. Should rule become too mild, ethnic acrimony would tear the state apart.[18] But this ethnic diversity is also a condition for what liberalization the country has achieved. The nationalities give a focus of loyalty in competition with that to the party, the ideology, or the artificial central state, and the existence of these alternative foci of loyalty gives rise to the cross-cutting cleavages political scientists used to be so enthusiastic about. The Dubček reforms in Czechoslovakia are sometimes said to have resulted from a coincidence of interests of the Czech intellectuals with the Slovak apparatchiks. Poland does not have the ethnic diversity of some other East European countries, but it does have a powerful and self-confident Catholic church. China lacks such particularistic social bases.

China will also have problems if the reforms, or something like them, are *not* institutionalized. A possible conclusion to this study is, again, that no liberalized political structure has formed, but the old totalitarian structure has decayed. A totalitarian system of the old style could perhaps now be restored only by an upheaval tantamount to revolution—and it is hard to see where support for such a revolution would come from. In the meantime, whether the regime continues to talk of reform without acting or whether the Teng group or its successors manage to consolidate a revisionist system, the Chinese rulers will face problems of legitimacy.

This issue of legitimacy is even deeper than that of institutionalization. Talk of the crisis of faith is evidence that the regime recognizes that segments of the population see the regime to be without moral foundation.

A past advantage of the radical tendency over the moderate has been its ability to produce a sense of moral commitment, at least as long as the radicals did not control central power. In practice many found radical moralism to give results grotesquely immoral, and both the Hua and Teng regimes derived moral advantage simply by presenting themselves as nonradical. This grows old fast, however, especially as alternatives to radicalism are seen to have their own blemishes; and denunciations of the Gang of Four are by now about as relevant to current conditions as continuing slurs on Chiang Kai-shek.

The Maoists seemed to think of virtue as adherence to a particular political line, and the last thing China needs is another power-imposed morality. It might need, however, some ethical system that defines the purposes, limits, and methods of political power. Such a system would be genuinely accepted by those with power, abuse of which will discredit them. It would embody the consensus of society and conform (in the old Confucian phrase) to universal human feelings. Within the moderate tendency, only the Marxian Confucian strain, the ancestor of the reform sentiment, attempted to develop such a thing (the radical position being, of course, that such a thing is impossible). Marxian Confucianism remained undeveloped, and the reformers have not seriously addressed the issue of the moral basis of power or at least have not gone much deeper than exhortations about "spiritual civilization." The moderates have in the past tended to define man's moral end as "happiness" and have defined happiness in terms of individual material comfort within a powerful state. This is an effective counter to Maoist cant about self-sacrifice and the like, but when Maoism is no longer the alternative it can be more than a little hollow.

## CONCLUDING UNSCIENTIFIC POSTSCRIPT

Totalitarianism in this work has meant revolutionary totalitarianism, the kind of system discussed by Hannah Arendt—the systems of Stalin, Hitler, and Mao. This was perhaps the dominant political fact of the first three-quarters of the twentieth century, just as liberalism was the dominant political fact of the nineteenth century. This kind of totalitarianism may be vanishing: in the early 1980s it may have lingered in Indochina and it may have been developing in Central America, but the larger states were either authoritarian, postliberal, or posttotalitarian. Revolutionary totalitarianism, however, may turn out to have been merely preparatory for a new kind of totalitarianism that is growing spontaneously in postliberal societies as well. This is the Moloch bureaucratic state and technological society, with political power divorced from human desires except insofar as power defines those desires. This new totalitarianism may be less terroristic than the old and less overtly brutal, but equally normless and perhaps more inhuman. If such is the trend, it is obviously generating resistance to itself, but it is not obvious that the resistance will be effective. The demand by both Chinese reformers and Chinese dissidents for law and democracy is testimony to the continued appeal of liberalism in its less technical sense. It may be, however, that forces in the world are making law and democracy obsolete, so that their advocacy is empty, as empty as Marcuse's critique of the technological society. Such forces may be in the last analysis the explanation of the limitations of Chinese dissent and reform (and an explanation of the limitations of reform and dissent elsewhere). Yet what the Chinese, so recently emerged from revolutionary totalitarianism, have to say may be of interest to others attempting to avert or moderate the dehumanizing tendencies in contemporary politics and society. The Chinese example is of more than parochial interest.

## NOTES

1. Peter R. Moody, Jr., *Oposition and Dissent in Contemporary China* (Stanford: Hoover Institution Press, 1977), pp. 167–84; Merle Goldman, *China's Intellectuals: Advise and Dissent* (Cambridge, Mass.: Harvard University Press, 1981), pp. 18–60.

2. Carl J. Friedrich and Zbigniew K. Brzezinski, *Totalitarian Dictatorship and Autocracy*, 2nd ed. (New York: Praeger, 1966); Hannah Arendt, *The Origins of Totalitarianism*, 2nd ed. (Cleveland: Meridian Books, 1958).

3. Robert Wesson, *The Aging of Communism* (New York: Praeger, 1980), pp. 6–8.

4. See Mab Huang, *Intellectual Ferment for Political Reforms in Taiwan 1971–1974*, (Ann Arbor: Center for Chinese Studies, University of Michigan, 1976).

5. Juan J. Linz, "Totalitarian and Authoritarian Regimes," in *Handbook of Political Science*, vol. 3, ed. Fred I. Greenstein and Nelson W. Polsby (Reading, Mass.: Addison-Wesley, 1975), pp. 266–72.

6. *Jen-min Jih-pao*, July 7, 1981. Emphasis added.

7. Linz, "Totalitarian and Authoritarian Regimes," p. 229.

8. Lowell Ditmer, "Chinese Communist Revisionism in Comparative Perspective," *Studies in Comparative Communism* 13 (Spring 1980): 3, 8, 12, 19–20, 23–24.

9. Seweryn Bialer, *Stalin's Successors: Leadership, Stability, and Change in the Soviet Union* (New York: Cambridge University Press, 1980), pp. 50–52.

10. George Konrad and Ivan Szeleny, *The Intellectuals on the Road to Class Power* (New York: Harcourt Brace Jovanovich, 1979), pp. 3, 10, 80, 84, 207, 209, 232.

11. Yen Kai, "Impressions of Hu Yaobang," *Cheng Ming* 46 (August 1, 1981) in Federal Broadcast Information Service, *Daily Report, China*, August 10, 1981, p. W2.

12. Compare Ly Singko, *The Fall of Madam Mao* (New York: Vantage, 1979).

13. Daniel Bell, *The Coming of Post-Industrial Society: A Venture in Social Forecasting* (New York: Basic Books, 1973), p. 114; Samuel P. Huntington, "Post-Industrial Politics: How Benign Will It Be?" *Comparative Politics* 6 (January 1974): 163–91.

14. Ronald Inglehart, *The Silent Revolution: Changing Values and Political Styles among Western Publics* (Princeton: Princeton University Press, 1977), p. 113.

15. Hsueh Min and Kuo Yung, "Discussing the 'Leftist' Tendency of 'Western Marxism,'" *Hsin-hua Wen-chai* 8 (August 1981): 38; from *Fu-tan Hsueh-pao* 2 (1981).

16. Konrad and Szelenyi, *The Intellectuals on the Road*, p. 216.

17. Compare Peter Kneen, "Why Natural Scientists Are a Problem for the CPSU," *British Journal of Political Science* (April 1978): 177–98.

18. Thomas Oleszczuk, "The Liberalization of Dictatorship: The Titoist Lesson to the Third World," *Journal of Politics* 43 (August 1981): 828.

# Appendix A

## Important Names and
## Special Terms

**Bourgeois liberalization**: A demand for the excessive loosening up of old practices; demands against the regime that take as their standard the practices of liberal democracy. The rulers as a whole accuse the democratic movement and intellectuals, particularly creative writers, who desire more cultural freedom of advocating bourgeois liberalization. Those opposed to the reform faction say Teng Hsiao-p'ing's policies encourage bourgeois liberalization.

**Chang Chih-hsin**: A party official in the northeastern provinces before the Cultural Revolution. She was arrested during the Cultural Revolution, tortured, and finally executed in 1976. In 1979 her mistreatment became the subject of a publicity campaign, whereby Teng Hsiao-p'ing was able to turn the tables on his leftist critics, many of whom were directly or indirectly implicated in the alleged injustice done Chang Chih-hsin.

**Chang Ch'un-ch'iao**: Before the Cultural Revolution, a party functionary in Shanghi. Later he became first secretary of Shanghai. The most able and intelligent of the Gang of Four, he was sentenced to death in 1981, with the execution of the sentence suspended for two years. The regime probably lacks the stomach to kill him, and, barring a major change, he will probably therefore spend the rest of his life in jail. He is alleged to have become a convert to political democracy while in prison.

**Chao Tzu-yang**: Before the Cultural Revolution, an official in Kwantung province. He was purged during the Cultural Revolution but reinstated in the early 1970s. Later he became first secretary of Szuchuan province, where he pioneered liberal economic policies. In 1980 he replaced Hua-Kuo-feng as premier of the State Council. He is one of the major reformers.

**Ch'en Hsi-lien**: A soldier, he was commander of the Shenyang military region until the early 1970s, after which he was transferred to become commander of the Peking military region. One of the more leftist of China's regional soldiers, he was purged in 1980 as a member of the "whatever faction."

**Ch'en Po-ta**: One of the major communist theoreticians in China, he served for many years as Mao Tse-tung's personal secretary. In his earlier years, he made a few attempts to find affinities between traditional Chinese philosophy and Marxism. Later he was one of the major theoretical elaborators of radical Maoism, particularly the cult of the individual. During the Cultural Revolution, he was a member of the radical leading core but was purged in 1970 for reasons still not entirely clear. He was convicted in 1981 of being part of the "Chiang Ch'ing, Lin Piao anti-party clique" but was given a relatively light sentence because of his great age and cooperative attitude.

**Ch'en Yun**: A long-time party organizer and economic policy maker. In the 1950s he advocated caution in economic policy and greater use of the market mechanism. Opposed to the Great Leap Forward, he was not purged but remained under a cloud until late 1977. He now may be, next to Teng Hsiao-p'ing, the second most influential man in the party hierarchy, and he is easily the most popular. He has taken a very relaxed attitude on matters of political opposition, Marxist dogma, and cultural freedom but may be having second thoughts about economic liberalization.

**Ch'en Yung-kuei**: A peasant from Shansi, he was appointed to the Politburo in 1969 because of his association with the Tachai brigade, an important Maoist agricultural model. His purge in 1980 symbolizes the regime's repudiation of the radical economic policies in the countryside.

**Chiang Ch'ing**: A one-time actress in Shanghai, later the fourth wife of Mao Tse-tung. The most colorful of the Gang of Four, she became famous during the Cultural Revolution for her shrill denunciations of the continued domination of Chinese intellectual life by feudal and bourgeois culture. She was jailed in 1976 and in 1981 was sentenced to death, with the sentence suspended for two years. Like Chang Ch'un-ch'iao, she will probably live out the rest of her natural life in jail.

**Chou En-lai**: A life-long communist revolutionary, he was premier of the State Council from the establishment of the People's Republic until his death in 1976. He was probably the architect of China's pro-Western policy of the 1970s. His domestic function was to follow along behind the radical Maoists attempting to pick up the pieces. His style embodied both suave urbanity and a flexibility often indistinguishable from lack of principle. A civilized, intelligent, and cultured man, he was popular both with intellectuals and with the population generally, although perhaps not as popular as the anti-Maoists later came to make him out to be when they were looking for someone to juxtapose against Mao.

**Chou Yang**: Before the Cultural Revolution, China's foremost literary inquisitor, he was purged in 1966 for being too liberal. He was rehabilitated in 1979, and in retrospect his alleged liberalism seems less of a joke than it once did: his prominence since 1979 has varied inversely with literary repression.

**Cultural Revolution**: A series of chaotic events beginning in 1966, involving a massive purge of the Chinese elite, an assault on the prestige and position of the party bureaucracy, and a questioning of all the "old" culture. It is common now to speak of the Cultural Revolution as lasting until Mao's death and the purge of the Gang of Four in 1976, but it is still more useful to consider it essentially ended by the time of the Ninth Party Congress in 1969, when superficial order had been reestablished in the country and the open power struggle had come to an end.

**Democratic movement**: A political movement most active in Peking and a few other Chinese cities in the winter of 1978–79. The participants, mostly students and former Red Guards, demanded that the Chinese political system be transformed into a constitutional democracy. Beginning in the spring of 1979, the major democratic activists have been placed under arrest, and the arrests have continued until the present.

**Fa-ch'üan**: "Legal rights." In 1975 the radicals denounced bourgeois legal rights on the grounds that these inhibited revolutionary development and laid the foundation for a new ruling class. The repudiation of the campaign against *Fa-ch'üan* in 1978 and later symbolizes the regime's new commitment to legality, at least of a sort.

**Four modernizations**: The modernization of agriculture, industry, science and technology, and national defense. Chou En-lai proposed these in 1964 and again in 1975. They became a major theme of the Hua Kuo-feng regime and, to a lesser extent, of the Teng Hsiao-p'ing regime, the point being that the Gang of Four had supposedly sabotaged the four modernizations because they did not want China to modernize.

**Four principles**: Words and actions must not depart from socialism, from proletarian dictatorship, from party leadership, and from Marxism-Leninism, the thought of Mao Tse-tung: limitations proposed on the free exercise of the public expression of opinion by Teng Hsiao-p'ing in the spring of 1979. Teng and the regime as a whole are most intolerant of any questioning of party leadership.

**Fu Yueh-hua**: A worker raped by her boss who, when she complained to the police and other authorities, was ignored. In the winter of 1979, she helped organize protests by persons coming to Peking to complain of poverty and mistreatment by officialdom. She was thereupon arrested and given a couple of years in jail for slandering her former boss.

**Gang of Four**: Chiang Ch'ing, Chang Ch'un-ch'iao, Wang Hung-wen, Mao Wen-yuan: in 1976 the surviving core of the Chinese radical establishment. They were arrested about a month after Mao died.

**Great Leap Forward**: A period of massive economic experimentation, lasting from 1958 through 1960, during which objective constraints on economic growth were largely ignored. The Leap policies brought the country to the brink of famine and economic collapse and were tacitly abandoned by 1961. The Leap Forward was not repudiated in principle, however, until around 1979.

**Hsu Shih-yu**: Formerly a powerful regional commander. He was the long-time head of the Nanking military region, transferred in the early 1970s to become head of the Canton military region. He allegedly protected Teng Hsiao-p'ing when the latter was purged for the second time in 1976 and probably was instrumental in bringing Teng back to power in 1977. Sometime thereafter, however, for reasons not completely clear but probably having ultimately to do with Teng's need to curb the power of the regional military, Teng and Hsu had become enemies.

**Hu Ch'iao-mu**: A party historian and propagandist purged in the Cultural Revolution. After his rehabilitation in 1978, he served as the head of the Chinese Academy of Social Science, Teng Hsiao-p'ing's most important think tank. Hu remains the reform faction's most prominent theoretician.

**Hu Yao-pang**: Before the Cultural Revolution, head of the Communist Youth League. Purged during the Cultural Revolution, he did not make a public comeback until 1978. In 1980 he became head of a revived party secretariat and in 1981 replaced Hua Kuo-feng as chairman of the Party's Central Committee. Upon the abolition of the post of chairmanship in 1982, he became the party's secretary general. Formally he holds the top position in the party hierarchy. Teng Hsiao-p'ing's right-hand man, he has the reputation of being a cultural liberal, although liberal statements by him are hard to come by since 1981.

**Hua Kuo-feng**: Prior to the Cultural Revolution, a relatively minor party functionary in Hunan province. After the Cultural Revolution, he became first secretary of Hunan and later minister of public security. In 1976 he succeeded Chou En-lai to the premiership. He led the purge of the Gang of Four and became a heroic and brilliant leader, chairman of the CPC's Central Committee. In 1980 he was replaced as premier by Chao Tzu-yang and a year later replaced as chairman by Hu Yao-pang. In 1982 he was removed from the Politburo. His political associations are with the nonradical left.

**Huang K'o-ch'eng**: A soldier, chief of staff under P'eng Te-huai, he was purged in 1959 with P'eng for arguing that the Great Leap Forward was insane and inhumane. Since his rehabilitation in 1978, he has served on the party's Disciplinary Committee. He has also functioned as a spokesman for the military left, possibly because he would be the most moderate member of that group.

**Hundred flowers**: In 1956 Mao sought critical advice from nonparty educated public opinion. He thought a hundred flowers should bloom, a hundred schools should contend. A hundred flowers did bloom in the spring of 1957, when intellectuals attacked the dictatorship of the Communist Party. This set the stage for a period of vicious party repression. Ever since then, however, the regime has consistently claimed that the hundred flowers is part of its basic policy, whatever the evidence of one's senses would seem to indicate.

**K'ang Sheng**: Long-time head of China's police and espionage system, part of the radical inner core until his death in 1975. He may have sponsored the careers of both Chiang Ch'ing and Hua Kuo-feng. He continued to be hailed as a great man after his death, only to be posthumously attacked in 1980. These attacks are part of the first visible evidence that Hua Kuo-feng's position was in danger.

**Keng-Shen reforms**: *Keng-shen* is one of the years in the Chinese sexegenary cycle. The year 1980 was *keng-shen*. That year there were proposals in the higher councils of the party to make power more responsive to popular opinion and to law and to set up some type of checks and balances on power in the party and the state. Attenuated versions of the *keng-shen* reforms began to be instituted in 1983, although it is impossible to say yet whether they will ever amount to anything.

**Kuang-ming Daily**: A national paper published in Peking that addresses itself primarily to the concerns of intellectuals.

**Li Hsien-nien**: A communist revolutionary, soldier, and economic manager. Although no radical, he survived the Cultural Revolution. Until the 1973 rehabilitation of Teng Hsiao-p'ing, he was the ranking vice-premier of the State Council under Chou En-lai and later the ranking vice-premier under Hua Kuo-feng. He is the major personality in the restoration faction.

**Li I-che**: A group of former Red Guards from Canton who in 1974 put up a wall poster advocating that China institute a system of law and democracy. Jailed at the time, they were released during the liberal period in early 1979, when the regime itself had in effect come over to their views. Apparently only one of the group, Wang Hsi-che, has continued to be politically active, and he was arrested for a second time in late 1981.

**Liberation Army Daily**: The national newspaper for the People's Liberation Army. It is hard to study systematically because it does not circulate abroad, and foreigners are not allowed to buy it. It has, however, on occasion taken a position different from that of the regime's other official media and can be treated sometimes as the organ of special groups or factions in the army.

**Lin Piao**: A communist soldier who succeeded P'eng Te-huai as minister of defense in 1959. He improved his position in the regime's hierarchy by playing up radical Maoism and the cult of Mao. His ambitions are at least in part responsible for the onset of the Cultural Revolution. In 1969 he was officially declared Mao's heir apparent. He was killed in 1971, allegedly while attempting to escape to the Soviet Union after a plot of his to murder Mao had failed.

**Liu Shao-ch'i**: The CPC's foremost organizational theorist, one of the major developers of Maoism. From well before the founding of the People's Republic, he ranked second to Mao in the party hierarchy. He was purged in 1966, accused of being a capitalist roader. In 1968 he was officially denounced as a renegade, traitor, and scab. He died in 1969 through a combination of mistreatment and neglect of long-standing illnesses. He was fully rehabilitated in 1980.

**Mao Tse-tung**: From 1935 until his death in 1976, leader of the CPC. Although in his early years he was identified more with the party's right wing than anything else, he became extremely radical in his old age. The official rewriting of party history still claims he was a great leader but blames him for serious errors from 1957 on, particularly the Great Leap Forward and the Cultural Revolution. The more thoroughgoing reformers would apparently prefer to say that the Great Leap Forward may have been an error, but the Cultural Revolution was a crime.

**May Fourth movement**: The movement proper was a series of student demonstrations in Peking and elsewhere on May 4, 1919, protesting the warlord government's acquiescence in Japanese demands made against China at the Versailles conference. More generally, the term refers to a whole period of intellectual ferment in which a generation of educated Chinese abandoned the traditional moral heritage in favor of what they thought to be science and democracy.

**Nieh Jung-chen**: A communist soldier and German-trained engineer, he was long in charge of supervising overall basic and applied scientific research in China. About a year after Mao's death, he became the first person within the leadership publicly to hint of a reevaluation of the former chairman's role.

**Pai Hua**: An army playwright, persecuted during the Cultural Revolution, who resumed activity in the late 1970s. His movie script, "Bitter Love," about the repeated disappointments of a patriotic Chinese educated abroad who returned home to serve the revolution, became the target of an attack from within the military in 1981. The regime's leadership first tried to blunt the criticism but eventually joined in, and Pai Hua was forced to make a public self-examination. He was not treated as cruelly as dissident writers used to be, but the campaign against him indicates at least a partial return to the old-style repression.

**P'eng Chen**: Before the Cultural Revolution, first secretary of Peking and second to Teng Hsiao-p'ing on the central Secretariat. He was the center of a core of party intellectuals dissatisfied with radical Maoism and became the first major victim of the Cultural Revolution. Many of his former followers later became active in the reform faction. P'eng Chen himself was rehabilitated in 1979 and has served as the regime's spokesman on legal matters.

**P'eng Te-huai**: Minister of defense in the mid-1950s and a communist soldier. He was purged in 1959 for opposing the Great Leap Forward and persecuted anew during the Cultural Revolution. His rehabilitation in 1978 is one of the first signs of an overt, rather than tacit, repudiation of the Maoist heritage.

**People's communes**: Huge collective agricultural enterprises established in 1958 during the Great Leap Forward. Originally they replaced the township, the smallest unit of local government in the countryside. Even by the early 1960s, they had lost most of their economic functions, and since 1978 agriculture has been even more radically decollectivized. In 1982 all administrative functions of the commune were abolished, and there was debate about whether the institution should be retained at all.

**People's Daily**: A national newspaper published in Peking, the official organ of the Central Committee of the Communist Party of China.

**Petroleum faction** (or gang): Officials associated with the petroleum ministry accused in 1980 of mismanagement and criminal negligence; a subset (or symbol) of the restoration faction.

**Politburo**: Elected by the party's Central Committee, the Political Bureau is charged with making major policy decisions while the Central Committee is not in session. Politburo membership is probably as good a measure as any of China's top ruling elite. The inner core of the Politburo is its Standing Committee.

**Practice faction**: An earlier term for the reform faction. The term is taken from Teng Hsiao-p'ing's slogan, that practice is the criterion of truth, a slogan that after 1980 had rather gone out of fashion.

**Red and Expert**: The regime has always demanded that those who hold important positions be both ideologically orthodox and dedicated (Red) and technically proficient (Expert). In practice at different periods it has stressed one aspect or the other, and the terms have represented a genuine tension within the rulership and in policy. This study hypothesizes that this tension is reflected in antiregime dissent as well: some dissidents stress democracy (and these are related to the regime's Reds), while others desire depoliticization (the Experts).

**Red Guards**: High school and college students who from 1966 through 1967 were encouraged by the radicals in the party center to run wild and "make revolution." Former Red Guards may well constitute the majority of lower-ranking party members now and are regarded with hostility by the dominant reform faction. These former Red Guards may demand either more radical policies or a more democratic style of policymaking.

**Reform faction**: A tendency affiliated with Teng Hsiao-p'ing. The top membership consists (mostly) of persons purged during the Cultural Revolution, most of these in turn not having been restored to power before Mao died. It appears they would be willing to push for radical and thoroughgoing changes in the structure of the regime, but they have also been willing to compromise their demands for reform in order to consolidate their power.

**Restoration faction**: A tendency consisting mainly of high-ranking cadres working in economic affairs. They were never sympathetic to Maoist radicalism, although most of the members, protected by Chou En-lai, avoided serious trouble during the Cultural Revolution. They are less liberal than the reform faction, and in particular more attached to management of the economy by command and direct administration. Their nickname refers to their notion that everything would be fine if the regime would simply restore the policies that held before the Great Leap Forward (whereas the reformers say mistakes have occurred ever since the founding of the state); the word also carries connotations of restoring the emperor (and the term, therefore, is used by their enemies, not by themselves).

**Secretariat**: The institution charged with the running of the routine work of the party bureaucracy under the supervision of the Politburo and Central Committee. It was headed by Teng Hsiao-p'ing until his first purge in 1966. The institution itself apparently ceased to exist at that time, until it was revived in 1980. The 1982 party charter, by making the head of the Secretariat the top ranking position in the party and abolishing the party chairmanship, probably increases the importance of the institution.

**State Council**: China's cabinet, headed by the premier; China's most important state executive institution.

**Szechuan experiment**: A set of liberal reforms involving allowing economic enterprises to make more of their own decisions, greater use of the market for economic allocation, and less collectivization of agriculture pushed by Chao Tzu-yang until he was first secretary of Szechuan province around 1978 and 1979. This became the model for the economic reforms of the country as a whole.

**Tachai**: An "advanced" agricultural unit in Shansi province, held up for years as the model of proper Maoist policy. It stood for the spirit of hard work, self-reliance, and dedication to collectivist principles. It was repudiated as a fake in 1980.

**Teng Hsiao-p'ing**: A communist revolutionary. From the mid-1950s, he served as secretary general of the Secretariat and was noted for being a relatively vocal critic of the cult of Mao. He was purged in 1966 as a capitalist roader and returned to office in 1973 under the sponsorship of Chou En-lai. He was purged again immediately after Chou died. Brought back to power in 1977, he backed, albeit ambivalently, proposals for radical reform of the structure and policies of the regime. In the course of the power struggle, he became the single most influential person in Chinese politics, although he has on the whole avoided taking the top position in the ruling institutions.

**Third plenum (of the Eleventh Central Committee)**: A plenum or plenary session is a meeting of the full Central Committee. The third plenum of the Eleventh Central Committee (that is, the Central Committee elected by the eleventh party congress) was held in December 1978 and marks the decisive but not yet complete victory of the Teng Hsiao-p'ing line. In the official Teng Hsiao-p'ing or reformer view, most things before the third plenum were pretty bad, while everything since then has been wonderful. Acceptance of the decisions of the third plenum constitutes a ritual of allegiance to Teng.

**Three Family Village**: A group of party intellectuals associated with P'eng Chen who wrote satires on radical Maoism in the early 1960s. Criticism of them became the pretext setting off the Cultural Revolution. They were rehabilitated (posthumously) at the third plenum in 1978.

**T'ien-an-men Square incident**: On April 5, 1976, a number of persons gathered at T'ien-an-men Square in Peking, ostensibly to honor the memory of Chou En-lai, but more to protest the purge of Teng Hsiao-p'ing—less, perhaps, because they liked Teng than because they hated the radicals who were persecuting him. Called at the time a counter-revolutionary incident, in November 1978 it was discovered to have been completely revolutionary. The reevaluation of the incident was one of the major blows against both Hua Kuo-feng and the Maoist tradition: Hua had been largely responsible for the suppression of the incident and the prosecution of those accused of fomenting it, and it was his handling of this incident that had allegedly earned Mao's full trust.

**8341 Troops**: A military police unit in Peking, formerly commanded by Wang Tung-hsing, responsible for the security of members of the Central Committee. In some ways it served as Mao Tse-tung's praetorian guard. This is the unit that carried out the arrests of the Gang of Four.

**Wang Hung-wen**: The youngest member of the Gang of Four and allegedly, since his arrest, the most cooperative. A former security guard at a Shanghai factory, he made a name for himself as a "revolutionary rebel" during the chaos of the Cultural Revolution. In the early 1970s, he rose to dizzying heights in the regime, only to be just as suddenly cast down.

**Wang Meng**: Possibly China's most outstanding new writer of fiction. In 1956, when he was only about 20 years old, he published a story, "The Young Newcomer in the Organization Department," detailing the bureaucratization of the revolution and its loss of idealism and élan. The story aroused much comment, and Wang Meng found himself spending a couple of decades in exile in Sinkiang. He resumed public activity in 1979 and has written several stories giving a realistic picture of the lives of ordinary people and officials in a totalitarian dictatorship. When officialdom once again began to take a repressive line, Wang said that censorship proves that someone is at least paying attention. In the spring of 1982 he took this line at a conference held in New York City, causing participants affiliated with Taiwan to jibe that Wang Meng is, fortunately, still a relatively young man— but he's become a young man from the Organization Department.

**Wang Tung-hsing**: Former commander of the 8341 Troops, he served for many years as Mao's personal bodyguard. He was instrumental in the purge of the Gang of Four and was perhaps the most sincere Maoist among the whatever faction. During 1978 and 1979, he controlled the party's theoretical magazine, *Red Flag*, and refused to give publicity to Teng Hsiao-p'ing's slogan that practice is the criterion of truth. His formal purge came in 1980.

**Wei Ching-sheng**: The most famous spokesman for the democratic movement. Once a Red Guard, in 1978 and 1979 he argued on wall posters and in underground journals that China could not completely modernize unless it became a democratic country. Technically because he had discussed China's invasion of Vietnam with foreign reporters but in fact because he supported democracy publicly, he was arrested and later given 20 years in jail.

**Wei Kuo-ch'ing**: For many years the first secretary of Kwangsi province, he was probably very influential in bringing Teng Hsiao-p'ing back to power. He became head of the army's General Political Department, the organization in charge of the political education and indoctrination of the troops and in that capacity voiced in the opinion that many of Mao's specific views on military affairs had become obsolete. Later, however, he became involved in the leftist revival in the military. In 1982 he participated in a challenge to Teng Hsiao-p'ing's authority and was removed from his army position, although he remained at least a nominal member of the Politburo.

**Whatever faction**: The nonradical left that participated in the overthrow of the Gang of Four. Thee are the persons politically closest to Hua Kuo-feng. Their name refers to statements they caused to have published to the effect that the regime was bound by whatever Mao had said or decided. They were defeated in the power struggle of 1979, and all but Hua Kuo-feng were formally purged the following spring.

**Wu Te**: From the Cultural Revolution until his purge, first secretary of Peking. He was Teng Hsiao-p'ing's most vocal critic and the most visible supporter of Hua Kuo-feng; he was a prominent member of the whatever faction. He was removed from his Peking positions in late 1978 and was dropped from the Politburo in 1980.

**Yao Wen-yuan**: The literary man among the Gang of Four. Before the Cultural Revolution, a propagandist in Shanghai noted mainly for the viciousness of his attacks on dissident writers, his criticism of the Three Family Village signalled the beginning of the Cultural Revolution. He rose to overall control of the regime's propaganda system. Since his arrest he is said, like Wang Hung-wen, to have become very cooperative with his persecutors.

**Yen Chien-ying**: Communist soldier and one of the regime's grand old men. He opposed the second purge of Teng Hsiao-p'ing and supported Hua Kuo-feng's overthrow of the Gang of Four. He was instrumental in bringing Teng back in 1977. Since then, however, he has become disturbed or frightened by the scope of Teng's reforms and functions as symbolic head of the restoration faction. At least since 1980, Teng has been hinting that Yeh should retire, and in early 1983 Yeh announced that this was now his intention.

**Yü Ch'iu-li**: An economic manager, one-time minister of petroleum industry, later head of state planning, and a long-time associate of Li Hsien-nien. He is a key figure in the restoration faction and the "head" of the petroleum gang. In 1982 he was made head of the army's general Political Department.

# Appendix B

## Chronology of
## Some Important
## Events

### 1975

**January**: Fourth National People's Congress convened. Chou En-lai proposes the four modernizations. The regime adopts a new constitution.

**March**: The radicals begin a new offensive against Chou En-lai, his policies, and his new constitution.

**Summer**: Teng Hsiao-p'ing, acting as premier for the sick Chou En-lai, causes an antiradical program to be drawn up and circulated within the party.

**September**: Publicity is given to Mao's criticism of the traditional novel, *Water Margin*—the first fruits of a radical counterattack on Chou and Teng.

**December**: The radicals purge the educational system. Covert but direct attacks on Teng Hsiao-p'ing begin.

### 1976

**January**: Chou En-lai dies and Teng Hsiao-p'ing is purged.

**February**: Hua Kuo-feng appointed acting premier.

**April**: The T'ien-an-men riots. Teng's purge is made public and official. Hua Kuo-feng is confirmed as premier. Mao tells him, "With you in charge my heart's at ease."

**July**: Terrible earthquakes in northern China.

**September**: Mao Tse-tung dies.

**October**: The Gang of Four, the radical Maoists, are placed under arrest. Hua Kuo-feng becomes party chairman and "heroic and brilliant leader."

## 1977

**January**: Beginning of a protracted media campaign glorifying Chou En-lai.

**Late winter, early spring**: Debate within the party on whether and how to restore Teng Hsiao-p'ing to honor.

**April**: Publication of the fifth volume of Mao's *Selected Works*, containing complimentary references to Teng Hsiao-p'ing.

**July**: Teng Hsiao-p'ing is brought back.

**August**: Eleventh Congress, Communist Party of China. Hua Kuo-feng says "First" Great Proletarian Cultural Revolution has come to an end.

## 1978

**January**: Short-lived talk of a "new leap forward": a split is beginning to develop between Teng Hsiao-p'ing and the "restoration" faction on the State Council.

**May**: The crimes of the Gang of Four are linked now with those of Lin Piao, signifying the beginning of a systematic and virtually explicit repudiation of Maoism. Publicity is given to Teng Hsiao-p'ing's slogan that practice is the criterion of truth.

**September**: The important regional military commander Hsu Shih-yu gives hints of his disappointment with Teng Hsiao-p'ing.

**October**: Purge of leftists of the Peking party committee and elsewhere.

**November**: Reevaluation of the T'ien-an-men Square incident. Amnesty for those named as rightists in 1957. Teng's group encourages public protests in Peking.

**December**: Third plenum, Eleventh Central Committee: the decisive victory for the Teng Hsiao-p'ing line. Hua Kuo-feng makes a self-criticism and repudiates the cult of the individual.

## 1979

**January**: China recognizes the United States, and Teng Hsiao-p'ing visits this country. The democratic movement is in full swing in Peking. Fu Yueh-hua is arrested.

**February**: China tries to punish Vietnam. Official censure of the democratic movement begins.

**March**: Wei Ching-sheng publishes "More About the Fifth Modernization." Teng Hsiao-p'ing criticizes the democratic movement and spells out "four principles" limiting the exercise of free speech.

**April**: Wei Ching-sheng is arrested. Leftists inside the party blame Teng Hsiao-p'ing and his people for encouraging chaos.

**May**: The campaign to celebrate the model of Chang Chi-hsin begins: Teng Hsiao-p'ing is launching a counterattack on the left.

**June**: Tensions between Hua Kuo-feng and the nonleftist rulers surface at a National People's Congress meeting. Hua announces there are no longer any antagonistic classes in China.

**August**: Brief revival of wall poster activity in Peking.

**September**: The leftists, now called the "whatever" faction, have been overcome by Teng's reformers. Yeh Chieh-ying admits that the CPC has made serious mistakes in line.

**November**: Wei Ching-sheng and Fu Yuah-hua are formally sentenced to prison.

## 1980

**February**: The Central Committee decides to eliminate the freedom to write wall posters from the state constitution. Liu Shao-ch'i is rehabilitated posthumously and the whatever faction is publicly removed from positions of influence. Hu Yao-pang becomes the head of a revived party Secretariat.

**March**: Hu Yao-pang begins to criticize China's economic performance during the Hua Kuo-feng years. The split between the reformers and the restorationists has become a breach. Public criticism of Mao intensifies, and reformers begin public criticism of the restoration faction for their feudal mentality.

**July**: K'ang Sheng is publicly criticized. Attack on the petroleum gang.

**August**: Chao Tzu-yang replaces Hua Kuo-feng as premier. Teng Hsiao-p'ing and other "old cadres" retire from the State Council. Teng continues to urge the need for radical structural reforms in the economy and the state.

**September**: High-ranking cadres attacked for corruption, their errors being attributed to the feudal arrogation of special privilege.

**Fall**: Publicity is given in the media to the *keng-shen* reform proposals, which would tend to decentralize and limit the exercise of political power by the party and the state.

**December**: Opening of the trial of the Gang of Four. The party leadership decides on a program of economic retrenchment, and further reforms are delayed. There is a minor purge of the economics systems.

## 1981

**Spring**: General atmosphere of reaction to the reformist zeal of the previous fall. The regime calls for patriotism and "socialist spiritual civilization." The army criticizes the liberal, bourgeois, unpatriotic behavior of certain creative writers. There are continuing arrests of persons associated with the democratic movement of 1978–79.

**June**: Sixth plenum, Eleventh Central Committee. The party formally reevaluates Mao's historical position and decides that from 1957 on he made serious errors (but does not say that he committed crimes). In the same reevaluation, Hua Kuo-feng is criticized for continuing leftist policies and the cult of the individual during the period following the overthrow of the Gang of Four. Hua-Kuo-feng is replaced as party chairman by Hu Yao-pang.

**August**: General crackdown on literary dissent and criticism of "bourgeois liberalization."

**Fall**: Massive military maneuvers in northern China.

**December**: Several ranking members of the reform faction allegedly make self-criticisms.

# 1982

**January**: Li Hsien-nien calls for activities against economic crime. This crime (that is, corruption) is now seen less as a consequence of "feudal" residues than as a result of Teng Hsiao-p'ing's liberal economic policies.

**March**: Counterattack by the reformers. Chao Tzu-yang speaks of the need for continued economic reforms and for structural reform of the state.

**May**: A reorganization of the State Council substantially undercuts the influence of the restorationists in the institution they used to dominate.

**August**: The military newspaper indirectly attacks Teng Hsiao-p'ing's reform program, particularly the influence that program gives to intellectuals.

**September**: Twelfth party congress. Hua Kuo-feng is expelled from the Politburo. The position of chairmanship is abolished, and Hu Yao-pang becomes instead the party's secretary general. The Advisor's Committee is set up. The new party charter stresses the party's obligation to operate only within the sphere of law.

**October**: Purge of military leaders opposed to Teng Hsiao-p'ing.

**December**: A National People's Congress session adopts a new state constitution stressing greater powers for the Congress and its standing committee and greater accountability by the State Council. The mass media become more outspoken in their attacks on leftism, by now a code word for opposition to reform.

# Bibliography

Apter, David E. *The Politics of Modernization*. Chicago: University of Chicago Press, 1965.

Arendt, Hannah. *The Origins of Totalitarianism*. 2nd ed. Cleveland: Meridian Books, 1958.

Bell, Daniel. *The Coming of Post-Industrial Society: A Venture in Social Forecasting*. New York: Basic Books, 1973.

Bernstein, Thomas P. *Up to the Mountains and Down to the Villages: The Transfer of Youth from Urban to Rural China*. New Haven: Yale University Press, 1977.

Bialer, Seweryn. *Stalin's Successors: Leadership, Stability, and Change in the Soviet Union*. New York: Cambridge University Press, 1980.

Bonavia, David. *The Chinese*. New York: Lippincott and Crowell, 1980.

Brodsguard, Kjeld Erik. "The Democracy Movement in China, 1976–1979: Opposition Movements, Wall Poster Campaigns, and Underground Journals." *Asian Survey* 21 (July 1981): 747–74.

Chang Ch'un-ch'iao. "On Full-Scale Dictatorship over the Bourgeoisie." *Hung Ch'i* 4 (April 1, 1975): 3–16.

Chang Ch'un-po. "Fake Criticism of Confucius, True Usurpation of Power." *Kuang-ming Jih-pao*, December 14, 1976.

Chang Hsien-yang and Wang Kuei-hsiu. "On the Nature of the Line of Lin Piao and the 'Gang of Four.' " *Jen-min Jih-pao*, February 28, 1979.

Chang P'en-ssu. "Does Truth Have a Class Character?" *Jen-min Jih-pao*, November 28, 1978.

Chang Sang-cho. "Theory and Practice of the Bourgeois Separation in Powers." *Jen-min Jih-pao*, October 7, 1980.

Chang Ta-k'o. "An Attempt to Discuss the Chao-Hsuan Restoration." *Kuang-ming Jih-pao*, October 2, 1979.

Chao P'u-ch'u. "The Revived Glory of Chinese Buddhism." *Chung-kuo-Chien-she* 10 (October 1980): 45–49.

Chao Tzu-yang. "The Exalted Virtues of a Communist." *Jen-min Jih-pao*, March 23, 1979.

————. "Study the New Situation, Fully Implement the Direction of Readjustment." *Hung Ch'i*, 1 (January 1, 1980): 15–20.

Ch'en Chung. "Put the 'Gang of Four's' Magazine *Study and Criticism* in the Prisoner's Dock." *Li Shih yeh-chiu* 1 (February 20, 1977): 29–39.

Chen Jo-hsi. *The Execution of Mayor Yin*. Bloomington: Indiana University Press, 1978.

Ch'en Pei-hsien. "Leading Cadres Must Let the Masses Speak." *Jen-min Jih-pao*, July 26, 1978.

Ch'en Yun. "Uphold Seeking Truth from Facts." *Jen-min Jih-pao*, September 28, 1977.

Cheng Lien. "The 'Gang of Four' and the Trotskyites." *Jen-min Jih-pao*, January 27, 1977.

Cheng Wen-lin. "Communist Morality or Socialist Morality?" *Kuang-ming Jih-pao*, September 18, 1980.

Ch'i Hsin. *Teng Hsiao-p'ing: A Political Biography*. Hong Kong: Cosmos Books, 1978.

Qi Xin (i.e., Ch'i Hsin) et al. *China's New Democracy*. Hong Kong: Cosmos Books, 1979.

Chin Wen. "Thoroughly Criticize the Bad Faith Implementation of the 'Left' Opportunist Line by Lin Piao and the 'Gang of Four' " *Kuang-ming Jih-pao*, January 23, 1979.

*China News Analysis*. Hong Kong.

*Christianity and the New China*. South Pasadena, Calif.: Ecclesia, 1976.

*Chung-kung Wen-t'i Tzu-liao*. Taipei.

*Chung-kuo Chien-she* [China, Reconstructs]. Peking.

*Chung-kuo-ien Yueh-k'an* [Chinese Monthly]. Taipei.

*Chung-yang Jih-pao* [Central Daily News]. Taipei.

Dahrendorf, Ralf. *Class and Class Conflict in Industrial Society*. Stanford: Stanford University Press, 1959.

————. *Essays in the Theory of Sociology*. Stanford: Stanford University Press, 1968.

Dittmer, Lowell. "Chinese Communist Revisionism in Comparative Perspective." *Studies in Comparative Communism* 13 (Spring 1980): 3–40.

Domes, Jürgen. *China after the Cultural Revolution: Politics between two Party Congresses*. Berkeley: University of California Press, 1977.

Doolin, Dennis J. *Communist China: The Politics of Student Opposition*. Stanford: Hoover Institution Press, 1964.

*Fan-mien Chiao-ts'ai "Shui-hu"* [A Negative Textbook, *Water Margin*]. Edited by Chinese Department, Peking National University. Peking: *Jen-min Ch'u-pan She*, 1975.

*Far Eastern Economic Review*. Hong Kong.

Feng Wen-pin. "On Questions of Socialist Democracy." *Jen-min Jih-pao*, November 24 and 25, 1980.

Feng Wu. "On Some Problems of Literary Creativity." *Jen-min Jih-pao*, February 11, 1981.

Foreign Broadcast Information Service. *Daily Report, People's Republic of China* (later: *Daily Report, China*). Washington, D.C.

Friedrich, Carl J., and Zbigniew K. Brzezinski. *Totalitarian Dictatorship and Autocracy*. 2nd ed. New York: Praeger, 1966.

Frolic, B. Michael. *Mao's People: Sixteen Portraits of Life in Revolutionary China*. Cambridge, Mass.: Harvard University Press, 1980.

Garside, Roger. *Coming Alive: China After Mao*. New York: McGraw-Hill, 1981.

Gelber, Harry G. *Technology, Defense, and External Relations in China, 1975–1979*. Boulder, Colo.: Westview, 1979.

Gold, Thomas B. "Back to the City: The Return of Shanghai's Educated Youth." *China Quarterly* 84 (December 1980): 755–70.

Goldman, Merle. *China's Intellectuals: Advise and Dissent*. Cambridge, Mass.: Harvard University Press, 1981.

*A Great Trial in Chinese History*. Oxford: Pergamon Press, 1981.

Hollander, Paul. *Political Pilgrims: Travels of Western Intellectuals to the Soviet Union, China, and Cuba.* New York: Oxford University Press, 1981.

Hsia Chih-yen. *The Coldest Winter in Peking.* Garden City, N.Y.: Doubleday, 1978.

Hsiang Hui. "Criticizing the Hunan Opera, the Gardener's Song." *Jen-min Jih-pao,* August 2, 1974.

Hsu Hsiang-ch'ien. "The Party Must Always Control the Gun." *Jen-min Jih-pao,* September 19, 1977.

Hsu Shih-yu. "Chairman Mao Will Always Live in Our Hearts." *Jen-min Jih-pao,* September 8, 1978.

Hsu Yun-hsi. "An Informal View of a Little Literary History." *Hsueh-hsi yu P'i-p'an,* August 1975, pp. 58–61.

Hsueh Min and Kuo Yung. "Discussing the 'Leftist' Tendency of 'Western Marxism.'" *Hsin-Hua Wen-chai,* 8 (August 1981): pp. 36–38.

Hsueh Mu-ch'iao. "Some Opinions on the Reform of the Economic System." *Jen-min Jih-pao,* June 10, 1980.

Hsueh Mu-feng. "How to Struggle against Bureaucratism." *Jen-min Jih-pao,* April 28, 1980.

Hu Ch'iao-mu. "Several Questions on the Current Ideological Line." *Hung Ch'i,* 23 (December 1, 1981): 2–22.

_____. "Work According to Economic Laws; Speed up the Realization of the Four Modernizations." *Jen-min Jih-pao,* October 6, 1978.

Hu P'ing. "On the Development of Diversity." *Jen-min Jih-pao,* August 8, 1980.

Hu Yao-pang. "Speech at the Meeting Commemorating Lu Hsun's Hundredth Birthday." *Hung Ch'i* 19 (October 1, 1981): 2–6.

Hua Hsiang. "Democratic Spirit and Revolutionary Order." *Kuang-ming Jih-pao,* March 18, 1979.

Hua Kuo-feng. "The Whole Party Should Mobilize, Do a Lot of Work in Agriculture, Fight to Make Universal Tachai-like Counties." *Jen-min Jih-pao,* October 21, 1975.

Huang Chen. "Welcoming a New High Tide in the Building of a Socialist Culture." *Kuang-ming Jih-pao,* May 21, 1978.

Huang Chih-chin. "How, After All, Should We Understand the Young of the Present Generation?" *Jen-min Jih-pao,* February 24, 1981.

Huang K'o-ch'eng. "On the Question of Party Style." *Jen-min Jih-pao,* February 28, 1981.

_____. "On the Questions of the Evaluation of Chairman Mao and the Attitude toward the Thought of Mao Tse-tung." *Jen-min Jih-pao,* April 11, 1981.

_____. "Pure in Heart, He Gazes at the Sun and Moon: His Moral Courage Will Endure a Thousand Autumns." *Jen-min Jih-pao,* January 3, 1979.

Huang Mab. *Intellectual Ferment for Political Reform in Taiwan, 1971–1974.* Ann Arbor: Center for Chinese Studies, University of Michigan, 1976.

*Hung Ch'i* [Red Flag]. Peking.

Huntington, Samuel P. "Post-Industrial Politics: How Benign Will It Be?" *Comparative Politics* 6 (January 1974): 163–91.

Inglehart, Ronald. *The Silent Revolution: Changing Values and Political Styles Among Western Publics.* Princeton: Princeton University Press, 1977.

*Inside China Mainland.* Taipei.

Jacobs, J. Bruce. "A Preliminary Model of Particularistic Ties in Chinese Political Alliances: *Kan-ch'ing* and *Kuan-hsi* in a Rural Taiwanese Township." *China Quarterly* 78 (June 1979): 237–78.

Jen Hsu-yu. "Study Religion, Criticize Theology." *Kuang-ming Jih-pao*, September 27, 1977.

*Jen-min Jih-pao*, [People's Daily]. Peking.

Jen P'ing. "A Gang of Pernicious Vermin Who Harm the State and Injure the People." *Jen-min Jih-pao*, November 14, 1976.

Johnson, E. H. "Christian Voices from the Church in China: April, 1975." *China Notes* 13 (Summer 1975): 26–30.

Kao, Michael Y. M., ed. *The Lin Piao Affair: Power Politics and Military Coup.* White Plains, N.Y.: International Arts and Sciences Press, 1975.

Kassof, Allan. "The Administered Society: Totalitarianism Without Terror." *World Politics* 16 (July 1964): 558–74.

Kneen, Peter. "Why Natural Scientists Are a Problem for the CPSU." *British Journal of Political Science* 8 (April 1978): 177–98.

Konrad, George, and Ivan Szeleny. *The Intellectuals on the Road to Class Power.* New York: Harcourt Brace Jovanovich. 1979.

Lee, Hong Yung. *The Politics of the Chinese Cultural Revolution: A Case Study.* Berkeley: University of California Press, 1978.

Lee, Leo Ou-fan. "Dissent Literature from the Cultural Revolution." *Chinese Literature* 1 (January 1979): 59–79.

Lei Chen-ch'ang. "Strengthen the Atheist Education of Young People." *Kuang-ming Jih-pao*, August 25, 1980.

Li Hsien-nien. "How to Look at the Reform in the Management System of Finance and Trade in Rural Areas." *Jen-min Jih-pao*, January 17, 1959.

Li Hung-lin. "Is Distribution According to Labor a Socialist or a Capitalist Principle?" *Jen-min Jih-pao*, September 27, 1977.

———. "What Does the 'Crisis of Faith' Show?" *Jen-min Jih-pao*, November 11, 1980.

———. "What Kind of Socialism Do We Uphold?" *Jen-min Jih-pao*, May 9, 1980.

Li I-che. "On Socialist Democracy and Legality." *Chung-kung Yen-chiu*, November 1975, pp. 117–31.

Li Shao-chun. "China's Ancient Feudal Despotism." *Kuang-ming Jih-pao*, August 14, 1979.

———. "The Eunuch Dictatorship of Ancient China." *Kuang-ming Jih-pao*, August 5, 1980.

Li Te-sheng. "Deeply Penetrate Reality, Link Up with the Masses." *Jen-min Jih-pao*, September 9, 1978.

Liang Hsiao. "Always Act According to the Directions Set by Chairman Mao." *Kuang-ming Jih-pao*, October 4, 1976.

Lieberthal, Kenneth. *Revolution and Tradition in Tientsin, 1949–1952.* Stanford: Stanford University Press, 1980.

*Lien Ho Pao* [United Daily]. Taipei.

Lin Ching-yao. "The Revelation of an Argument between Marx and Engels." *Kuang-ming Jih-pao*, July 29, 1978.

Lin Feng. "The Struggle of Marxism against the Vulgar Theory of Nothing but Production Forces." *Jen-min Jih-pao*, September 7, 1977.

(Lin Li-kuo). " '571' Engineering Outline." *Chung-kung Yen-chiu*, July 1972, pp. 98–102.

Lin Wei. "Uphold Historical Materialism in the Relation between Economics and Politics." *Kuang ming Jih-pao*, May 15, 1980.

Linz, Juan J., "Totalitarian and Authoritarian Regimes." In *Handbook of Political Science*, vol. 3, edited by Fred I. Greenstein and Nelson W. Polsby, pp. 175–411. Reading, Mass.: Addison-Wesley, 1975.

Liu Hsi-sheng. "Discussing a Few Questions about the Way Short Stories Should Be Written." *Kuang-ming Jih-pao*, March 30, 1979.

Liu Men-chieh. "Preliminary Discussion of the Mainstream of Literary Development in 1980." *Hung Ch'i* 3 (February 1, 1981): 30–34.

Liu Ping-yen. "Between Man and Devil." *Jen-min Wen-hsueh*, September 1979, pp. 83–102.

Liu Shao-ch'i. *On Inner Party Struggle*. Peking: Foreign Languages Press, 1952.

Liu Tso-ch'ang. "Comments on Thomas Jefferson's Democratic Thought." *Li-shih Yen-chiu* 4 (August 15, 1980): 149–64.

Lu Hsun. *A Brief History of Chinese Fiction*. Peking: Foreign Languages Press, 1964.

Lu Li. "Leadership in Agriculture Must Begin from Reality." *Jen-min Jih-pao*, November 12, 1960.

Ly Singko. *The Fall of Madam Mao*. New York: Vantage, 1979.

Ma Jia-ju. "A Pioneering Work on Economic Reform—Notes on Sun Yefang's *Theoretical Questions of the Socialist Economy*." *Social Sciences in China* 1 (March 1980): 216–27.

Mao Chih-yung. "Earnestly Allow the Party's Economic Policy to Take Root and Fully Mobilize the Peasants' Socialist Activism." *Jen-min Jih-pao*, August 30, 1978.

Mao Tse-tung. "A Great Leap Forward Will Appear in China." *Jen-min Jih-pao*, December 26, 1977.

––––––. *Mao Tse-tung Hsuan-chi* [Selected Works of Mao Tse-tung]. Vol. 5. Peking: *Jen-min Ch'u-pan She*, 1977.

––––––. "On Uninterrupted Revolution." *Jen-min Jih-pao*, December 26, 1978.

Mao Tun. "Some Shallow Opinions on the Study of Lu Hsun." *Jen-min Jih-pao*, October 19, 1977.

Mehnert, Klaus. *Peking and the New Left*. Berkeley: University of California Press, 1970.

Meng Fan-hsing *et al.*, *Ti-chen yü Ti-chen K'ao-ku*. Peking: Wen-wu Ch'u-pan She, 1977.

Moody, Peter R., Jr. "Law and Heaven: The Evolution of Chinese Totalitarianism." *Survey* 24 (Winter 1979): 116–32.

––––––. "The New Anti-Confucius Campaign in China: The First Round." *Asian Survey* 14 (April 1974): 307–24.

––––––. *Opposition and Dissent in Contemporary China*. Stanford: Hoover Institution Press, 1977.

———. *The Politics of the Eighth Central Committee of the Communist Party of China.* Hamden, Conn.: Shoestring Press, 1973.

———. "Power and Policy: The Career of T'ao Chu, 1956–1966." *China Quarterly* 54 (April/June 1973): 167–93.

Mu Chia. "This Topic of 'Capitalist Restoration' Is Worth Studying." *Jen-min Jih-pao,* July 17, 1980.

Nakane, Chie. *Japanese Society.* Berkeley: University of California Press, 1970.

Nathan, Andrew J. "A Factionialism Model for CCP Politics." *China Quarterly* 53 (January/March 1973): 32–66.

Nieh Jung-chen. "Restore and Develop the Party's Excellent Style." *Jen-min Jih-pao,* September 5, 1977.

Oksenberg, Michael, and Sai-cheung, Yeung. "Hua Kuo-feng's Pre-Cultural Revolution Hunan Years, 1949–1966: The Making of a Political Generalist." *China Quarterly* 69 (March 1977): 3–63.

Oleszczuk, Thomas. "The Liberalization of Dictatorship: The Titoist Lesson to the Third World." *Journal of Politics* 43 (August 1981): 818–30.

Onate, Andres D. "Hua Kuo-feng and the Arrest of the 'Gang of Four.' " *China Quarterly* 75 (September 1978): 540–64.

Pao T'ung. "A Few Opinions on Opposing Bureaucratism." *Jen-min Jih-pao,* October 30, 1980.

Parenti, Michael. *Democracy for the Few.* 2nd ed. New York: St. Martin's, 1978.

Parish, William L., and Martin King Whyte. *Village and Family in Contemporary China* Chicago: University of Chicago Press, 1978.

P'eng Hsiang-fu and Cheng Chung-ping. "On 'Monolithic Leadership.' " *Jen-min Jih-pao,* December 12, 1980.

Pfeffer, Richard M. "Serving the People and Continuing the Revolution." *China Quarterly,* 52 (October/December 1972): 620–53.

Popper, Karl R. *The Open Society and Its Enemies.* 2 vols., 3rd ed. London: Routledge and Paul, 1957.

Pye, Lucian. *The Dynamics of Chinese Politics.* Cambridge, Mass.: Oelgeschlager, Gull & Hain. 1981.

Rawski, Evelyn Sakashida. *Agricultural Change and the Peasant Economy of South China.* Cambridge, Mass.: Harvard University Press, 1972.

Ren Tao. "Investigation Report: Enterprises in Sichuan Province Acquire Greater Independence." *Social Sciences in China* 1 (March 1980): 201–15.

Rush, Myron. *How Communist States Change Their Rulers.* Ithaca, N.Y.: Cornell University Press, 1974.

Schapiro, Leonard. *Totalitarianism.* New York: Praeger, 1972.

Shao Yne-hsiang. "Eliminate the Influence of Feudal Residues." *Jen-min Jih-pao,* November 12, 1980.

Shen T'ao-sheng. "The 'Gang of Four' and Lin Piao." *Jen-min Jih-pao,* May 18, 1978.

Shih Ch'un. "A Certain Professor's Ambush Historiography." *Jen-min Jih-pao,* April 19, 1978.

Shirk, Susan L. "Going Against the Tide: Political Dissent in China." *Survey* 24 (Winter 1979): 82–114.

Simon, Julian L. "Global Confrontation, 1980: A Hard Look at the Global 2000 Report." *The Public Interest* 62 (Winter 1981): 3–20.

Skinner, G. William. "Marketing and Social Structure in Rural China." pt. 1, *Journal of Asian Studies* 24 (November 1964): 3–43.

Solzhenitsyn, Aleksandr. "The Courage of See." *Foreign Affairs* 59 (Fall 1980): 186–210.

Starr, John Bryan. *Continuing the Revolution: The Political Thought of Mao.* Princeton: Princeton University Press, 1979.

Strong, John, and Sara Strong. "A Post-Cultural Revolution Look at Chinese Buddhism." *China Quarterly* 54 (April/June 1973): 301–30.

Sung Jen-ch'iung. "Use the New Party Charter to Educate Party Members: Make a Good Ideological Preparation for Party Rectification." *Jen-min Jih-pao*, December 18, 1982.

Teng Hsiao-p'ing. "Report on the Rectification Movement." *Jen-min Shou-ts'e*, 1958, pp. 33–42.

_____. "Report on the Revision of the Party Constitution." *Jen-min Shou-ts'e*, 1957, pp. 26–37.

*Teng Hsiao-p'ing and the "General Program."* San Francisco: Red Sun, 1977.

Teng Li-ch'un. "The Voice of Truth Cannot Be Smothered." *Jen-min Jih-pao*, June 24 and 25, 1980.

*The Third World: Premises of U.S. Policy.* San Francisco: Institute for Contemporary Studies, 1978.

T'ien Ch'ing. "Part of the Record of the 'Gang of Four's' Failure in Their Struggle to Usurp the Party." *Jen-min Jih-pao*, November 14, 1976.

*T'ien-an-men Shih-chien Shuo-ming-le Shen-ma?*. Peking: *Jen-min Ch'u-pan She*, 1976. *New York Times*.

Tsu Wei. "Oh, Fathers and Brothers." *Jen-min Jih-pao*, November 8, 1970.

Tu Mo. *Chung-kuo Ta-lu T'ien-chu-chiao Chen-hsiang* [True Picture of the Catholic Church on the China Mainland]. Hong Kong: Chiu-Chen Hsueh-she, 1966.

Tucker, Robert C. *The Marxian Revolutionary Idea.* New York: Norton, 1969.

Tung Tung. "One Baby for You, One Baby for Me." *American Spectator* 14 (January 1981): 15–17.

Unger, Roberto Morgibeira. *Knowledge and Politics.* New York: Free Press, 1975.

Vogel, Ezra. "From Friendship to Comradeship: The Change in Personal Relations in Communist China." *China Quarterly* 21 (January/March 1965): 46–60.

Waley, Arthur. *Three Ways of Thought in Ancient China.* Garden City, N.Y.: Doubleday Anchor, n.d.

Wang Chao. "A Critique of the Centralized System of the Sung Dynasty." *Kuang-ming Jih-pao*, October 21, 1980.

Wang Hsueh-wen. *Chung-kung Wen-tzu Kai-ko yü Han-tzu Ch'ien-t'u* [The Chinese Communists' Reform of the Writing System and the Future of Chinese Characters]. Taipei: Kuo-chi Kuan-hsi Yen-chiu-so, 1970.

Wang Hui-te, "A Counterrevolutionary Quack." *Jen-min Jih-pao*, January 22, 1977.

Wang Jen-chung. "Unify Thought, Earnestly Rectify Party Style." *Hung Ch'i* 5 (March 1, 1982): 1–13.

Wang Jo-shui. "Marxism and the Liberation of Thought." *Jen-min Jih-pao*, August 1, 1980.

Weng Meng. "The Butterfly." *Chinese Literature*, (January 1981): 3–55.
―――. "The Voice of Spring." *Jen-min Wen-hsueh* 5 (May 1980): 10–16.
―――. "The Young Newcomer in the Organization Department." *Jen-min Wen-hsueh* 9 (September 1956): 29–43.
Wang Ssu-cih. "Feudal Autocracy and Eunuch Dictatorship." *Kuang-ming Jih-pao*, August 5, 1980.
Wei Hua and Tung Hsiao. "Iron Proof of a Plot to Usurp the Party." *Jen-min Jih-pao*, December 13, 1976.
Welch, Holmes. *Buddhism under Mao.* Cambridge, Mass.: Harvard University Press, 1972.
Wen Shan. " 'To Encourage Sounds of Praise—How Can That Do Us Any Good?' " *Jen-min Jih-pao*, August 13, 1979.
Wesson, Robert. *The Aging of Communism.* New York: Praeger, 1980.
White, Lynn T., III. *Careers in Shanghai: The Social Guidance of Personal Energies in a Developing Chinese City, 1949–1966.* Berkeley: University of California Press, 1978.
Whitehead, James D., Yu-ming Shaw, and N. J. Girardot, eds. *China and Christianity: Historical and Future Encounters.* Notre Dame: Center for Pastoral and Social Ministry, 1979.
Whitson, William. "The Field Army in Chinese Communist Politics." *China Quarterly* 37 (January/March 1969): 1–30.
Whyte, Martin King. *Small Groups and Political Rituals in China.* Berkeley: University of California Press, 1974.
Womack, Brantly. "Politics and Epistemology in China since Mao." *China Quarterly* 80 (December 1979): 768–92.
Wu Hsu. "Welcoming a New Leap Forward." *Jen-min Jih-pao*, January 3, 1978.
Wu Te. "Liberate Thought; Greet the Technological Revolution." *Jen-min Jih-pao*, May 24, 1958.
Yang Ch'eng-wu. "Greatly and Particularly Establish the Absolute Authority of the Great Supreme Commander Chairman Mao, Greatly and Particularly Establish the Absolute Authority of the Great Thought of Mao Tse-tung." *Jen-min Jih-pao*, November 13, 1967.
Yang I-chen. "To Extirpate Chaos and Restore Rectitude It Is Necessary to Liberate Thought." *Jen-min Jih-pao*, August 23, 1978.
Yao Wen-yuan. "On the Social Base of the Lin Piao Anti-Party Clique." *Hung Ch'i* 3 (March 1 1975): 20–29.
Yeh Chien-ying. "Great Strategy Decides the War." *Jen-min Jih-pao*, August 30, 1965.
―――. "Raise High the Red Banner of the Thought of Mao Tse-tung and Manage Schools after the Style of Resist-Japan University." *Jen-min Jih-pao*, August 2, 1966.
Yeh Tzu. "Is There Absolute Freedom of Speech?" *Hung-Ch'i* 8 (April 1, 1981): 31–35.
Yih-tang Lin, comp. *What They Say: A Collection of Current Chinese Underground Publications.* Taipei: Institute of Current China Studies, n.d.
Yu Ch'ing. "Thoroughly Smash the Gang System of the 'Gang of Four.' " *Jen-min Jih-pao*, August 6, 1977.
Yuan Fang. "*Bitter Love* and the Patriotism of Intellectuals." *Hung Ch'i* 9 (May 1, 1981): 27–33.

# Index

# About the Author

PETER R. MOODY, Jr. is a member of the Department of Government and International Studies at the University of Notre Dame and is also director of the Asian Studies program at Notre Dame.

Dr. Moody has been a Peace Fellow at the Hoover Institution. He is the author of *Opposition and Dissent in Contemporary China* and articles on Chinese affairs, international relations, and comparative politics in various scholarly journals.

Dr. Moody has an A.B. degree from Vanderbilt University and an M.A. and Ph.D. from Yale.